THE
ICE MUSEUM

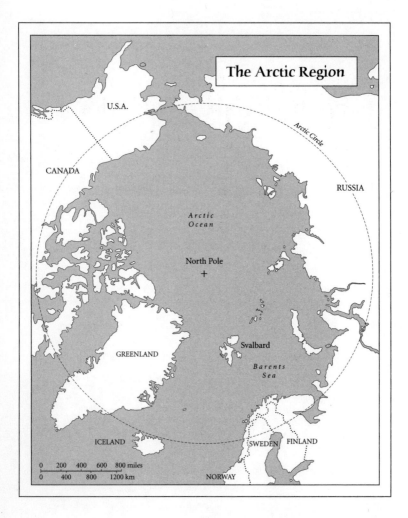

The Arctic Region

U.S.A.

Arctic Circle

CANADA

RUSSIA

Arctic
Ocean

North Pole
+

Svalbard

GREENLAND

Barents
Sea

ICELAND

SWEDEN   FINLAND

0   200   400   600   800 miles
0   400   800   1200 km

NORWAY

THE
ICE MUSEUM

IN SEARCH OF THE LOST LAND OF THULE

Joanna Kavenna

VIKING

VIKING

Published by the Penguin Group

Penguin Group (USA) Inc., 375 Hudson Street, New York, New York 10014, USA
Penguin Group (Canada), 90 Eglinton Avenue East, Suite 700, Toronto, Ontario,
Canada MP4 2Y3 (a division of Pearson Penguin Canada Inc.)
Penguin Books Ltd, 80 Strand, London WC2R 0RL, England
Penguin Ireland, 25 St. Stephen's Green, Dublin 2, Ireland
(a division of Penguin Books Ltd)
Penguin Books Australia Ltd, 250 Camberwell Road, Camberwell, Victoria 3124,
Australia (a division of Pearson Australia Group Pty Ltd)
Penguin Books India Pvt. Ltd, 11 Community Centre, Panchsheel Park,
New Delhi—110 017, India
Penguin Group (NZ), Cnr Airborne and Rosedale Roads, Albany, Auckland 1310,
New Zealand (a division of Pearson New Zealand Ltd)
Penguin Books (South Africa) (Pty) Ltd, 24 Sturdee Avenue, Rosebank,
Johannesburg 2196, South Africa

Penguin Books Ltd, Registered Offices:
80 Strand, London WC2R 0RL, England

First published in 2006 by Viking Penguin,
a member of Penguin Group (USA) Inc.

1   3   5   7   9   10   8   6   4   2

Copyright © Joanna Kavenna, 2005
All rights reserved

ISBN 0-670-03473-8

Printed in the United States of America

Set in Berkley Book • Designed by Elke Sigal

*For my parents
and B. H. D. M.
with love*

CONTENTS

LIST OF MAPS

FLIGHT

. . . Only the past is immortal.
Decide to take a trip, read books of travel
Go quickly! Even Socrates is mortal
Mention the name of happiness: it is
Atlantis, Ultima Thule, or the limelight,
Cathay or Heaven. But go quickly . . .

"Personae," Delmore Schwartz (1913–1966)

Seen from above, the ice sounds a ceaseless warning. A vicious blankness emanates from the white expanse below. The shadow of the plane falls on fleeting clouds. The ice smothers forests and mountains under a thick pall. Nothing moves across the whiteness.

The plane is drifting downwards, falling towards the glazed countryside. The ice is a vista of emptiness, like a paradox, a symbol expressing the inexpressible; here is the vivid realization of absence. As the plane descends, the warning sounds insistently: LEAVE. A single syllable resounding across the smothered land. No point in coming here. The country is closed for the ice deluge, to be opened in the spring. The plane is plunging through a white sky, into banks of drifting cloud. The trees below are bleached, their branches bent under the weight of the snow. As the plane skids across the runway the trees blur into lines of whiteness.

Shaking their heads, the passengers disembark. A pale sun shines onto the rigid arms of the trees. I step slowly onto the frost-coated runway. A thick wind blasts at my body, forcing me to bend against it. A woman is signalling frantically, pointing at a bus. We all board, obediently.

In this icy landscape, it is hard to discern distance and gradient. Complex layers of vegetation are simplified into one dense line of thick snow-bound forest. Only the most violent features of the landscape remain—the most jagged and stark. Trees seem to be locked in the ice, bowed by the weight of their casing, like statues struggling to become free of a block of stone. The sun trembles above the horizon, casting squat shadows on the snow, waiting to sink into darkness again. It is a landscape ripe for fantastical embellishment; the silence invites it. Something about the brute simplicity of the nature outside—cold, white, blank—sends me into thoughts of the remote and atavistic—stumbling monsters, shambling old trolls, vast footprints in the snow.

Under the snow, the ice land is an anonymous world, the trees stripped of colour. The frost breath of the wind makes me blink, the frigid air rips at my lungs. The fjord is frozen, the trees are silver splinters.

I was travelling through northern lands, compelled by the endless indeterminacy of a myth: the land of Thule—the most northerly place in the ancient world. Before the regions north of Britain were mapped, there was a dream of a silent place, where the inhabitants lived under darkened skies through the winter, and enjoyed constant sunshine in the summer. A land near a frozen ocean, draped in mist. Thule was seen once, described in opaque prose, and never identified with any certainty again. It became a mystery land, standing by a cold sea. A land at the edge of the maps.

A Greek explorer, Pytheas, began the story: he claimed to have reached Thule in the fourth century B.C. He had sailed from the sun-drenched city of Marseilles to Britain. He sailed up to the north of Scotland, and then sailed onwards for about six days into the remote reaches of the ocean, until he sighted a land called Thule. There, so the story goes, the inhabitants showed him where the sun set on the shortest day. In the winter, the land was plunged into darkness. Near Thule, the sea began to thicken, and Pytheas saw the sea, sky and land merging into a viscous mass, rising and falling with the motion of the waves. He turned away from the seething semi-solid ocean, and sailed back to Marseilles.

Where was Thule? The question perplexed the ancient geographers, as they fashioned their fantastical maps—imagining the known world encircled by an impassable river, or crisscrossed by vast belts of water from Pole to Pole and around the equator. There were contenders throughout history—Iceland, Scandinavia, Britain—but the precise location of Thule was never categorically determined. Thule remained a mystery—an island, shrouded in a mist, standing on the edge of a frozen ocean.

Pliny the Elder described Thule as the 'most remote of all those lands recorded,' a place where 'there are no nights at midsummer when the sun is passing through the sign of the Crab, and on the other hand no days at midwinter, indeed some writers think this is the case for periods of six months at a time without a break.' Virgil called it Ultima Thule—farthest Thule—emphasizing its remoteness, its status as the shadowy last country of the northern world. Strabo poured scorn on the idea. Pytheas—a charlatan, wrote Strabo—had made up a load of fiction about the north, and Thule was just one among the mass of lies and fables he had spun. He had said that Thule was six days' sail north of Britain, which was absolutely impossible, Strabo insisted. It was obvious that Britain was the most northerly inhabited land in the world, a place where the inhabitants lived in misery because of the cold. Only Ireland was more miserable, Strabo thought, where everyone lay with their sisters and ate their parents.

With each new discovery in the north the name of Thule was evoked. The Romans reached the north of Britain, and claimed they had conquered Thule. The scholar Procopius thought Thule was in Scandinavia, and wrote garbled anthropologies of the Thulitae, the inhabitants of the vast country of Thule. In search of a retreat, clerics from early medieval Ireland sailed to Iceland—a land they thought was Thule—and brought back stories of a place where hermits clung to sea-lashed rocks, and cried for the forgiveness of their God. The Venerable Bede called Iceland Thule, as did King Alfred of England. The medieval German poem "Meregarto" described Thule as a place where the sun never shone, and the ice became as hard as crystal, so the inhabitants could 'make a fire above it, till the crystal glows.' Petrarch mused on where it might be; the cartographer Mercator fixed Thule at Iceland. Christopher Columbus claimed he had been there, long before he arrived in America. As the lands of the north were mapped—Iceland, Scandinavia, Britain, Greenland, the Baltic coast—the name of Thule was moved around, from Iceland to Norway, from northern Britain to the tip of Greenland. Northerly latitude was enough, a midnight sun and a frozen ocean still more persuasive.

Ultima Thule, distant island, place of dreams, but disconcerting and somehow strange—writers flung the words into their verse and prose, drawing on their resonance. A few scholars tried to find the solution in the meaning of the word "Thule," stacking up their definitions, squabbling about Old Norse and Phoenician meanings. Some said Thule might have come from the Old Norse for frozen earth or tree or from the Old Irish for silent or from the Old Saxon for limit or from the Arabic for far off. But no one could decide for certain; eventually most seemed to agree that the origin of the word was unknown. The spelling of Thule was inconsistent through the ages: Thule, Thulé, Thula, Thyle, Thile, Thila, Tyle, Tila, Tylen and Tilla, among others. Faced with the subject of the pronunciation of Thule, the scholars shrugged their shoulders. Some said 'Toolay,' some said 'Thoolay,' a very few said 'Thool.' Poets rhymed Thule with newly, truly and unruly, but never, it seemed, with drool.

Mist, sea and land, a frozen ocean, a midnight sun in the summer, a twilight sky throughout the winter. Pytheas's account of his journey was lost, and no one could decide where Thule might have been. It left the story of Thule as a glimpse of a distant land. It was an empty page, its silent rocks inviting interpretation. Gradually, through countless verses and learned hypotheses, Thule became a symbol of remoteness, of the shadowy world of the north. Nothing could be known for certain about Thule, and so the word was drawn into imaginative histories, poems, novels and explorers' accounts. It was worshipped and parodied, cited in stanzas and used for rhetorical phrases. Thule was entwined with thousands of years of fantasies about what might lie beyond the edges of the maps. As the maps came to cover the world, Thule was bound up with the crusades of modern exploration.

In the nineteenth and early twentieth centuries, as more and more travellers set off for the remote north, Thule recurred in explorers' accounts: Fridtjof Nansen from Norway, Richard Burton from Britain, Vilhjalmur Stefansson from Canada, Knud Rasmussen from Denmark all sounded the cry Thule, as they travelled across the Arctic. Imaginative explorers filled in the blank moment of arrival with a devout incantation. Where the ice stretched away, and the birds plunged and dived, crying into the cold air, the explorers remembered Thule, pinning the word to the empty wilderness.

I found Thule as a curious footnote, a detail that enticed me. I was working in an office in London, dreaming of escaping the city. The crowds were grinding me down; it was a common complaint, but I found I could hardly board a tube. I had lost the will to push myself forward, and as spring broke across the grey-fronted houses I knew I had to leave. I was not vehemently anti-city; in the evenings when the crowds had become more shambling and slow-paced I liked to wander through the centre, from the South Bank to the City, along the Strand, past the fractured façades of the old buildings. I liked the incongruous noises outside my window in the mornings—a solitary bird trilling like a soloist, above an accompaniment of cars and trains. At weekends I sat in parks, reading the papers, staring at the city shimmering under smog. But I was tired of standing in an endless sea of people. I wanted to walk through empty serenity and hear nothing but the thump of my feet on the rocks.

I knew about the idea of Thule from earlier reading. I remembered it as a plain white place, a land that was startling and strange. But I hadn't known there was a US air base called Thule, and it was this that set me thinking about the far north. Thule Air Base was in northern Greenland, and had been a staging post for nuclear bombers during the Cold War. It was—when I read the article—being upgraded, as part of America's new missile defence system. It had seen off one threat, the threat of war between the USSR and the USA, and now it was part of a new sense of security concerns. Thule Air Base was the most northerly listening post of a vast military empire. A military base called Thule, nuclear bombers in the remote north, military waste spreading across the silent ice. It was a potent idea; it intrigued me as I read. I thought of this camp, at nearly eighty degrees north, in the most northerly land in the world.

It was around that time that I regained an earlier obsession with polar exploration. It was an old interest of mine; I had always enjoyed an Arctic saga, but I began to buy them in bulk. There was something about the starkness of life in the snow, the terrible risks of travelling across ice plains, that seemed to supply a release from the sameness of my days, the relentless round of my hours. Leafing through explorers' accounts, I read about Thule again. The old fantasy of a remote northern land appeared in a book by the Norwegian explorer Fridtjof Nansen, the story of his attempt to reach the North Pole in 1893. As a way to draw the reader in, to emphasize the significance of his journey, its place in polar history, Nansen added Thule to the narrative. For Nansen, Thule meant the grandeur of the ice, the pure beauty of the northern landscape. It was a land obscured by mists, standing somewhere in the northern ocean.

Each day, I took another explorer into the packed carriages, flicking through another attempt to shade in a few more blanks on the maps. My mounting fascination supplied a sense of purpose, something I had lost in my dislocated progress round the city. I thought of plains of ice, snowscapes and glaciers shining under a pale sun. As the crowds swelled into the underground, I thought of emptiness, barren rocks washed by a clear blue sea, the long shanks of ancient mountains. I had travelled and lived in the far north; I knew that the ragged mountains and cold fjords still supplied the consolations of a perfect view, the tranquillity of slowness, and I longed to set out for them.

On this theme of Thule, I started compiling notes, scribbling down quotations as I read through books. A long line of philosophers, poets, advocates and detractors referred fleetingly to Thule, from Boethius to Percy Bysshe Shelley. Mostly they cast it in a cameo, adding the word to a line of their prose or verse, using it to evoke pallor and the north. Alexander Pope wrote a slapstick interlude in "The Dunciad," in which a fire was extinguished with a dank and clammy page of a poem about Thule. Charlotte Brontë put Thule into a gothic scene, as Jane Eyre sits, abandoned by her relatives, dreaming alone on a rain-drenched afternoon. She is reading a book about the Arctic; a reference to the lonely rocks of Thule sets her off into a wild transport, as she conjures the bleak shores of Lapland, Siberia, Spitsbergen, Nova Zembla, Iceland, Greenland, with 'the vast sweep of the Arctic Zone, and those forlorn regions of dreary space,—that reservoir of frost and snow, where firm fields of ice, the accumulation of centuries of winters, glazed in Alpine heights above heights, surround the Pole, and concentre the multiplied rigors of extreme cold.' Thule was the symbol for all of this, Brontë thought, all these dreams of beauty and fears of desolation. From Julius Caesar to Edgar Allan Poe, Thule suggested cold silent plains, the blank spaces of the remote northern lands, awaiting discovery and interpretation. '. . . To the west, to Hesperian darkness, and the shores of barbarian Thule,' wrote William Godwin, in *Caleb Williams*. 'A wild weird clime,' Edgar Allan Poe called it, a land on the way to night, a strange unworldly place.

Thule appeared in fairytales, in children's fables. Through the years, a complete cast of fantasy Thulean inhabitants appeared in verse: there was a 'King of Thule,' a 'Lord Archbishop of Thule' who preached to 'elfin legions,' there were 'children of wild Thule' who lived in the deep caves of the northern sea, and there was the Queen of Bubbles living in her caves on the coast of Thule. Thule came to stand in for anything superlative, any finest example of its type. So e e cummings wrote of the 'Ultima Thule of plumbing,' and Cecil Day Lewis wrote of trains drawing out from a terminus, 'snorting towards an Ultima Thule.' It could be anywhere remote, so Thomas Hardy talked about Thule as the geographical antithesis of London, and Anthony Trollope described Penzance as 'your very Ultima Thule.' By then, Thule was so hoary and established that you could play with it, laugh a little at its antiquity and resonance.

In the twentieth century, Thule told a changing story. For thousands of years, no one had known what lay in the ice around the North Pole. During the twentieth century the most northerly places had been mapped and seen, a slow line of explorers with sledges and planes had arrived onto the ice. Lands draped in shadows for thousands of years had been drawn into the light. Fantasy had been replaced by knowledge. It was a desperate struggle, filled with uncertainty. For generations it was thought that the American Robert Peary had been the first man to reach the North Pole by land, arriving there in 1909. Later, Peary's account was questioned: his skiing was too fast; his diary had perhaps been doctored. In 1926, the Norwegian Roald Amundsen, with his companions Lincoln Ellsworth and Umberto Nobile, flew above the Arctic ice in an airship, dropping flags onto the North Pole. They saw the Pole, but they didn't land on the ice. In 1948, a Russian expedition, led by Alexander Kuznetsov, landed an aircraft and walked the last steps to the North Pole. If Peary's detractors were right, Kuznetsov's team would have been the first to stand at the Pole, fifty years after Nansen had come home. And if Peary had never arrived, it would have been as late as 1969 that the first overland ski and sledge expedition reached the Pole, led by a British explorer, Wally Herbert. It was in the same year that Neil Armstrong walked on the moon. The northerly regions remained distant and inaccessible throughout most of the twentieth century, even as the focus turned to space travel.

Now, you could fly to the North Pole if you had the resources and mass tourism had made incursions into the northern lands. You could take a tour of Greenland and Svalbard, for the pleasures of the white mountains, the Northern Lights or the midnight sun. Wilderness treks set out across the interior of Iceland. Norway was a winter playground, offering dog sledging, reindeer herding, skiing; and in the summer the coast was full of slow-moving ferries, bringing tourists to the north. These mysterious lands, once untouched, then barely known, were now trading on their ancient credentials: their purity, their emptiness, their beauty. There was an industry in Thules—Thule tours, Thule gear, Thule knitwear shops, Thule cruises. Typing in Thule on the Internet released an array of Thule companies touting for trade, offering the sublime experience of northern wilderness. I knew that things were changing in the north. I knew there was a sombre theme in reports from the Arctic—the suggestions of climate change, the glaciers haemorrhaging ice into the fjords, the heat of the sun scalding explorers. The dour predictions hardly stopped the Thule tours; the intimations of pending destruction failed to dampen the longing for empty nature.

Further reading on the subject revealed another strain to the story, another fantasy cast onto the receptive blankness of Thule. In Munich at the end of the First World War, a sinister group met in secret under the name of the Thule Society. Members and guests of the Thule Society had included Adolf Hitler, Rudolf Hess, Alfred Rosenberg and Dietrich Eckart. The uncertain provenance of Thule meant that the word could be used by anyone who found it. It could be tied to any cause, any deranged perspective on the history of the north. For these Germans, Thule suggested the lofty origins of the Germanic race; it was from the mists of Thule that the Germans had come, they thought.

A century of wars and technological revolutions separated my sense of Thule from that of nineteenth-century explorers like Nansen, as they dabbed the word onto the scenery. The former lands of Thule had been invaded by the Germans and the Russians, sparred over in world wars. The ambiguity of the myth had been drawn into interwar hatred and extremism, though Thule was an ancient mystery, thousands of years old, and could never be reduced to a single definition, a single set of ideas. From the age of modern exploration to the contemporary age of mass travel, Thule had lingered on, a potent symbol of empty lands and silence. But what had happened, I started to think, to the idea of remoteness, the sense of magisterial nature embodied in the word "Thule"? In a hundred years explorers had mapped the most remote regions. In a hundred years, it seemed that we had passed from imagining the far north to imagining its future destruction. We had passed from the age of modern exploration—when Fridtjof Nansen, Roald Amundsen and Robert Peary set out for the northern blankness—to the age of scientific warnings about the melting of the polar ice. The subject engrossed me; it kept me in a trance, as the spring sunshine flickered across the London parks and everyone lounged through their lunch hours, reading papers in Soho Square, massing in Hyde Park at the weekends. What had happened in this wild and forceful century to an old idea like Thule? When B-52s flew across the Pole, when nuclear waste rotted in the depths of the Arctic Ocean, what had happened to a dream of a pure place, a place apart from the ambiguities of the world below?

The questions and the northern lands themselves summoned me. Thule was a traveller's account; in its first appearance, Pytheas claimed he had really been there. And though the name became a mystery, it was a mystery intricately entwined with ideas of a particular sort of place, identified in relation to the midnight sun, to the frozen ocean. It was a word suggesting the rocks of the north, whiteness and space. It was a word suggesting innocence, a prelapsarian place. I did a faintly foolish thing. I gave up my job, a job everyone had told me I was lucky to have, and I prepared to travel through the lands that had been named Thule—from Shetland to Iceland, then to Norway, Estonia, Greenland and finally to Spitsbergen.

FORWARD

THE MAN OF BONE CONFIRMS HIS THRONE
IN CAVE WHERE FOSSILS BE
OUTDATING EVERY MUMMY KNOWN,
NOT OLDER CUVIER'S MASTODON,
NOR OLDER MUCH THE SEA:
OLD AS THE GLACIAL PERIOD, HE;
AND CLAIMS HE CALLS TO MIND THE DAY
WHEN THULE'S KING, BY REINDEER DRAWN,
HIS SLEIGH-BELLS JINGLING IN ICY MORN,
SLID CLEAN FROM THE POLE TO THE WETTERHORN
OVER FROZEN WATERS IN MAY!

"THE MAN OF THE CAVE OF ENGIHOUL," HERMAN MELVILLE (1819–1891)

By way of prelude I made a trip to Oslo, to look at Nansen's boat, the
boat he made to sail beyond Thule in. I wanted to start my trail with
him, with his polar ambitions and his sense of the far north. Of all
the polar explorers, he was the most compelling to me. He had lived
through a crux time, when a great surge of explorers was coming
closer and closer to the unknown edges of the globe: the North and
South Poles. Once these points were reached, thousands of years of
fantasy and speculation about what lay at the extremes of the earth
would be replaced by concrete knowledge. Nansen was born in
1861, when Norway was a poor country, its inhabitants struggling to
survive on fishing and farming. Powered from an early age by ravenous ambition, Nansen stared intently out of early photographs, a
man with blond hair and a powerful jaw, tall and strong. He looked

excellent on a horse; he cut a fine figure in a uniform, but was equally suited to the rags and beards of Arctic exploration. He was a neurologist, he was awarded a doctorate; he hunched himself over microscopes in Norwegian research laboratories, but became restless. Yearning for grand vistas, the empty spaces of the north, he set off for Greenland, making the first known crossing of the ice-bound country in 1888. He returned to Norway a national hero, hailed as an explorer in the Viking tradition. In 1889, still short of thirty, he decided he needed another challenge and opted for the North Pole, a place still taunting explorers, lingering out of sight in the shadows beyond the maps. Nansen decided he would build the perfect Arctic boat, and end the ancient argument about the far north.

Writing an account of his journey towards the North Pole, a brilliant and egomaniacal description called *Farthest North*, Nansen reached for a way to attach his expedition to the ancient history of exploration in the far north. He rummaged in his remembered store of tales, and found the old idea of Thule. He used lines from Seneca as the epigraph to the book, creating a symbolic focus for his journey: 'A time will come in later years when the Ocean will unloose the bands of things, when the immeasurable earth will lie open, when seafarers will discover new countries, and Thule will no longer be the extreme point among the islands.' The extract from Seneca's *Medea* hinted at it all, entwining the longings and optimism, the silence of the Arctic night and the terrible beauty of the drifting ice with the old story of the land of Thule. Nansen had been much preoccupied with the deathly kingdom he planned to enter and by the presumptuous nature of his enterprise. By opening his account with Thule he claimed a victory against the old superstitions, the dusty old pile of fantasies about the far north. Thule had been the most northerly place for the early geographers, but Nansen was aiming to clear up the lingering mysteries, and sail even beyond Thule.

The mountains were coated in frosted trees and on the streets of Oslo the snow was stacked up. The tramtracks were slender pencil lines on a white page. The pavements were coated in layers of sludge snow and ice, trampled down during the winter. Everyone shuffled on the ice, a city of people wrapped in winter clothes. Snow fell, white swirls from a blank sky. The mountains loomed into the whiteness. There was a castle, glazed with ice, and a port with boats lined along the quayside, secured by frozen chains. The city was smothered, the noises of the cars softened by the snow; the pedestrians were looking down, heads bowed against the wind, preoccupied with the ice beneath their feet. It was a city concentrating on the mechanics of motion, where everyday activities had become absorbing and difficult. I walked from the central station in a cold wind, wet snow falling onto my clothes, into my eyes and mouth.

I slid away from the city centre, over fields and along summer footpaths transformed into a ridge of packed-up snow. The frozen ground stretched up a hill flanked by ice-trees. A dim sun was drifting towards the horizon. Occasionally I caught a glimpse of the pasty waters of Oslofjord, glinting in the afternoon semi-light. Nansen's beached boat was an hour's walk across the Bygdøy Peninsula, a spit of land curving away from the city. It would have been a gentle stroll in any other weather conditions, but I was wishing I had packed crampons, instead of shabby notebooks that weighed me down. I passed slowly up a hill, breathing in cold air, shuddering into my coat. I walked through streets of perfect wooden houses, with elegant old Norwegians sliding past on their daily circuit; glad of the cold, they skied slowly through the tranquil afternoon. The buildings on Bygdøy were the homes of the affluent and influential: ambassadorial residences with security gates, flying Norwegian flags like recent settlers.

Nansen's boat was kept under a roof—a tight-fitting canopy, built above the masts. When I arrived I saw what looked like an enormous icy tent standing in a car park, with the pallid fjord on the other side. Across the fjord container ships were waiting at Oslo's city harbour, while passenger ferries turned slowly to head for Sweden and the Baltic. The Kontiki Museum, a memorial to the resilience of Thor Heyerdahl, stood next to the icy tent. A few families were walking through the doors.

The white compound housed the low-slung hull of Nansen's boat. Pushing inside, feeling the coldness of the room, I saw a boat with its sides swelling outwards, a creation of curved wooden planks, immaculately painted in red and black. I stared up at the relic, a boat cleared of barnacles and debris, its neatness emphasizing its obsolescence, dried out, never to be launched again. And I thought how Nansen had planned the ship, how he had stalked across its polished boards, galvanizing his crew against the long polar night. He named her *Fram*—meaning 'forward' in Norwegian. It was a challenge—forward into the onslaught of the elements, beyond the land of Thule to somewhere still more distant and strange. *Fram* was fitted for Arctic exploration alone. The tub-shaped hull, the hulking thickness of the sides, had been lovingly crafted by Colin Archer, a Norwegian-Scot, on specific instructions from Nansen. It was the physical weight of the ice that had obstructed previous attempts to reach the Pole, Nansen thought. 'Everywhere the ice has proved an impenetrable barrier, and has stayed the progress of invaders on the threshold of the unknown regions,' Nansen told his audience at the Christiania Geographical Society in 1890. At the time, he had just returned from making the first crossing of the Greenland ice cap, and he was generally regarded as something of an expert on jagged vistas of ice. Despite the overwhelming evidence that it was impossible to reach the Pole by ship, Nansen thought it was worth continuing to try.

Nansen saw the history of Arctic exploration as an epic quest for knowledge. He laced his own exploration with a sense of myth and mystery. 'Unseen and untrodden under their spotless mantle of ice the rigid polar regions slept the profound sleep of death from the earliest dawn of time,' he wrote. 'Wrapped in his white shroud, the mighty giant stretched his clammy ice-limbs abroad, and dreamed his age-long dreams. Ages passed—deep was the silence.

Then, in the dawn of history, far away in the south, the awakening spirit of man reared its head on high and gazed over the earth. To the south it encountered warmth, to the north, cold; and behind the boundaries of the unknown, it placed in imagination the twin kingdoms of consuming heat and of deadly cold.'

He wrote in unapologetically baroque prose, spilling out references, everything wrapped in poetic phrases. 'When our thoughts go back through the ages in a waking dream,' wrote Nansen, 'an endless procession passes before us, like a single mighty epic of the human mind's power of devotion to an idea, right or wrong—a procession of struggling, frost-covered figures in heavy clothes, some erect and powerful, others weak and bent so they can scarcely drag themselves along before the sledges, many of them emaciated and dying of hunger, cold and scurvy; but all looking out before them towards the unknown, beyond the sunset, where the goal of their struggle is to be found.' Ignorant of what they might find, they cast illusions onto the silent ice, patterning the unknown regions with dark fantasies, expectations, dreams of grail treasure.

With this lacy patterning of myth, Nansen had sailed north.

Walking up to the deck I passed through an exhibition of stuffed birds and animals, set against an Arctic stage set—a painted backdrop of craggy Arctic rocks, dotted with pink tundra flowers. A thick sheet of polystyrene represented ice, where a bleached Arctic fox was standing, gazing into space. There was the obligatory polar bear sniffing a path towards a ringed seal. They all stood posed in a parody of motion: paws raised, legs extended. On a fake mountain, balanced on rock ledges, there were fat-bellied kittiwakes, a pair of puffins, an assortment of Brünnich's guillemots, and a scattered collection of little auks. Against another backdrop stood a colony of lost penguins, wings outstretched, standing on a painted plank.

I passed more glass cases, crammed with the flotsam and jetsam of polar exploration—the penknives, matchboxes, violins, dogs' bells, compasses in wooden boxes, the pictures of dour polar explorers staring pensively towards the camera, their features blurred. There were notes scribbled from explorer to explorer, pages torn from diaries, mundane objects rendered interesting by the person who had used them—'Roald Amundsen's teapot,' 'Fridtjof Nansen's cufflinks,' no object too small, no function too insignificant for the glass cases. This museum had its freaks and particular sights: a lock of Nansen's hair 'cut by Mr. J. F. Child at Cape Flora June 1896,' stuck to a piece of card. It seemed to betray a mindset lost to history, the curious world of Mr. Child who, stationed in a frozen Arctic camp, confronted by a renowned explorer, chose to commemorate the meeting by slicing a piece of hair from his visitor and neatly mounting it. There were menus from dinners at 84° N, feastings of cloudberry pie and reindeer steak with coffee and cigarettes to follow. Only lacking were the hypnotic tape recordings of aged explorers, which I had sometimes heard in other Arctic exhibitions, voices repeating themselves on looped tapes: 'Ice, the cold floes, we walked for hours. The ice around us, a strong driving wind. We walked for hours. Ice, the cold floes. . . .' In the *Fram* museum the exhibition was confined to objects, but these were redolent enough—the tattered bits of cloth and leather, the belt buckles, sledges, pipes, tobacco tins, hardened biscuits and skis—like a white-elephant stall selling curios from the tundra.

Hesitantly, I approached the ship. A gangplank led onto the deck, a piece of dark polished wood. There were masts without sails, their booms neatly tied lengthways down the ship, the rigging stretched out to each side. Ropes hung in coils at the base of the masts. A lantern dangled from the front boom. There was a compass in an ornate brass case, mounted on the deck. I stood by the wheel, a wooden piratical object, with 'Fram—Polarskipet'— 'Fram—The Polar Ship'—engraved on it. Everything had been immaculately restored and polished; the ropes hung in meticulous rows, the brass shone brightly. But there was something wretched about the ship. It was made for a purpose never fulfilled: to reach the North Pole. It had done better in the south when Roald Amundsen sailed it down to Antarctica for his successful attempt on the

South Pole, in 1911. Now it sat, neatly trimmed and cleaned, awaiting a re-launch that would never happen, its wide wooden belly
long deprived of the soothing lick of the ocean. Instead, the shaved
planes of its decks supplied a playground for a couple of children,
running free of their parents to fumble with its ropes.

And when the children had been scooped up and taken away, I
walked down the steps to the cabins. The solitary entrance gave me
a bout of the shakes, which might have been caused by the atmos-
pheric sub-zero temperature of the museum, or perhaps the clear
vision of the past, the props without the people, arrayed before me.
There was a dusty old piano ahead, in a communal room, with seats
and tables arranged beside it. And all around were the cabins of the
long-dead crew, with names engraved above their doors. Names
once spoken by awed admirers, now part of polar history: Hassel,
Sverdrup, Wisting, Juell, Nordahl. Some of them went with Nansen
when he tried to reach the North Pole; some of them went with
Roald Amundsen when he sailed *Fram* south. I imagined the creaking of the boards under their feet, as they moved heavily through
the boat—stocky, weather-hardened men, born into Arctic darkness, bred in thick snow and long winters.

Cabin One, on the starboard side, was Nansen's. As I peered
through the glass door, I could see a cramped cell, barely large
enough for a bunk and a chest of drawers. The walls were anachro-
nistically decorated with commemorative plates ('The North Pole
Expedition 1893–6') and tacky souvenir portraits of Nansen and
his crew. A few pieces of woollen clothing had been strewn on the
sofa; two guns leaned against the wall. There was a thermometer, a
map, and a large bronze bust of Nansen perched on the bunk. A
microscope stood on the chest of drawers. Other than that, little remained of the diverse obsessions of the former occupant.

Nansen was a biologist by career, but he dabbled in many of
the Arctic arts, and developed a personal theory of oceanography.
As early as autumn 1884, at the age of twenty-three, Nansen read
an article in the Norwegian newspaper *Morgenblad* which referred

to various pieces of wreckage found on the south-west coast of Greenland. The wreckage was thought to have come from the *Jeannette*, a ship that set out in 1879 under the command of George Washington De Long of the American Navy. De Long thought that if he ran the ship up the Bering Strait he would profit from a warm current along the east coast of Wrangel Land, which might help him towards the North Pole. Whalers had recorded that their ships generally drifted northwards whenever they were set in the ice; De Long set off with this in mind. His ship was trapped in the ice at 71°35' N and 175°6' E. The *Jeannette* drifted in the ice from Wrangel Land to the New Siberian Islands until it was crushed in June 1881, north of the New Siberian Islands, at 77°15' N and 154°59' E.

A few years later, wreckage from the ship had been found off the southern coast of Greenland at Julianehaab; a battered collection of objects including a pair of oilskin breeches belonging to one of the crew and a list of provisions signed by De Long. There were many at the time who thought it was quite impossible that these pieces of explorers' debris should have ended up in Greenland; doubts were raised about the genuineness of the items, accusations of forgery were levelled at the locals. Yet there were others who thought the pieces must have been taken on an ice floe across the Arctic Ocean. Nansen was firmly in this second camp, and, moreover, he thought this ice floe must have passed across the North Pole. Nansen jumped to an optimistic conclusion—if wreckage could drift from the New Siberian Islands to Greenland, then so could a boat.

In February 1890, Nansen stood in front of the Christiania Geographical Society, and proposed that he and his audience might solve the problem of Arctic transport by paying strict attention 'to the actually existent forces of nature and seeking to work *with* them and not *against* them.' De Long had been right, even though his ship had been smashed by the ice.

'The distance from the New Siberian Islands to the eightieth degree of latitude on the coast of Greenland,' Nansen began, 'is 1,360 miles, and the distance from the last-named place to Julianehaab was 1,540 miles, which together makes a distance of 2,900 miles. The floe traversed this distance in 1,100 days.'

He started with numbers, seeking to stress the scientific process, the careful mathematical calculations he had applied to the question.

'It may be assumed then,' Nansen continued, 'that the ice floe travelled at a rate of 2.6 miles per 24 hours. Knowing as we do the speed of the current along the east coast of Greenland, the speed of the wreckage drifting along this coast can be calculated with a certain amount of precision—it would have taken 400 days at least to traverse this distance. So 700 days remain, as the longest time the drifting articles can have taken to travel from the New Siberian Islands to the eightieth degree of latitude. Supposing that the pieces of wreckage on their ice floe or floes went the shortest and most direct route, via the Pole, they would have averaged a speed of 2 miles every 24 hours. But if the floe had taken a less direct route, say, it went, for example, south of Franz Josef Land, and south of Spitsbergen, then the floes must have drifted at a faster rate.'

Spitsbergen—now called Svalbard—is an archipelago of islands, lying in the Barents Sea. If the current flowed south of Spitsbergen, then Nansen would never reach the Pole. It was vitally important that Nansen could establish that those ice floes had drifted north of Spitsbergen. Nansen had a further suggestion. The wreckage was not the only proof. There were the throwing sticks. The Inuit had found throwing sticks on the western coast of Greenland, which must have come from the Alaskan coast. And, added Nansen, there were the trees. The trees clinched the argument. Dead trees that drifted from Norway and Siberia to Greenland. Anomalous trees, *Picea obovata*, Nansen added, flaunting his credentials, the Siberian species of alder and poplar, were frequently found on beaches in Greenland, and used to make boats. There were no such trees in Greenland. It was impossible, Nansen thought, that this driftwood floated south of Franz Josef Land and Spitsbergen. Siberian driftwood was regularly found north of Spitsbergen. All this wood, drifting around in the polar ice, proved categorically that the implacable whiteness of the polar ice was being dragged in turn by its own imperative—the force of a sea current. A current flows from the Siberian Arctic Sea to the east coast of Greenland, Nansen concluded. It flows north of Spitsbergen. It flows, he sincerely hoped, via the North Pole.

It is here that the polished flanks of *Fram* take their part in the story, returned to their original function, not to stand memorialized in a boathouse, surrounded by an assortment of indignant stuffed animals, but to push away the ice, to rise above its clutching tightness. Nansen proposed to build a ship, as small and strong as possible, just big enough to carry coal supplies and provisions for twelve men for five years. The boat would need sloping rounded sides, strong enough to withstand the violent force of the ice. When the ice came to crush the boat, drawing it down under the mounting pressure of frozen water, *Fram*'s curved bathtub of a body would push the ice down, and the ship would rise upwards. Nansen intended to sail up through the Bering Strait and along the north coast of Siberia towards the New Siberian Islands as early in the summer as possible. Then he would head into the ice and moor among the floes. He would let the ice take the ship, and, trapped in the ice, he would drift towards the North Pole.

While formerly the ice had prohibited, now it would facilitate. Nansen's idea was to work with, not against, nature. In defiance of the humanist raging of the likes of John Stuart Mill, the rallying cries against the insensible force and random cruelty of nature, Nansen saw nature as a perfect system. Instead of making significance and order of chaos and emptiness, Nansen accepted the internal rules of the space around the Pole. Imagining the Pole as a sort of compelling whirlpool, drawing everything towards it, Nansen intended to sit in his boat, and wait to arrive. It was exploration through compulsory inertia. Nansen would not set himself apart from the limitless expanse before him, he would seek to become inherent to it—the sea and sky would envelop a small, tub-shaped boat.

The critics bayed, in print and in the learned clubs of international polar exploration. General Adolphus Washington Greely, Sir Francis Leopold McClintock, Sir Allen Young, all distinguished in their fields, were united in their fears that Nansen would perish. They predicted various deaths for the Norwegian: his ship would run aground on lands hidden in the ice around the Pole; he would cut off his escape route and lose his ship to the force of the ice. They conceded that his plan was audacious, it might just work, but the risks were too great. The finest of Victorian exploration briefed against the young Norwegian—as if the nineteenth-century figures in the National Portrait Gallery descended from their frames, to mutter condemnations.

The rotund hull of *Fram* signalled a new approach, which drifted where the Arctic current ran, making a strategy of impotence. It was a broad-hipped boat, with frame timbers made of choice Italian oak. The outside planking, now so scrubbed and sanctified, was an intricate barrier of three layers, the inner one made of oak three inches thick. Outside this, there was another oak layer, four inches thick, and outside this there was the 'ice-skin of greenheart,' wrote Nansen. The aim was to ensure that the ice could claw away all of the ice sheathing, and yet leave the hull untouched. The 'Achilles' heel' of an ice ship, the rudder, was to be built so low down as to be invisible below the waterline, so if a floe collided forcefully with the stern it would shatter against the strong stern part and not hit the rudder itself. *Fram* was fitted out with everything they might need: a well-stocked library—protection against the boredom of the Arctic night—a self-registering aneroid barometer, a self-registering thermometer, a large theodolite, a spectroscope especially adapted for the Northern Lights, an electroscope for measuring the electricity in the air. Sledge dogs from Siberia whined below-decks.

Fram could carry coal for four months' steaming at full speed, but Nansen imagined there would be little cause for steaming. It was the perfect ship to sit and wait in. With this precision, this attention to every detail he could find, Nansen proposed to travel into the unknown regions around the North Pole.

After roaming *Fram* for hours, I began to imagine that I had sailed in it, that I had felt the smash of the ice against its bow, had been thrown from my bunk by the pressure of the bergs. I came to a halt in the communal area, standing by the piano, imagining the festive occasions, the moments of release from the cold business of exploration, with someone pounding the piano while the crew sang. But, there was a small child tugging at the companion ladder, calling for her father, and my head was reeling from the dank below-decks air. Shaking the past from my heels, I clambered up to the deck and crossed the gangplank back to the present.

Fram had drifted perfectly, resisting the force of the ice, but she drifted insufficiently. The moving ice moved too far south, and at 84° N Nansen decided to leave the ship, and head for the Pole by ski and sledge. In mid-March 1895, Nansen set off with another member of his crew, Frederik Hjalmar Johansen, a lieutenant who had been so keen to come on Nansen's ice expedition that he dropped into the only position available—the stoker. *Fram*, trapped in the ice, but defending herself against its clutches, was left in the care of Commander Otto Sverdrup, who had followed Nansen before on the ski-trip across Greenland. Now Sverdrup was left with the crew, looking nervously at the ice stacked around the ship. The first refractions of the sun against the ice were visible as Nansen set off; it would soon return to lurk low in the sky. Nansen and Johansen had sledges and dogs; they wore woollen clothes, camel-hair coats, socks made from sheep's wool and human hair, knickerbockers, 'what is called on board ship an anorak,' wolf-skin gloves, snowshoes and felt hats. They carried a reindeer-skin double sleeping bag, little knowing they would be sleeping in it together for a year, a strong tent made of undressed silk, and a recent innovation in Arctic camping, a Primus stove from Sweden. They each took two double-barrelled guns.

Swift on their skis and extremely fit, Nansen and Johansen were forced to turn back, after only three weeks of struggling through the ice. 'The ice grew worse and worse,' Nansen wrote, 'and we got no way. Ridge after ridge, and nothing but rubble to travel over. We made a start at two o'clock or so this morning, and kept at it as long as we could, lifting the sledges all the time; but it grew too bad at last. I went on a good way ahead on snowshoes, but saw no reasonable prospect of advance, and from the highest hummocks only the same kind of ice was to be seen. It was a veritable chaos of ice-blocks, stretching as far as the horizon. There is not much sense in keeping on longer; we are sacrificing valuable time and doing little.' On 8 April 1895, Nansen decided to give up, and turned southwards. The ice, the barrier he had hoped to surmount by the careful construction of the perfectly passive ship, had defeated his active attempts to move across it. They turned away from the Pole, and moved painfully over the uneven ridges of ice, towards land. They got lost; they spent a winter holed up in a frozen hut, shooting bears to survive. They were bored, frightened at times, when they almost lost their guns in the water, or when a bear crashed towards the hut. After days and nights together, deprived of other company, they ran out of things to say, so they fantasized together about soft clothes, a Turkish bath, cakes, chocolate, bread and potatoes. By July 1896, Nansen was camped on an expanse of permafrosted land—he was not sure where he was. The clouds of mist that had obscured the land the previous day were beginning to lift, when Nansen heard the distant sound of dogs barking. 'It seemed incredible, and yet—out of the shadowland of doubt, certainty was at last beginning to dawn,' he wrote.

Certainty came in the embodied form of a Mr. Frederick Jackson, an Englishman, who was wandering around on Franz Josef Land, an island north-east of Svalbard. This was, Nansen discovered, where he had camped. The two men met. Jackson was a well-dressed Englishman in a checked suit and high rubber water boots, smelling strongly of soap, raising his hat to say 'How do you do?' Nansen was a man dyed black with oil and soot, with a long, shaggy beard, wearing foul-smelling rags and something roughly akin to a hat, but he extended a dirty hand, shaking Jackson's recently scrubbed and perfumed one, soft to the touch. Their conversation was brief, confused at first by Jackson's failure to recognize Nansen. Nansen recorded it in his notes:

> 'I'm immensely glad to see you,' said Jackson.
> 'Thank you, I also,' replied Nansen.
> 'Have you a ship here?' asked Jackson.
> 'No, my ship is not here,' replied Nansen.
> 'How many are there of you?' asked Jackson.
> 'I have one companion at the ice edge,' replied Nansen.
> And then Jackson suddenly stopped talking and looked the oil-stained man in the face.
> 'Aren't you Nansen?' he asked.
> And Nansen answered, 'Yes, I am.'

Seizing the soot-encrusted hand again and shaking it still more vigorously, Jackson said, 'I am very glad to see you!'

A well-washed Stanley to Nansen's blubber-greased Livingstone, Jackson supplied a hut to sleep in, water to bathe in and letters from Norway, which he had taken in case of just such an unlikely meeting. Nansen and Johansen were swiftly released from the elements; their oil and soot encrustations were washed away. 'The troglodyte has vanished,' wrote Nansen, 'and in his place sits a well-favoured, healthy-looking European citizen in a comfortable chair, puffing away at a short pipe or a cigar, and with a book before him.' The dark heart of the Arctic night had been washed from their bodies, Nansen seemed to say; they were reclaimed by civilization. Nansen had tried to harness the power of nature to achieve his ends, but he was forced in the end to admit defeat. 'Nature goes her age-old round impassively; summer changes into winter; spring vanishes away; autumn comes, and finds us still a chaotic whirl of daring projects and shattered hopes,' he wrote. He had managed a distance of 86°13.6' N, the furthest north so far reached by any explorer. He had spent three years of his life in the far north, leaving his wife, his child and his job. He had proved his theory of the drift of the ocean, he had returned without losing a man, but he had failed to reach the North Pole.

For many it would have been a triumph, but Nansen was disappointed, a dark secret disappointment. He continued dining and dancing with the international explorers' set, turning up in British society, later immaculate in ambassadorial robes, charming, a courteous dining companion, an elegant dancer. Internally, he was raging and melancholy, desperate for solitude, fearful of its effects. He was hardly pitiful; he was robust and strong, hailed as a hero by the Norwegians, showered with praise, paraded along the streets of Oslo and invited to lecture the formerly sceptical experts of the London establishment. Yet he was a moody Viking hero, his long moustache dragged down by the turn of his mouth, his fierce blue eyes expressive in later photographs of despair barely contained.

As I walked away from *Fram*, I was thinking again of Nansen's quotation from Seneca. There were hundreds of stirring Thule quotes Nansen could have used. Nansen had used the lines at the start of his account of the journey on *Fram*; he wrote for a captive audience, and his book was an immediate bestseller. The words seemed to spell out a sense of glory. Nansen had been to lands beyond Thule: the barren island he wintered on, a place beyond the earlier limits of the world. He had proved his theory that the Arctic regions would succumb to laws, to scientific calculation. If he hadn't reached the Pole, he had gone further than anyone before him, and he had formed a reasonable idea of a portion of the globe that formerly lay in darkness.

But something in Nansen's fixed stare made me think his Thule quotation might mean something else, something more ambiguous.

There was a chance his quotation from Seneca was more like a personal code, a phrase that was only superficially jubilant. The play the quotation comes from, *Medea*, is a gory sequel to the story of Jason and the Argonauts, showing Jason and Medea at home, after they had eloped when Jason took the Golden Fleece. At the opening of *Medea*, Jason has found that living with a sorceress no longer suits him and is erring towards a dynastic marriage with the daughter of the King of Corinth. The marriage, Jason hopes, will bring him back into the establishment, away from the marginal brutality of Medea, who murdered half of her family to secure their escape. The characters are mostly unsympathetic—Jason is an unappealing hero and Medea is unhinged to a degree notable even in classical tragedy. When Seneca's Medea realizes Jason is about to abandon her, she murders their children and hurls the bodies to him on the street below as she flies away in a chariot.

Interspersed with the bloodbath, a nostalgic Chorus intones about how much simpler it was when everyone stayed at home, happy on their own shores, living to a ripe old age on the fields of their ancestors, knowing only their home soil. No one then, the Chorus says, was able to navigate from the stars, but a time came when sailors began to understand the winds, and could spread their sails or bind them at the top, in order to speed themselves around the world. Jason's ship, the *Argo*, which he took on his Fleece-quest, was one such nature-defying vessel. The *Argo* moved past Scylla, past the tempting songs of the Sirens. Since the *Argo* made this voyage, the Chorus says, things have become easier still, and a great ship like the *Argo* is no longer even required. Sailors are setting off in any ship they can find, wandering at will on the previously mysterious deeps. The Chorus complains that all the boundaries between nations have been removed, cities have set their walls in new lands, and nothing has been left where it previously stood. Everything has been mixed up, joined by the boats crossing the oceans, and 'the Persians quaff the Elbe and the Rhine.'

After these observations, the Chorus presents its prophecy, as

Jason and Medea's marriage spirals into further destruction. The Chorus's moral seems to be that no good comes of hubristic curiosity, from this haphazard mapping of the world. It makes Thule part of a strange premonition: 'A time will come in later years when the Ocean will unloose the bands of things, when the immeasurable earth will lie open, when seafarers will discover new countries, and Thule will no longer be the extreme point among the islands.' Set against the murderous finale of the play, the words suggest that the acquisition of knowledge and the craze for exploration have their dark side. With knowledge comes a terrible loneliness, as humans realize they are alone in the world, alone with their laws and cracked civilization. The last words of the play are Jason's cry after Medea: 'Go on through the lofty spaces of high heaven and bear witness, where thou ridest, that there are no gods.' Jason's triumph over the Ocean ends in a bloody flight from Pelias, and the bloody end of his marriage to Medea. There are no more mysteries, and no more gods in Jason's world, after the Ocean has been crossed.

It was something of this that Nansen, a polymath who would have known the play he quoted, expressed in the Seneca line. Nansen's use of the Seneca quotation could have been a simple rallying cry, a simple expression of optimism—the old mysteries would be outlawed, man would be supreme and lord of all he surveyed and so on. Daring insouciance, absolute confidence— Nansen's party persona. But behind the quote, as under the slick surface of Nansen's charm, lurked something more complex. Nansen asked what progress meant, what this surge of explorers struggling towards the north might mean for the old sense of mystery and wonder.

Standing beneath the boat again, I gazed at the gentle sides of *Fram*. A beautiful bow-legged bison of a boat, she sat squatly, surrounded by the ranks of stuffed animals. In the glass cabinets, the relics gathered dust; the discarded trappings of the early struggle for the North Pole.

Outside, dusk had fallen, a three o'clock dusk spreading darkness over a cold shore. Stumbling across the ice, through the twilight, I cast a glance across the fjord towards the city. The lights of Oslo twinkled blissfully up the mountainside. There were no ferries across the fjord, so I waited for the bus, which rambled through the evening streets back to the National Theatre. The bus passed a statue of Henrik Ibsen, jowly with huge whiskers, staring towards the Storting—the parliament building. The main street, Karl Johans Gate, curved upwards like a ski-jump, flying towards a modest palace. There was an outdoor ice rink, with skaters performing tentative turns, the occasional expert turning centrifugally, arms outstretched, a leg raised. In the shops along the street, people were buying hot dogs spread with luminous sauces, which they were eating with gloved hands. I stepped off the bus and turned the corner towards my hotel on Rosenkrantz Gate, not far from the Grand Hotel, where Ibsen used to dine. One of the many photographs on the walls of *Fram* was of Rosenkrantz Gate in September 1896, decked in flags, thousands of people streaming along the street saluting Nansen and his crew, who had just returned from their voyage. The faces of the celebrants are cast in shadow, but the buildings—large, solid blocks, in white and yellow stone—are gaudy with bunting and flags.

It was a clear, cold night, and the streets were full of shrouded figures, moving along the ice pavements. The bells from the Town Hall clock chimed, atonally. The town spread up the mountainsides, casting a haze of streetlights into the forest. In the hotel I sat in the polished bar, watching a table of Norwegians toast themselves through the evening, huddled round a fire. They had been skiing in the mountains above the city, I heard them saying. Great conditions. Wonderful snow. Their skis were propped by the door, bleeding ice onto the wooden floor.

The barman passed me a glass of aquavit, which I drank slowly,

sitting outside the circle of light from the fire. I found I was thinking about the past, about my childhood fascination with polar explorers, and the simple sense I had of things at the time. As a child
I merely loved the cold; winters were never cold enough, even
when the snows fell and blocked the roads, and there was sledging
on the low hills of Suffolk. Sometimes the river at Flatford was
crusted with ice; the church at East Bergholt surrounded by
whitened graves. When it snowed the morning was muffled, footfalls faded into the whiteness outside, cars slid along the roads. It
was a time when car engines failed in the cold mornings; the rising
street was a chorus of spluttering seventies' cars, struggling to hit
the high note, when the engine would spark to life. A series of em-
physemic coughs came from each drive, with the contrapuntal
sound of rising frustration, keys jangling in the ignition, the slam of
the door. The windows were patterned with hieratic displays of ice,
crystals glistening on the other side of the glass.

These earliest memories were focused around small novelties—
the spectral phenomenon of visible air, as I breathed out on a cold
day, the sharp sensation of chilled oxygen entering my lungs. The
infant games, the fresh snow like a blank page, waiting for the im-
print of child shoes, the crisp whiteness cold and damp in my
hands. In the snow branches were beautiful, like the ghosts of trees,
haunting the edges of the village where the streets became fields.
And there were the long evenings, when I thought the roads looked
like dark rivers, between the shores of streetlights.

When I read stories of polar exploration, I lingered over the descriptions of intense cold; and when my brother and I played at explorers we were always lost in the storm, beaten by frigid winds. To
me, the tales of exploration were more mesmerizing than the fairytales I was supposed to enjoy. Dutifully, with mounting boredom
and confusion, I read through the tales of princesses, princes, the
whole range of fairytale royals, choking on apples, pricking their
fingers, sleeping, waking with dwarfs, generally misbehaving. Dis-
carding the multicoloured child-friendly books, I pored over the

explorers' diaries, the immaculate records of pemmican eaten, pemmican stored, oil cans squandered to the frost, gloves dropped on the snow, never recovered, the sighting of a seal, six o'clock, gun jammed.

It was the chill of the stories that made them appeal to me. I never responded with such excitement to adventures from deserts or lukewarm places. There was something in the stillness of the ice which gripped me, stillness like suspense, an empty stage ready at any moment for the grand entrance of another explorer, struggling against the snow. I liked the shifting illusions of the Arctic—the bergs which hid their depths in the sea, rising like drifting mountains, the crevasses under a thin surface of ice. I memorized lists of countries, lists of explorers: Britain, Norway, Iceland, Greenland, Wilson, Oates, Bowers, Scott, Shackleton, Bjaaland, Johansen, Amundsen. An exotic pantheon, to me. The ships ploughing a furrow through the pallid ocean, towards the great walls of ice. The explorers sounding the refrain—death or glory, a heroic return to a bunting-festooned quayside, or a fading away into the silence of the snow. Some sailed in ships doomed to founder, their wreckage found drifting on floes; men who would become mysteries themselves, never seen again, never heard of. Or years later, a diary would be found at a frozen last camp; they lugged their diaries to the end, recording the dwindling strength of their colleagues—the death of the first officer from a malady which swelled his limbs, the death of the oceanographer who had eaten rotting seal flesh. I imagined these explorers as a series of shadows, stumbling over brilliant white snowfields. Pitching another flag, in the middle of an interminable nowhere, leaving it fluttering against the snow.

The famous names of British exploration went south: Captain Robert Scott, Ernest Shackleton, 'Titus' Oates. Yet I somehow preferred the stories about the north. When, aged eight, I first read about Scott's race with Roald Amundsen for the South Pole, I pitied Oates, who disappeared into the ice, in the howling storm: I pitied them all, Scott and Wilson and Bowers, lying in their tent, the sides lashed by the gales, writing their farewells, struggling to grip their pens. Later, I felt my sympathies sliding towards Amundsen, who packed abundant supplies, and raced on skis towards the South Pole, returning without losing a man. Amundsen was a wiry man with a great beak nose, fascinating and grotesque to a child. He had seemed to me like an exotic creature, found only on crazy polar trips. With slick thrusts of his skis, pushing across the ice, following the dogs dragging sledges, he had made Scott's exhausted labours look like wilful masochism. He had skied to the South Pole, joyfully, brilliantly, with a pack of sliding ace skiers around him. Then, after the thrill of the Antarctic race, he had sailed to the Arctic, and disappeared for seven years, into the ice around the North Pole. It intrigued me that a man could disappear for so long, refusing the applause of the crowds, shrouding himself in the silent ice.

When I first read about the explorers, I knew almost nothing; I relied on imagination to understand their accounts. I accepted their diaries as literary works, creating a world with its own rules. I absorbed the set paragraphs about preparation, fund-raising, skis, sledges, dogs, ponies, tents and supplies of pemmican. I made up polar vistas in the garden: a ragged tent became shelter from an Arctic storm, domestic objects could be transformed entirely. It was a turning-in of the senses, as if sensory signals came most forcefully from the imagination. The idea of the strange, as distinct from the everyday, was unintelligible to me, as a child; the two worlds constantly coincided. There was nothing unusual about my childhood fascination. I recall days with friends, spent in a sort of collective hallucination, entirely absorbed in a polar world we had created. We would imagine we were on a ship in a storm, sitting in a playground with a few swings. Or I would wake in a pensive mood, thinking of snow plains and rocks, and drag my brother into the garden to perform a chaotic series of imaginary expeditions.

There was a formulaic element to the explorers' accounts that made them understandable, and they were written in a simple pared-down prose easy enough for a child to read. Only Nansen was aloof and baffling, a little cranky, given to floating phrases, phrases which took off into something I had no knowledge of at all, references to remote places, to strange people: Pliny, Seneca, Geminus of Rhodes, Pomponius Mela.

But the descriptions of colours, of the myriad colours of the ice, were clear—the pack ice, the play of light against frozen water, the vivid rainbows, the ice crystals shining in the mist, like a halo. Knowing nothing of the places the explorers went to, I responded to the force of their words—to Scott's poetic soliloquy, one man in an icy tent, writing notes with a trembling hand, hoping they might be found later. I responded to Nansen's endlessly floral prose, to Bjaaland's caustic diary entries, to Amundsen's brisk phrases. The explorers did not know exactly what they would find at the extremities of the earth, though there were dozens of theories—from the fashionable to the dismissed—most of them inaccurate. When Nansen sailed it was still a matter of debate whether he would emerge onto ice or land. They saw the world in a different way from us—their maps were incomplete, furnished at their edges with question marks and hypotheses. As I grew up, I wondered what exploration meant at this time, when vast areas were still truly unknown, untouched by humans. It must have been disorienting, I thought, to live in the world when its edges were vague, falling into shadows. When nothing was known, imagination was the only option—and this made the experts like children, creating fictional worlds to compensate for ignorance; lacking experience, they dreamed of what might lie in the silent wastes. The nineteenth-century theories of treasures at the Pole, of an ancient island blanketed with ice and gold, were eventually as discredited as the fantastical outpourings of medieval clerics, or classical geographers who claimed that the far north was inhabited by unipeds and immortals.

NOSTALGIA

FATHOMS DEEP BENEATH THE WAVE
STRINGING BEADS OF GLISTERING PEARL
SINGING THE ACHIEVEMENTS BRAVE
OF MANY AN OLD NORWEGIAN EARL;
DWELLING WHERE THE TEMPEST'S RAVING
FALLS AS LIGHT UPON OUR EAR
AS THE SIGH OF LOVER, CRAVING
PITY FROM HIS LADY DEAR,
CHILDREN OF WILD THULE, WE
FROM THE DEEP CAVES OF THE SEA
AS THE LARK SPRINGS FROM THE LEA
HITHER COME, TO SHARE YOUR GLEE

"SONG OF THE MERMAIDS AND MERMEN," SIR WALTER SCOTT (1771–1832)

In the quiet hotel room in Rosenkrantz Gate, the pallid morning light began to drift across the room. I heard atonal bells striking eight outside. There were soft sounds from the corridors; people were beginning to walk up and down the stairs. As it grew lighter and lighter I flicked through the pages of a tourist magazine. 'Come and see the beautiful Holmenkollen ski jump,' I read, and when I had finished this, I rose and got dressed. I opened the window and peered out, onto the street beneath. The streets were deserted; the city workers had already reached their offices. I leant forward with my elbows on the windowsill. I stared at the sky. It was cloudless; it looked like the day would be fine. The snow lay stacked up in piles on the streets where it had been pushed out of the way of the cars

33

and trams. The snow was muddy, old snow from the winter living on into the spring; it would melt in the next month.

The air was crisp; the sun shone dimly. I walked out onto the streets behind the hotel, away from the centre. I passed through a part of town called Majorstuen and began to stumble slowly uphill. Cyclists slipped along the slope, scuffing their heels on the snow. I moved across the ice, making glacial progress, until I could see the silvery sea below, heavy and becalmed. It was a still day, and the ships were hardly moving at all. I noticed as I walked that there were places where the snow was turning to water and the ice was breaking up. A slight fragrance was rising from the earth, where it had been released from the winter layer of snow: a smell of dust and grass, unfamiliar in the sterile air. Across the fjord, I could see a ferry arriving from Denmark, a huge ship with DANSEBATEN on its side. It sounded its horn.

It took a while to walk up the hill. In the suburbs, the whitewash had made everyone vanish into their houses. A few four-wheel drives ground slowly along the ice roads. I passed through a patch of forest, until I arrived at a main road. I padded on for a few more minutes, and then turned left, sliding across the ice until I reached a row of small brown wooden houses, like chalets. Kicking the snow from my boots, I hammered on the door of one of the houses. There was a movement from within, and then, after a long pause, a wiry, slightly hunched man opened the door. He looked astonished to see me, astonished and not yet delighted.

'Hallo! Are you from the United States?' he asked.

'No, Britain.'

'Britain! Hah! How many of you are there?'

'Just me.'

He peered around me to check.

'You have come up the hill?'

'I walked from Rosenkrantz Gate.'

'Yes, of course. Come in, come in.'

He welcomed me into a small, cold room. Everything was made of polished wood. There was a sofa, with a small cuddly pig sitting on it. A few books lay on a table—William James's *The Varieties of Religious Experience*, Spinoza's *Ethics*, Schopenhauer's *Essays and Aphorisms*. The old man read in English, shoring these fragments against his decline. He had a face of crags and lines, chiselled cheeks and a high brow, a shock of grey hair, and pale blue eyes. He was Arne Naess, the ageing conscience of an oil-rich nation, a philosopher almost as old as the century, born the year after Amundsen arrived at the South Pole. He was a philosopher of the pending eco-apocalypse, sitting it out in a snowfield, waiting for the global thaw, the great change to the climate that would destroy everything. Like an environmentalist Cassandra, he wailed his prophecies to the masses, and they carried on driving around in cars, his government continued exporting rivers of oil. This old philosopher had discerned a threat, stretching as far as the empty lands of the north. The wildernesses stood imperilled. Drastic solutions were required, bold definitions: 'enlightenment,' 'apocalypse'—the big guns of social change. Arne had been living in the mountains, trying out the life of a solitary seer, making his philosophy from scraps of Gandhi—'self-realization' through universal realization, minimalism, self-discipline. But now he lived in the suburbs of the city, at the edge of the forests.

Arne was wiry and strong, despite his ninety years, lively and eloquent, despite the fact he seemed to have forgotten that I was coming. I removed my shoes, which were damp from the snow. He sat down on the long, low sofa, wearing a snug woollen jumper, looking extremely warm. A low flame crackled in the grate. The wood on the walls and floor was immaculately polished. He gestured to me to sit near him.

'This is a beautiful house,' I said, politely.

'Yes, yes, beautiful. But so expensive to have all this polished wood. It cost a lot. My wife did it all. Beautiful though, I agree. You are kind,' he said. And then he looked slightly worried, and said: 'You have something special to talk about?'

There was a note of challenge to his voice. In Norway, Arne was notorious, a national legend. When I said to the hotel manager that

I was going to visit him, he had told me that Arne used to climb up the buildings in the University of Oslo. Students would wait for him in a lecture room, and he would appear through the window. I wanted to ask this old man in the thick jumper if it was true, but something more substantial seemed to be required. He had cocked his head to one side, and his eyes had glazed over entirely; he was staring at a stain on the floor.

I had gone to him to mark the parameters of my enquiry: from the explorers struggling towards the frozen ocean to contemporary concerns about the melting of the ice, the loss of Thule. I was talking about remoteness, the changing sense of the limits of the world, and I said that Thule had once been the last land in the north, a beautiful and forbidding place. A wild place.

He interrupted with sudden enthusiasm, smiling as if I had pleased him.

'Yes!' he said. 'Yes, that's right. I have used the term "free nature"—it's a grey area in a sense. In Europe, we should not talk about wilderness—because we can never have this again. We cannot talk of wild nature. We can have small patches—I call them patches—of nature that is not obviously dominated by human activity. When I was young, in Norway, there was a real big difference there—you could see people on the coast of Norway sitting and looking into the water—there was so much to see, so much to see. And also the experience of water—I had a great time sitting and looking at tiny waves—very big ones also—but tiny waves, just little wrinkles. I walked into the water, I was amazed at all the living beings I could see—but not today. Yes, everything is dead. All the things are contaminated, all spoilt. But when I was a child, it was amazing, I was amazed. For instance, there would be little flatfish; little flatfish would be getting away when I was nearly stepping on them, these little flatfish used to get under here'—and he pointed to the bottom of his foot—'finding it was a nice place to hide.'

The flatfish were quite enchanting him, and his face creased into a smile.

'I found they liked very much that there was some place they could hide, hiding under me, not really understanding what was going on. But anyhow, in my time all children were experiencing the coast of Norway—an enormous coast—standing in water, finding endless interest in the tiny things of nature—and they got a firm . . . what do you call . . . love of nature.'

There was a pause. He stared at the floor again.

'So you feel everything has changed?' I asked.

'Yes,' he said, firmly. 'And when we ask will things ever be like that again in the future, so far as I can see it will be very different—and it will take a long time, a very long time, before our nature gets back to this wildness, but it was marvellous and it was one of the pillars of the Norwegian sense of nature—these things that we were experiencing, in the water. Because it seems that we have a special relationship to nature in Norway—even in Sweden, it's not even the same in Sweden—there is something, something there. And so many Norwegians when they are . . . what is the word . . . wanting to commit suicide—I call it voluntary limitation of life—then they go into nature, and they die. Strange, isn't it?'

Arne was in mourning for the lost past, the pure past of his country, when the landscape was pristine, he said. In the century Arne had lived through, the remote north had become accessible by plane, by icebreaker. But Arne thought something had happened to the lands closer to home, even to the fjords of Norway, to the empty places of Europe. Even here the century had shifted the scenery, he was saying. There was a pause, and then he said: 'For many many hundreds of years in Norway you didn't have neighbours, there were no neighbours, because there were quite big distances between people—so they had either to find themselves lonely or to relate more personally to the nature around them. Otherwise they would be very lonely, thinking, "Oh my God we are so lonely."' And he laughed quietly.

'But, they didn't feel lonely, because they had this personal intimate relation to nature. Now people have for the last fifty years or more, more and more gone into cities, and there are very few, mostly old people, who are living out in the rural areas, mostly old people. I am sorry for that, of course,' and he shook his head. 'Really,' he said, 'it is OK that they get neighbours, but they should continue to have this very personal relationship to nature.' He nodded slowly. He seemed to be thinking.

By Arne's standards, Nansen lived in benighted immaturity, seeking to claw a path across the indifferent wilderness, to perch his flag on a piece of ice. But Nansen also lived in the golden age that Arne was mourning, 'when we had so much light, you could see the stars, and children were there under the heaven of stars. You didn't get smaller, by that, you got greater by that, by being together with the stars—you were greater by being together with the stars.'

'So have people lost this experience?' I was asking.

Arne never answered a question directly. It made him slightly gnomic, with his head cocked to one side and a slight smile curling his lips.

'I want to tell you about mountains,' he said. 'I have seen a lot of mountains. In the mountains you have a basic sense of upward, ascent. And this is positive,' he was adding. '"Ascent" is a positive word. Up and up. A great increase. And so on. So you have feelings there which are satisfied without you knowing it. You see, there is the sky. The bigness of mountains, that's one thing, and then you have the greatness. There are some mountains in western Norway which are just as great as Mount Everest. But they are not so big, but that is not the essence of mountains, it's not the bigness, it's the up, the getting higher, and the broadening of the outlook, seeing vast areas.'

When this wizened philosopher could still climb, he refused to reach the tops of mountains, renouncing the quest for domination over the natural world, he claimed. A sense of the smallness of the self, the vastness of nature, he seemed to be saying, was somehow revitalizing, a healthy experience to have from time to time. Arne thought that the only goal of his submission was to find unity with nature, and he started to tell a story about when he climbed a series of peaks, across the Mediterranean.

'I started getting to the summit of each mountain, but after about thirty summits, I could go just because of the beauty and the greatness. And even though the summit was only ten metres from me, I would not take those ten metres, to include that summit also in my list of summits. I would just go where it was great to go. I was getting more mature. Going for days and days and days, I got more mature. What is really here? What's the greatness, what's the greatness? What's the greatness in my experience of these mountains? And then of course the summits were not counted any longer, at all.'

Arne was winding up, his words no longer falling into sentences, instead he was sounding a little like a hippie Beckett— 'When you have something like this, you know this is—I will be in this, yes I am at this moment, no more, you are—what I do now— breathing deeply, breathing deeply, and feel this different relation to time; something gets away from you—time-bound no longer—it's just timelessness. You get a little feeling of timelessness. Slower, slower, take time, take time.' Like Krapp's last tape, he was concluding, a tone of determined finality to his voice.

'I invite people to be more aware of the sense of timelessness,' he said. Then he stopped talking, and smiled at me.

It seemed to be a hint that I should disappear, and I stood up. 'And now we must hug,' he said. 'For three seconds only. To fully engage with each other.'

He put his arms around me, and counted to three loudly. Then I was moved quickly onto the steps of the house. He smiled, and waved, his wave like a child's, emphatic and staged. Then he shut the door.

There will come a time, Nansen had thought, when the goal that was the Arctic wilderness will have been explored, and there will be nothing left to find. But our longing for a simple life will be unsatisfied; we will continue to search for silent places. Even as everyone set off on their wilderness holidays, Arne and the prophets were telling them it was doomed. Wherever they went, they would find traces of humanity and signs of future destruction.

It made for a forbidding doctrine. It was nostalgic; it preferred things as they were a hundred years ago. Nansen had seen the beginning of the descent, Arne was saying; nature was now measurable, the furthest north was barren and hostile but somehow less mysterious. But there was a guarded optimism to Arne's talk. He refused to believe it was over; he shied away from sounding the final mournful chord. Even as he talked of a wake for the wilderness, Arne was preaching the consolations of emptiness. He couldn't let go of the dream of Thule, even as he said the northern wilderness was endangered.

I walked along the snow-mountain, with the lights of the city like distant fires lining the fjord. The trees were hissing and the wind felt harsher than before. The sun was sinking towards the horizon. The snow coated my feet, and the darkness in the forest made me hurry towards the incandescent platform. I stumbled under the bridge, running to beat the sunset, as the air grew colder.

Because I grew up in the countryside, in a verdant part of Britain, my early memories were entwined with the seasonal change of the fields, the fires which purged them after the harvest, the smoke lingering along the streets, the sound of tractors sowing new seeds, the corn turning golden and then being harvested. Before I understood anything about time, I was aware that things recurred, that there was a pace to nature, a particular sort of process, immutable, reassuring in its regularity. I knew that as leaves fell from the trees combine harvesters would churn through the fields; I knew that an acrid taste in the morning meant that winter was coming. The cornfields were at the end of my street; it was a walk of a few minutes to the first line of trees, with the fields stretching beyond, immense to a child. There was a dust track through the fields called the Donkey Track, with a stream running alongside, and I used to run along there with friends, dimly aware of the colours of the crops, the foliage of the hedgerows, the sound of the birds. We made dens in the streams, piling up hay to dam the water; rummaging around by the sides of the streams we would find field mice, quantities of baby rabbits, curled in small huddles. Because I was young, it seems when I remember that the skies were a particularly brilliant shade of blue, the summers particularly hot, the evenings particularly long, the shadows still lengthening along the garden when I was summoned to bed, my bedroom a dim orange as I put my head under the pillows to sleep.

My village was hardly a rustic idyll. It was more of a rustic commuter belt, a strip of suburbia disguised as villages and fields. The village feigned pastoral autonomy; there was a commune, which grew vegetables, and every year an Albion Fayre was set up on the fields around the village—stalls selling rosehip wine and home-baked cakes, to the soundtrack of Steeleye Span. People had boats on trailers parked in their drives through the winter, which they towed away to marinas for the summer. The daily momentum went towards London; each morning people stepped into their cars and commuted away, down the A12, arriving in the evening again. It was a compromise, too subtle for a child to understand. I saw only the winding lanes and the green banks of trees, the yellow ripeness of the corn, the blueness of the sky against the vivid fields. I knew nothing about the commuting files to London, cars moving bumper to bumper, hold-ups and jams, the tailbacks from Kelvedon to Capel St. Mary. I walked with my grandmother around the village as she pointed out the flowers in the hedgerows and made me listen to the different songs of birds.

I can't remember when I first understood that there were worlds outside my village, places which moved to a pace of their own, irrespective of the seasons. My other set of grandparents lived on the Wirral, which supplied a holiday experience of somewhere else. These grandparents lived on a street opposite a bank of factories, in an interwar house. I remember staring through my grandparents' kitchen window at a line of railings separating their road from the factory grounds. A broken umbrella had been hung on the railings, like a black rook, fluttering in the wind and the rain. The wind had blown piles of litter against the railings: cigarette packets with their shiny foil papers, crisp packets softened by rain, and lines of cans and bottles. My grandmother and I would sometimes take the bus into Birkenhead, sitting on the top floor staring at the traffic. There were days when we took the ferry to Liverpool, watching the churning wake and the gulls behind the boat. Liverpool would appear ahead, and I remember my grandparents telling me about the Liver Birds looking across the city, turned green by the weather.

I associated the Wirral with my grandparents specifically, as if it was their land, a land run under their rules, as distinct from those of my parents. This was why the houses were grey, and the umbrella rook hung from the railings, and why the factory had a gas container, shaped like an immense golf ball, which my grandfather said would take the whole of Merseyside with it should it ever explode. When I saw the golf ball, and the corrugated iron of the factory buildings, I knew I was near my grandparents' house, and these decaying pieces of industrialism became a part of their world, serving only as signposts to their home, the final stage of a long journey. Everything in their house was novel: the shape and feel of the beds, the creak of the stairs, the smell of dust on the bars of the electric fire, the cupboard under the stairs, where my grandfather kept a World War Two flying suit. The cigarette lighter hidden under a model of Dick Turpin. The tins of barley sugars and mint imperials. The miniature forklift truck on a stand, which had been presented to my grandfather when he retired. The garage with the trapdoor, which opened onto steps going down to a shelter they had built during the war, tunnelled out under the garden. The urban environment was the exotic landscape of my grandparents' lives, and of my mother's past.

When I was ten, my parents moved to the Midlands, to a market town near Nottingham. It was the first time I remember disliking the view around me, noticing its plainness. The lines of interwar housing seemed limitless—buildings with ugly brick archways, hedges pruned into shapes, ornamental jugs and stools. The houses were crushed together, separated by brutal little walls, overgrown fir trees which looked like the fringes of graveyards. The surrounding countryside was undulating and forested, but I was too young to know what lay beyond the grey streets of our part of town. There was something tacky and bland about our house; the ceiling of my bedroom was covered with polystyrene, occasionally chunks would fall onto my bed, and I would cut them into shapes, the roof of the living room was flat, and fell to pieces one day. The garden was organized in neat rows, a fifties' patio, rows of rhubarb plants, apple trees. I survived the transition, writing it out in a diary, quietly defiant: It is A.W.F.U.L., I wrote, a dozen times, across an entire day. The woods were too far away and I was never allowed to walk there. The only area worth spending time in, I had decided, was a field behind our house, a patch of grass which my brother and I shared with football teams on Saturdays, burly blokes shouting as they churned into the mud, sparse crowds cheering from the sidelines. One night, after staying for dinner at a friend's house, I took a shortcut across the field, back to my parents' house. The field was dark, muddy and uneven underfoot, and the stars were vivid in the sky. I stood for a while in the centre, furthest from the patches of light, looking at the shadows of the darkened grass, the ditches appearing as chasms in the darkness, the trees rustling gently. I was intrigued by the unfamiliar look of the field, the empty darkness, the quietness of the evening.

Because I never lived in the countryside again, I retained an image of the small Suffolk village, decked in the rich remembered colours of childhood, with the endlessly running soundtrack of the birdsong at dawn, the whirring of farmyard machinery. These memories were inevitably mingled with nostalgia, for the vivid sensations of early childhood, the blueness of the sky, bright yellow cornfields, the dim twilight of the winter evenings, when the streetlights became pale red at three in the afternoon. I idealized my childhood in the countryside, imagining it like a secret garden, remaining beautifully tended, should I ever return. In childhood, in the countryside, I had been free. At midnight when the house was quiet, I often thought of the village as I remembered it, the languid pace of the evenings, the slow rising of the sun across the fields.

United Kingdom and
the Shetland Isles

SHETLAND
ISLANDS

ORKNEY
ISLANDS

*Atlantic
Ocean*

SCOTLAND

• Aberdeen

*North
Sea*

Edinburgh •

NORTHERN
IRELAND
Belfast

*Irish
Sea*

York •

IRELAND

Dublin •

WALES

ENGLAND

Cardiff

Oxford •

London •

FRANCE

| 0 | 50 | 100 miles |
| 0 | 50 | 100 | 150 km |

THE UNCANNY

～∞∞～

And when the Morn shall spread with dawning Day
Her purple Loom, and shoot her early ray,
You'll Thule and th'Orcadian Isles descry
Which scatter'd o'er the Ocean's bosom lie.

"King Arthur," Sir Richard Blackmore (1650–1729)

I flew back to London, and the next morning I was on the way to Scotland. Even at the time Nansen sailed north, even in Arne's Golden Age, there was a holiday industry in remote and empty Thules. The British travellers of the nineteenth century worked their way along the British coast, heading first for Shetland, a former Thule, and then onwards to Iceland, another former Thule. There were fleets of tourist ships ploughing through the seas towards the north, taking their occupants away from their more cluttered countries. London lay under a thick coating of coal pollution, but the northern lands were pristine retreats for the city-sore. Richard Burton, British explorer, translator of the *Arabian Nights*, sailed along the British coast in 1872, carrying the idea of Thule like hand luggage. In the 1870s, William Morris—Socialist reformer and designer of tasteful patterns, who loved the Sagas— took the same route to the north. Anthony Trollope, author of baroque yarns, had sailed in a society horde, keeping to the main sights.

They were serious men, their beards spilling over their smart jackets, who all left England between 1870 and 1900, sounding the Thulian mantra, beguiled by the early stories of the far north. For

45

them, even then, Thule was a metaphor for a receding world—an innocent world, where nature was unadulterated by human inventions, by the cranking pistons of industrialism. Everything was being dragged into the light, as technology moved relentlessly towards a world of rules and visible processes. But Thule remained—a place where the brute forces of the natural world were so unbridled that they threw up wild entertainments, inexplicable and extraordinary.

And the journey to Thule was a next-best to the Pole for Victorian women like Mrs. Alec Tweedie. Mrs. Alec Tweedie, sometimes known as Ethel, was a second string on the polar stage. She had a fashionable list of explorer friends, Nansen among them, and she waved off Frederick Jackson from Cannon Street Station, when he set off for the North Pole in 1894. Jackson was even carrying a letter when he met Nansen, from Mrs. Alec Tweedie, addressed in waggish style to Dr. Fridtjof Nansen at the North Pole. Mrs. Alec Tweedie had waited for Nansen, looking forward to waltzing around ballrooms in London with the triumphant explorer, as he had promised. Tweedie's Ultima Thule, Burton's Ultima Thule, was a holiday in emptiness for the Victorians, the northern lands a playground for summer trippers in crinolines and smart collars. 'The next best thing to being at the North Pole itself, and far more comfortable!' wrote Mrs. Tweedie, like a brochure. The Victorians in search of something a little extraordinary set off on steamships, preparing themselves for the discomfort of the crossing, the surliness of the ocean, and the inevitable bouts of seasickness. It was voyage enough for the Victorian afflicted with the nature craze, accessible for society types, in search of a retreat from their satin shoes and their long white gloves.

Everything was processed through a wild chorus of hyperbole, every detail of the voyage laced with myth and interest. Feeling the epic past, the Victorians made much of the journey up the coast of Britain, even though they travelled along a tourist trail. They took steamers from Edinburgh. Edina, Dun-Edin, Quebec of the Old World, the Grand Chartreuse of Presbyterianism, Modern Athens they cried, passing out of the port. Adieu, O Edinburgh! they sighed, looking out towards the ocean, the ocean wearing an azure and gold robe, they wrote. Smoke was rising from the many steamers ploughing a path through the sea; smoke was forming a thin canopy, drifting across the pale blue waters. Their steamships were crowded, carrying dozens in a state of misery, making slow progress through the waves. The passengers complained bitterly, finding that their ships had no bath and the food was greasy—and they listed it all, writing it all out in their immaculate diaries: giant tureens of oleaginous soup, fish which could not be kept quite fresh, and chunks of greasy meat. Like an explorer, checking supplies, Mrs. Alec Tweedie provided a list of the clothing required for the journey: a thick serge dress, short and plain for rough wear, with a cloth one as a spare; a tight-fitting thick jacket, good mackintosh, and very warm fur cloak; one pair of high mackintosh riding boots (like fishermen's waders), necessary for crossing rivers and streams; a yachting cap or small tight-fitting hat, with a projecting peak to protect the eyes from the glare; blue glasses, a great comfort; and thick gauntlet gloves.

The steamships passed along the Scottish coast, the passengers were hypnotized by the sea, feeling slightly sick and apprehensive about the crossing. They steamed past Fifeness, past the fjord-like gaps in the cliffs, past a coast fretted into shallow bays, fronted by stunted sandy beaches and vistas of yellow shingle. They stood on deck, listening to the wheezing of the wind. There were ruin-shaped rocks of brown sandstone streaked with white layers of guano. Daylight blazed until 10 P.M., the smoke from the chimneys of the boat obscured the view, and they lost the outlines of the rocks. They stood in the raw and rainy morning, looking at the steep and frowning headlands. They passed the edge of Scotland, admiring the grand profile of the cliffs, their sides streaked by golden sunshine. When the weather was warm they sat on deck watching the sea; when the winds grew stronger they became squeamish and lay below-decks, prostrate but resigned. In the nights they took chlorodyne and tried to sleep, but the lurch of the ship made them nervous; they thought it was about to sink, they lay awake smelling the sweet smell of the bilge water.

They stopped at Kirkwall on Mainland, the largest island of the Orkneys. They visited a curious small museum, where there were exhibits of natural stone knives, specimens of pots, a two-handed scraper of whale's bone, and a human skull with four rabbit teeth. They admired the old cathedral, staring up at the rude and ponderous Norman-Gothic, the red sandstone mixed with whitey-grey *calcaires*. One of the finest remains of Catholicism in the north, they wrote, unduly neglected by strangers. Then they returned to their boats, and prepared to sail further north.

I took the ferry from Aberdeen to Lerwick, on Shetland. Like a belated hanger-on, unpunctual by more than a century, I sat in the bar listening to the grinding of the ferry as it prepared to leave Aberdeen, as the bloated gulls circled above the decks. These ferries are even less picturesque than the crowded Victorian steamships. Mostly empty, at the time I sailed. Rows of quiet corridors, silence slung like a winter canopy across the ship. I was meant to be sharing a cabin, but no one arrived to claim the other beds. I wandered along the deck. A few tourists with video cameras were filming the wash of the wake behind the ship. I heard the sound of laughter, distant on the wind. I sat at the bow, feeling the lunge of the boat, watching the sea. The ship was called the *Hrossey*, the Norse name for Orkney, and it was a lumbering ferry, licensed to carry hundreds in neat cabins, licensed to serve them champagne over dinner in the luxury restaurant, to wash down the salmon steaks. The scattered passengers were those who had chosen not to fly, taking the slow route across the sea. They were travelling on weekend breaks to the austere beauty of Shetland, lugging cameras and binoculars. The church spires and grey terraces receded; the ferry passed through a narrow stretch of water and moved along the wreckage of the docks. The ship moved out into the northern ocean.

In the chiaroscuro hours, a fog swept across the sea, and coiled around the boat. The horizon disappeared into the matted whiteness. The waves were full-bodied, crested with white flecks. But the mist made them monochrome; the whiteness fell on the waves, blurring the distinctions between sea and sky. The ship moved slowly through the swirling fog, juddering to a halt in the harbour of Kirkwall, the town a string of lights, dim in the mist, with the greyness of the fog mingling with the dark blue of nightfall. The night was thick and damp; the mist sank onto the deck of the ship. I watched the deckhands uncoiling the ropes, sliding them onto the quayside. The cars drove off in a long line, their wheels bouncing over the ramps. There was a pause while the cars disappeared into the mist, and the water churned around the ship. Soft sounds came from the quayside, subdued motion, dulled in the whiteness. The engines began to rise in pitch, the walls juddered, and the ship moved out again into the mist-ocean. The lights of Kirkwall faded into the darkness.

The Victorian steamships made a detour to Shetland, so their passengers could see the peat island, the cliffs blasted by gales. There was a possibility that Shetland was the island Pytheas found, when he sailed north from Britain in the fourth century B.C. and brought back the name Thule. A Greek ship might have found the crossing to Shetland arduous, and the mists sweeping across the ocean might have made Pytheas think the sluggish tides had congealed. It was unlikely, because Pytheas seemed to have mentioned a frozen ocean and the midnight sun, attributes not readily available in Shetland, but if you were really determined that Shetland was Thule you could argue that Pytheas had only heard about these aspects and had added them to his story of Thule, spicing up a trip to a rocky archipelago with bizarre elements. More certainly, northern Britain had been Thule to the Romans, when they moved around Britain after the invasion of Caesar in 55 B.C. Tacitus, writing in the first century A.D., seemed to have named Shetland Thule, or somewhere like Shetland. The conquest of the last land of the world was the culminating triumph of Caesar's reign, wrote Florus: 'Having traversed all land and seas, Caesar faced Ocean and, as if the Roman world were no longer enough, contemplated another.' In a satire, Juvenal scoffed at it all, at the relentless marching towards the barren wastes of the north, and at the attempts to Romanize the natives, suggesting that the Britons were beginning to learn eloquence, and even Thule was thinking of hiring a rhetorician. The conquest of Britain was a triumph, the poets agreed, but it brought the Romans to a gruesome place, where the terrible tribes of Britons lived.

The ship moved slowly through the matted whiteness of the North Sea, which the Romans had called Ocean, after the mythical Ocean of the Greeks. The briny sea, the resistant waves, convinced them they had found Thule, when they arrived in Britain. It was near Thule, they thought, that Pytheas saw the sea congeal, and become a thick paste. There was a poem by Pedo—a man admired by Seneca—which described the sinking of the Roman Germanicus's fleet in the North Sea, a fleet that had dared to pass through the shadows towards the final shores of the world. The fleet had been destroyed, Pedo thought, by the force of Ocean, a sea scattered with sea beasts. Tacitus agreed: Germanicus had succumbed to Ocean, a sea so wide and deep that it was thought to be the final one, unbounded by land.

On the maps of the Ancient Greeks the inhabited world was drawn in the shape of a dinner plate, surrounded by water. An idea more ancient than Thule, Ocean surrounded the known world. Beyond Ocean, the Hesperides, the progeny of Dark Night, tended the golden apples, and their trees. Ocean spilled out off-spring, beginnings and ends; it was the origin of life and the nothingness surrounding the boundaries of the known world, the creating force and the void. A people called the Cimmerians lived a miserable life on the shores of the deep and endless stream of Ocean, near the entrance to the Underworld, their city covered with mist and cloud, constantly under dismal night. One of Ocean's daughters was Styx, the river the dead crossed to reach Hades; Ocean was a force of nature incorporating foul decay and blackness, as well as generation and lightness. In the *Odyssey*, the path to Hades went through Ocean, to a narrow strand where there were tall black poplars and willows with wasted fruit on their branches.

Even after Pythagoras proposed that the earth must be a sphere, the idea of the gaping emptiness of Ocean was not dispelled. Water was a powerful and prohibiting element to the Greeks; they devised maps depicting a vast sea crossing the world like a belt, running through both the Poles, and another belt of water round the earth between the tropics. But there were Greeks, like the early historian Herodotus, who denied the existence of Ocean altogether. Herodotus thought Homer or some earlier poet had invented the name Ocean. It was absurd, he wrote, that the mapmakers added a fiction to their maps, showing Ocean running like a river round a perfectly circular earth.

The Romans believed that nothing could be beyond the reach of their empire, even the strange land of Thule. It was inter-civilizational one-upmanship, thinking they had outdone the Greeks by solving the mystery of Thule. But the Romans stopped too soon, at the first remote land they found in the torpid ocean. As the Victorians sailed through the stormy northern ocean, Shetland seemed too far south to be Thule. It was too much like home for the Victorians, who were sailing north in search of the *unheimlich*—the German word which means uncanny but which contains within it the sense that the uncanny is anything 'unhomelike,' anything unfamiliar. Shetland was a beautiful island of cliffs and peat scapes, but the Victorians found it insufficiently strange to be Thule. They were brutal where Thule was concerned, refusing to let national sentiment intervene in a myth trail. But they were thorough, so they enjoyed the detour, as a nod to former empires.

They arrived in Lerwick, the main town on Shetland; they walked dutifully around the port, looking at the houses with crow-stepped gables. They made careful notes in their diaries. The bogs stretched across the low hills; the snowy quartz-veined rocks shone against the yellow fields of oats and barley. There were willows and maple planes, hanging their shade over the broken ruins of cottages. There were ducks and geese everywhere, gulls more numerous than the cocks and hens, and salt-fish lying piled on the sands. The industrious women crowded the markets, some carrying crates of peat, some spinning yarn and knitting stockings.

I arrived in Lerwick under a cold sky, the wind blasting through the sallow streets. The town was a series of stone houses, a main street and a road snaking towards the harbour, where the sea splashed against the docks. Beyond the outskirts stood the dark green cliffs, and the long valleys stretching inland. The mist hovered low on the rocks around the town, on the matted grass hills, breathing across the plains. There was an old fort at the end of the main street, with a set of cannons pointing out to sea, pointing towards the passenger ferry I had arrived on, still looming above the buildings, waiting to leave. The wind whipped in from the sea, racing between the buildings, ripping at the awnings on the boats in the harbour. A gaff-rigged boat moved past, its sails stretched by the wind.

There was a bar called Thule by the quayside, which looked like an extension to a prison, its exterior dank and salt-stained. It sat on the harbour road, a torn notice taped to the window, addressed to Norwegian sailors. VELKOMMEN TIL THULE! the notice read. Welcome to Thule. An ancient land, and now a bar, far more convenient for the weary sailor recently arrived on a ship from Norway. Inside were chrome walls and stools, in Scando-minimalist design. A Nordic home-from-home. Hammering on the window, I persuaded the barman to open the door, and asked him why the bar was named Thule. He propped himself up against the frame, looking tired. Perhaps it was too early in the morning, perhaps the wind was whipping my words away, but he was reluctant to talk. 'Don't ask me, I just work here,' he said.

He was a strawberry blond, pulling on a jumper as he stood in the doorway, squinting in the cold light. The skin around his eyes creased into intricate lines as he spoke. He grimaced at the wind, which gusted against the door, almost slamming him back inside. I raised my voice, as the wind became a howl echoing around the quayside buildings. 'What do you think?' I tried to shout. 'Do you think Shetland was Thule?'

He shrugged again. 'I really couldn't say,' he replied, his face blank. And then, more hospitably, 'Come back later, you'll see a real old get-together.' And he waved me back into the wind.

In a chorus, Greek in its fatalism, the locals I spoke to mourned the recent refurbishment of Thule, the turning of everything to chrome. The Thule Bar had once been a place of character, they said, where you might have bumped into a business lunch, a drunks' party, and a wedding reception, all on the same day. But in the evening the bar was always full, the chrome walls slick with sweat, and the shining floor sticky with beer.

The morning was cold and gaunt and the streets were jaundiced, stained by the pale sun. I lingered under the grey terraces, as the gulls circled and the rain slammed onto the slate. At noon the ferry moved slowly out of the port. The streets grew busy, and I walked past the Crystal Shop, the Harbour Café, with its stream of damp sailors waiting at the window for chips, the shop selling Shetland knitwear, which was also called Thule. Thule was having a quiet time of it in Shetland—the people I asked were polite but baffled, as anyone might be, stopped by a stranger on a windy street, and asked about a land called Thule. Thule was elusive, even in a former Thule, and the people of Lerwick weren't setting too much store by it.

But they lived on a quiet island, a ragged and wild island, a place where winds gusted across the harbours and battered the buildings. It was a land of moss plains, peat stretches and bright green islands lapped by sea froth. A place of gashed mountains, inky tarns and streams. The rain drew a rich smell of peat from the drenched valleys. A short walk out of Lerwick, I found a deserted coastal path winding across slippery stones, from where I watched the surge of waves across the beach. My only company was a shy cat stalking along the path, which squeezed under a fence and disappeared. As the day drew on, the sun grew stronger in the sky, drying the sides of the houses, gleaming on the rocks.

Shetland was a place where the peat plains had preserved traces of the distant past, the shapes of houses and forts embedded in the soft ranges. At the edge of Lerwick, beyond the grey pebbledash buildings and the painted wooden housing estates, there was the Loch of Clickhimin and a low knoll. On the knoll were stone ruins, older than the Roman tales of Thule, older than Pytheas's first sighting of the mystery island in the north. The first settlers came to Shetland thousands of years before the Roman invasion of Britain. Long before Pytheas sailed, these settlers came from Orkney in skin-covered open boats, across the blistered sea. Remains were found near Sumburgh, in the south: smashed bones and fragments, hammerstones and beads.

These settlers lived quietly in small stone houses, growing grain, fishing, tending cattle, leaving their litter across the peat plains—their ploughshares, discs and stone balls, pendants, pins, rings in bronze, glass beads, bone pins and antler neck-

laces. They left ruins scattered across the land, the cracked remnants of their houses, preserved in the spangled cotton-grass and
the low plains of moss. There was one wall at Clickhimin,
sunken in the earth, and the circular walls of a stone tower, built
around the time the Romans came to Britain. The stone tower
had supplied protection against enemies, but no trace remained
of the reasons for their wars. Grass had grown around the rim of
the tower; the roof lay open to the sky. For millennia, these
brochs stood, scattered along the coasts, turrets on wind-lashed
islands. Looking out at the sea or across the hills and bogs gashed
with deep earth cracks.

Stones lay littered across the fields: low walls that were once
houses, built thousands of years ago, overgrown with moss. Driving through soft valleys, where the sun chased the shadows across
the hills, I found a gate singing in the wind, and an oval-shaped
ruin a few feet high, which might have been a temple, or a village
hall, or a burial chamber. To the eerie song of the gate, I stood at
the edge of the building, finding I was reluctant to walk inside.
The external outline was almost complete, the shape of the building preserved in the ruined walls. All the forgotten worshippers,
dancers, villagers, or farmers would have seen were the matted
green hills, stretching away. The sea was invisible, making the site
unusual in Shetland, where the sea is never more than a few miles
away. But the significance of the location was lost, and nobody
knew for certain what the building had been used for, what forgotten protocol or practices it had embodied. These islands were covered with these low walls of stone, the moss-coated debris of
thousands of years ago. The people lived quietly along the coasts,
and the winds blasted symphonies across the rocks and the waves
drummed on the sands.

Later, I went back to the Thule Bar, running into the bunker
building as the rain fell in sheets. I sat on a chrome stool by the bar,
my clothes dripping on the floor, but no one minded. The locals
were jovial and polite, speaking in their thick Scots-Scandinavian

accents, but even after a few beers, they still weren't sure that Shetland was Thule. Like a consortium of pedants, they were careful with the past, refusing to leap to a conclusion.

'But what about the Romans?' I said, speaking above the sound of the bar. 'What about the Romans arriving two thousand years ago, saying that the north of Britain must be Thule?' They were nodding politely, looking blank. 'The Roman historian Tacitus,' I said, causing a Shetlander to upset his glass, 'said that Thule was Shetland.'

'Tacitus!' someone bellowed across the bar, as if he were proposing a toast.

Tacitus placed Thule north-east of the Scottish mainland, and gave the credit for finding it to his father-in-law, Agricola. Agricola sent out the fleet which found Thule, wrote Tacitus, on a mission to circumnavigate Britain, and his fleet had seen Thule across the torpid waves of Ocean. Britain, wrote Tacitus, was the largest land known to the Romans: its northern shores had no lands opposite them, but were beaten by the wastes of a vast empty sea. In A.D. 77, Agricola became governor of Britain, taking up the post at a time when the land remained uneasy. In the years after he arrived, Agricola moved his armies north. The soldiers, wrote Tacitus, were prone to bragging, claiming that their battles against the local tribes were as mythical as the conquest of Ocean.

There were skirmishes between the Romans and the Caledonians, and then the armies faced each other for a major battle. Tacitus reports the speech one of the Caledonian leaders made, a speech curiously laden with a Roman sense of Britain as the last land to the north: 'There is no land beyond us and even the sea is no safe refuge when we are threatened by the Roman fleet,' he said, according to Tacitus. 'Today the furthest bounds of Britain lie open—and everything unknown is given an inflated worth. But now there is no people beyond us, nothing but tides and rocks and, more deadly than these, the Romans . . . They have pillaged the world: when the land has nothing left for men who ravage every-thing, they scour the sea.'

And Agricola's rallying cry to his troops drew similarly on no-tions of remoteness, invoked in order to emphasize Roman su-premacy: 'The furthest point of Britain is no longer a matter of report or rumour; we hold it, with forts and with arms. Britain has been discovered and subjugated . . . And it would not be inglorious to die at the very place where the world and nature end.' The Ro-man Army had found out the coward Britons, he said, the Britons who hid in the furthest reaches of their remote country: 'They have not made a stand, they have been trapped.'

Tacitus claimed that the battle was won by the superior tactics of the Romans; some thousands of Britons were killed, and only a few hundred on the Roman side, he wrote. 'The Britons dispersed, men and women mingling their cries of grief, dragging off the wounded, calling out to survivors, abandoning their homes and in their rage even setting fire to them, choosing hiding places, and then leaving them again at once.' The Romans passed a joyful night, delighted at the 'outcome and the booty,' and in the morn-ing, under the dawn light, their victory could be seen across the land: 'the silence of desolation on all sides, the hills lonely, home-steads smouldering in the distance, not a man to encounter the scouts.' As the summer was over, Agricola decided to stop the bat-tle. He instructed the prefect of the fleet to sail around Britain; forces were allocated for the purpose. Agricola settled the cavalry and infantry in their winter quarters. When he left Britain, he 'handed over to his successor a province peaceful and secure,' wrote Tacitus.

The Roman fleet Agricola sent out discovered the islands called Orcades, and 'Thule also was surveyed; their instructions taking them only so far: besides, winter was approaching.' Thule was seen, across the capricious Ocean, before the ships sailed southwards.

Thule for Tacitus might have been the Shetland Isles. The Roman fleet found their ships were impeded by the sea, as Pytheas's had been centuries earlier. The obstinate waves, slowing their oars, were further proof, they might have thought, that they had found Pytheas's Thule—the land in the congealed Ocean.

Through the windows of the Thule Bar, this beer-stained corner of antiquity, I saw only the folds of the mist, and the baroque patterns of the churning ocean, as the rain lashed the glass, and the fog coiled tighter round the town. There was a local who had a fistful of theories, none of them about Thule, and he seemed in a conspiratorial mood. He was wearing a greasy pair of jeans, a crumpled shirt, and his face was ruddy and chapped. 'I've got a good story for you,' he said. 'Better than that Thule story you're talking about.' He asked the barman for two whiskies, and handed me one. 'Drink that, it's a cold gale outside,' he said.

His name was Douglas, and he had worked in a fishing institute for years. His mother had met his father here during World War Two, he said. His father had come from occupied Norway on a boat.

'It was called the Shetland Bus,' he said. 'The resistance in Norway arranged for people to sail their small boats over. If they were caught by the Germans they were killed or imprisoned. My father—he came from a small fishing village, north of Bergen on the western coast of Norway—he couldn't stand living under the Germans. He was a fine man. His name was Olav, like the kings of Norway, you know. So he set off with his brother in a boat—they were terrified. They were stuck in storms and they thought the boat would go under. But they arrived in a port further north from here, on the island of Unst. Their boat couldn't take them further, so they just settled where they landed. The people welcomed them, glad to help. My father always talked about how grateful he had been, that the people were so kind. And my father got some work with my mother's father. He didn't know her then, of course.

He said the first day he was there, he was working away in the yard, trying to fix some piece of machinery, and this woman appeared—she was the most beautiful thing he'd ever seen. But he was shy, quite young of course, and didn't want to bother the boss's daughter. He thought he'd lose his job, and then what would he do? Straight back to Norway and to the Nazis, and after all that rocking around in the sea, it would have been a terrible thing. So he did nothing. He just worked hard every day, and every time he saw her he said he almost dropped the hammer, or whatever he was using, she was so beautiful.'

'It has a happy ending,' said the barman, who was listening. 'Don't you worry yourself, it's a great ending.'

Douglas smiled, gripping his pint between rough fingers. 'The ending is me and my sister and brother. So you could say it's happy. Finally, my poor dad plucked up the courage. You can imagine the lad, speaking with his Norwegian accent, trying to ask her if she would marry him. He thought that was the best thing to try. Everything or nothing. Turned out she was in love with him. Had loved him the moment she saw him. He stayed on Shetland for the rest of his life. They were always happy.'

And Doug smiled again, swilling his whisky round his glass. 'Something in the peat,' said another man at the bar.

Later, I drifted out of the conversation at the bar, as a group listed the Top Ten Drunks of Thule, and I thought how the Romans had taken the elements as their evidence. The briny sea, the resistant waves convinced the Romans they had found Thule when they arrived in Britain. It was all tenuous. I sat in Lerwick, with the wind wailing outside and the mist swirling at the windows. A more self-effacing collection of people was impossible to imagine; the regulars at the bar hardly laid claim to the place at all. A couple of guide books ran the story out, mumbling briefly about the Romans, before sliding into something else entirely, but that was it for Shetland-Thule. A collection of cautious locals, a bar and a knitwear shop. A ragged, empty place, with its crusted peat bogs and bright green islands. It was affecting and slightly strange. Strange to find this outpost at the edge of Britain. Strange to find it so littered with ancient stones, ancient houses, all alluding faintly to the past.

In Shetland, I drove up and down the islands, sitting on car ferries as the evening fell, crunching the gears on the coastal paths. Green hills slipped away in the rear-view mirror. Most of the time I was alone on the coasts, at the peat ruins and the brochs. But there was a ragged collection of Viking stones, called Jarlshof, in the south of Shetland, where the car park was full of buses and German and Norwegian tourists queued at a ticket office. Jarlshof was a composite site, the accumulated ruins from thousands of years of habitation on the island, and a shattered house on a cliff, left by the Stewart earls of Orkney and Shetland, abandoned since the seventeenth century. Sir Walter Scott, who found the hills of Shetland a perfect retreat, had given Jarlshof its name. Scott thought the cragged castles, derelict stone lashed by waves, made for a romantic backdrop, though all he saw were the surface ruins, the storm-smashed house on the cliff. He knew nothing about the middens, piled with leftovers from earlier settlements. It was only in the last century that the surging of the storm waters revealed stone walls, and the layers of ancient foundations.

I stood on a viewing rostrum above Jarlshof as the wind screamed across the bay. The ruins looked like a stunted maze, every crumbling wall grown over with grass and moss. I walked around the site, deafened by the gale. The tour groups sheltered from the wind in the round-house ruins, listening to German guides. Jarlshof was a vast and significant pile of ruins—the broken foundations of Norse settlements, the stone walls of a Pictish farmhouse, the outhouses and barns. There had been bone pins, clay bowls, steatite pots, iron sickles, fishhooks and iron scissors, dropped in the earth. The earliest settlers collected cockles, mussels and limpets, and kept a few sheep, cattle and pigs. They built a cluster of oval stone houses among the sand dunes, and they caught fish and hunted seals. Surrounded by other buildings stood the half-eroded shape of a broch, built of smooth stone slabs.

There were people who had wanted Thule for Shetland, Scottish patriots some of them, Albion-worshippers some of the others, casting Thule in the national drama. I had the quotations running through my head, as I stared at the shattered ruins, under a pearl-white sky. They chimed in, with their stanzas, their sonnets, their odes to the monarchs of Albion and Thule. Scotland and Thule were entwined, in rhetorical couplets, for the sake of a decent rhyme, for a rousing chorus. In "The Seasons," James Thomson described the 'utmost isles' of Thule, somewhere off the coast of Scotland. Eighteenth-century wig-maker, bookseller and poet Allan Ramsay made a rousing cry to 'Britain's best blood,' all those living 'From utmost Thule to the Dover rock,' the limits of Britain. In another poem, he imagined John Gay praised 'frae Dover Cliffs . . . to Thule's shore,/Where Northward no more Britain's found/But seas that rore.' Nineteenth-century Scottish poet and physician David Macbeth Moir wrote about the Battle of Flodden Field, mourning the 'nameless dead,' imagining the laments sounding from 'northern Thule to the Tweed.' It was a floral way of saying from north to south, making the phrase as epic as he could. At the end of Scotland, they wrote, Thule lay, the last land of the Romans, a place with an epic past.

In the nineteenth century this sense of an ancient outpost enticed the Victorians, though they were unsure of Shetland's claim to the title of Thule. They commandeered boats and sailed out to brochs lashed by waves. They darted around the peat hills near Lerwick, staring across the cliffs towards the ruined castles and the small ports. They found a museum full of old pots, picked them up with a brisk air, and made a few notes in their diaries. For William Morris, Shetland was the beginning of the remote north. Shetland was where the sea became a great 'glittering green and white wall,' where the ships first met the 'roll of the Atlantic,' he wrote. For Burton, it was a place where the people changed colour; 'the blondes,' he wrote, 'wear that faded and colourless aspect which especially distinguishes the Slavic race. The look is shy and reserved, and the voice is almost a whisper, as if the speaker were continually nervous.' The muddiness of their complexions, he thought, derived from all the peat water they drank.

Driving into the evening, I crossed the purple hills of the island of Yell, on the way to Unst, the most northerly island in Britain. I drove through miles of empty rock. The sun was fading across the treeless hills. The islands along the coast were green and bulbous, lying in the sea like inflated handkerchiefs. The few small villages sprawled around the firths. There were ruined houses on the cliff tops, open to the wind. A single-lane road spanned the island of Yell. Arriving at a café by the shore I waited for a ferry to the island of Unst. The sun cast a dying light across the water. And the island of Unst was nearly empty; the stark cliffs stood deserted, as a handful of cars moved under their blankness towards the north. At intervals, the road passed through pebbledash towns, council rows in the middle of nothingness, spreading around the bays. Muness Castle, Britain's most northerly ruined former fortress, stood in a field, a slab of crumbled stone tapered into turrets. Laurence Bruce had begun it, an inscription over the entrance said, in the year 1598. The castle stood incongruously among the low stone cottages, protesting its former grandeur, though its roof had fallen in, and there was no one else there to visit it.

The sea was pale; the rocks were jagged at their edges, rising to plateaus. At Skaw, where the island stopped, I walked on the rough grass towards the beach, as the birds whirled above the cliffs. There was a marquee on the beach with nothing inside it, and an empty car parked by a stream. I walked to the edge of Britain, once the last land of the world. The moss was a cold green shade, spectral in the half-light, and the stark cliffs rose to empty grass plains. As the evening fell I stood on the empty cliff, looking at the sea stretching away towards the horizon. A frigid wind raced in from the sea. There was a brilliant, wine-rich sunset.

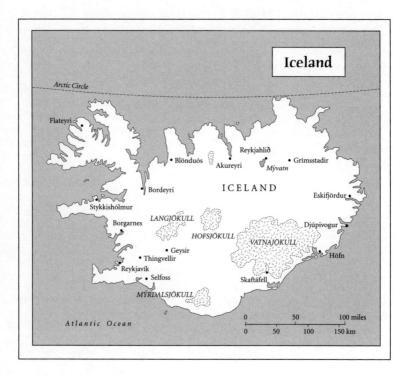

ANOTHER WORLD

⎯⎯⦕∞⦖⎯⎯

By a route obscure and lonely
Haunted by ill angels only
Where an Eidolon, named Night,
On a black throne reigns upright,
I have reached these lands but newly
From an ultimate dim Thule
From a wild weird clime that lieth, sublime
Out of Space . . . out of Time!

"Dreamland," Edgar Allan Poe (1809–1849)

I left this outpost of my country, this luminescent set of islands, and travelled further north. It was an inevitable momentum. The idea of Thule expanded with the maps. As knowledge of the north increased, so the ends of the world shifted, and a land beyond the limits of the known world had to move with changes in cartography. It was a story about unbounded curiosity; as new northern lands were found, so Thule was reapplied, sometimes for rhetorical effect, sometimes from a sense that a recent discovery must be the last land, the mysterious land sighted by Pytheas. The idea of Thule was entwined with mysteries and gaps. It was intriguing to imagine Pytheas arriving in a northern land, finding a midnight sun, and sailing home. But it was an act of imagination even to think about Pytheas's journey; from the surviving fragments it was hardly possible to say for certain where Thule might have been. Any discussion of Thule as a particular place was an elaborate piece of reconstruction. It was like rebuilding an ancient temple from a few scattered stones. A hypothetical version of Thule could run along, certain of a few things, plunging into vagaries on others. Thule was a land where the sun shone through the summer nights, and where the winters were dark. It might have been near a congealed ocean, or near a sluggish ocean, or near a frozen ocean. It might have been a place inhabited by barbarians of some sort, though this was uncertain. It might have been six days' sail north of Britain, but this could have meant due north, or north-east, or north-west, and Pytheas had previously found it difficult to calculate distances with accuracy. It was a land with a curious array of qualities—not exactly like anywhere, but redolent of many places. All the lands of the north contained elements of Thule—from Shetland to Svalbard. Even as I travelled, they were lands still valued for their beauty and emptiness. Pure in parts, with the soft sunshine gleaming across their ancient rocks.

For the Victorians on their steamers, Shetland was hardly a contender. Iceland was the only plausible Thule. They stayed stubbornly on their ships, passing the Faroe Islands in a flurry of excitement, pointing out the turf houses of Tórshavn and admiring the great circling crowds of seabirds. Then they waited for Iceland to appear on the horizon. Mrs. Alec Tweedie, William Morris, Anthony Trollope, Sir Richard Burton, understood that the rough outline of the north was almost complete, the pencil lines were convening on the maps. But they wanted Ultima Thule to be a land unlike any other, a land weird enough for a mystery lasting thousands of years. They imagined travelling to Thule as a ride to a Gothic Utopia. They travelled with Edgar Allan Poe in mind, reciting his fantasy verse on the theme of Thule:

> I HAVE REACHED THESE LANDS BUT NEWLY
> FROM AN ULTIMATE DIM THULE
> FROM A WILD WEIRD CLIME THAT LIETH, SUBLIME
> OUT OF SPACE . . . OUT OF TIME!

They wanted to see nature in its weirdest outfits, performing its most hysterical tantrums and fits. In the lands of the Icelandic Thule, the eternal works of nature were grotesque, and scarcely even eternal. The land shifted throughout the ages, birthing new mountains and islands, the rocks were constantly shattered and flooded with steaming waters. Iceland was a land where flames burst from the ice and burning lava spread across the land. A land in a state of flux: the volcanic flames flickering above ancient glaciers, red on white, the fires fading into the purple blackness of the lava fields. A land where ice mountains melted and flames cooled to rock. Bold, callous colours, crazy stretches of whiteness lurking in the gaps among the barren mountains, savage darts of flame in the dusk. The Victorians came for the mountain of Hekla, once thought to be the entrance to hell, or for Snaefellsjökull, Jules Verne's entrance to the centre of the earth. They came for the view over the ragged lava piles, and the moon landscapes. They came for the thousand cones and spikes of volcanic ground, forged in successive eruptions. A place like Thule: an interim point between the familiar and the outlandish.

When the Victorians arrived, there was a living convention of perorations to the ragged lava plains, the devil holes, the sulphur pots, the lairs of Beelzebub, each bubbling spring or jagged rift representing a different aspect of the Dark Prince. Most of the travellers' hysteria focused around the Geysir, though a few amazed words were reserved for the volcano Krafla in the north of Iceland and the terrible former Viking capital of Thingvellir, where the earth cracked in two. In the late eighteenth and early nineteenth centuries Dr. Uno von Troil, Mr. William Jackson Hooker, Sir George Steuart Mackenzie, and Ebenezer Henderson had vied for exploratory firsts. They were frequently astonished, like Dr. Von Troil, who travelled in 1772, finding a devastated land of barren mountains, eternal snow and vitrified cliffs. Sir George Steuart Mackenzie, Baronet, Fellow of the Royal Society, travelling in 1810, found that despite his various titles he could not convey the mingled raptures of wonder, admiration and terror with which his breast was filled, and that was just at the sight of the Geysir, the exploding hot spring. These early visitors divided their bemusement into sub-headings: 'On the Pestiferous Effects of the Air,' 'Of Steeped or Macerated Fish,' or 'Of the Peculiar Instinct of the Horses in this District.' They were transfixed by the fantastic groups of hills, craters and lava, the distant snow-crowned glaciers, the mists rising from a waterfall, the profound silence, glowering clouds, the crazed element of fire ravaging the land.

The Victorians gathered coats and hampers, and arrived in the capital, Reykjavík, buying up horses, trotting out to the sites—the Great Geysir, Thingvellir, or the lava plains in the north. They stood in the rain, reciting the Sagas, as William Morris did; they came in genteel tour groups, like Anthony Trollope and his party, spilling slippers and smoking jackets onto the lava fields, in a procession of nearly a hundred horses. Through repetition in their diaries, the arrival became a ritual, a moment of recited stanzas and set phrases. The boat would dock, after a lurching voyage of some weeks, the passengers sick at heart, longing for the shore. They saw mountains standing out sullen and forbidding against a grey sky. They admired the scorched lava fields stretching away. In the summer the nights were dark blue, and the sky was always tinted with daylight colours. The interior stretched away, an inhospitable waste at the time, almost entirely unknown.

The banner still hangs, LAND OF FIRE AND ICE, across the rain-doused country. Iceland touts its wares. The tourists come for the natural pyrotechnics, as the Victorians did. Everyone is dragged to Iceland on a tractor beam of hyperbole, lured by stories from the constantly mutating island. The tourist brochures breathe visions of the earth's crust, spewed liberally across the land. A land like a disaster film, a natural gore-flick—the country scattered with the innards of the earth. Keflavík Airport, outside Reykjavík, was overrun with tourists jostling towards the luggage carousel. Tourists decked in climbing gear, preparing to hike through the lava plains, across the spacescapes, across the brilliant orange pastel sands of the sulphur bays. They stood, watching backpacks turning circles, everything stamped with a sticker: the Volcano Experience Inc., Arctic Tours, TM.

I had been travelling for a day, from Aberdeen to London, and then from London to Iceland. But it still seemed indecently fast, when I thought of the Victorians in their cramped steamships, bitterly seasick, finding the arrival in Iceland an enormous relief. I had landed into a rainstorm, but I was wrapped in waterproofs, sitting in a bus to Reykjavík. The rain slapped against the windows. The tourists were slightly sodden; we were all sitting wetly on our bags, rustling in waterproof layers. As the bus moved across the lava plains, the country was grey. The sea was blanched and tepid. The dry grass stretched to the sea; there were flatlands where horses grazed. Low shrubs took the place of trees. A white stone church stood on a hill. The road ran past the serried stacks of flat-topped mountains, rising from the shrublands and the rock plains.

A plain of cracked earth stretched away, littered with black ash rocks, coated with thick moss. The ground was always uneven; it looked like an immense sculpture, representing sultry waves. A crazed piece of national art, it was motion petrified, retaining something of the dynamism of rocks that have succumbed to the force of the lava burning beneath them. Above the spikes of the lava plain, the mountains rose and the grey clouds moved slowly above. There were mountains shaped like explosions, extruding sharp points. There were long-backed ridges, draped in cloud vapour, and clear cones, their sides neatly chiselled.

The land was rain-drenched; the afternoon was cloaked in mist. On the bus I stared through the smeared windows at the lava fields. The city of Reykjavík stretched languidly along the coast, dwindling into low-rise concrete at the edges, crowded in the centre around a small lake. The suburbs were full of American-style diners, mall-strips interspersed with trees. The sea was cold white, hammered flat by a grey sky. The centre of the city was made of corrugated iron, its small houses pressed closely together. The streets were teeming with drenched travellers, shuddering at bus stops in their wax jackets and woollen hats, or staring damply into lighted shop windows. Stepping off the bus, I walked through Reykjavík into the Parliament Square, where there was a Café Paris, an art nouveau hotel and a green-stained statue. The light shook across the city; the pink tips of the mountains were silhouetted against the cold sky. Hallgríms Church was brightly lit, its main tower decked with flashy lighting, looking like a pushy cousin of the Chrysler Building in New York. There was a revolving restaurant, balanced on a great stack of towers, like a stylized sculpture of a mushroom. I reached the Town Hall, built in glowering space station style, its black form reflected on the waters of the Pond, a lake in the centre of the town.

I walked through the evening. The wind swept across the waters of the lake, distorting the reflection of the buildings. Arctic skuas shrieked across the water. There were signs to Viking sites, to the Saga Museum, to the National Gallery, to the Volcano Show: 'You will be amazed as the earth explodes before your eyes.' As the whine of planes above the city died into the damp evening I followed the sign to the Volcano Show. The Volcano Show was offering a glimpse of the natural weirdness of Iceland. It was like a circus sideshow, the sort of grotesque turn the Victorians might have enjoyed. 'Fire and Ice!' said the sign. 'You will not believe your eyes!' In a small building there was a projector and a wizened man with wild greying hair and a gaze of intense frustration. He saw me, fixed me with a disconsolate stare, and said slowly: 'The Volcano Show has followed the same timetable for seventeen million years, and it will follow the same timetable for the next seventeen million years.'

'So are you the person who films the volcanoes?' I asked.

'No no,' he shook his flimsy beard. 'That man is older than God.'

'And how long has the cinema been running?' I asked.

'The cinema is also older than God. Step back please.'

And another person stepped up to buy a ticket.

'The Volcano Show,' he said to her, 'has followed the same timetable for seventeen million years, and it will follow the same timetable for the next seventeen million years.' And she smiled and paid, moved along, preparing the stage for the next recipient of the same gag, repeated to fade, to the end of time, or until Iceland consumed itself in a vibrant explosion of fire.

The cinema was a small dirty room, with bits of dismembered projector scattered across the floor. Dozens of tourists had been shoe-horned in here by the Volcano Man, who was shuffling in and out, muttering about technical hitches. The show was an hour late, but he seemed not to care; he knew he was doomed to another evening of cracking the same old jokes, and he couldn't quite get up the impetus to start. There was an entire busload of English schoolchildren, inexplicably dropped here, a crowd of Italians, a few Germans, and a quiet Dutch couple at the front. 'Dutch people!' said the Volcano Man. 'You have a wonderful country. A wonderful country. I once knew someone from Holland—' And then he stopped mid-sentence, gripped by a crashing sense of futility.

With an enormous effort of will, struggling against overpowering lassitude, he cleared his throat and stumbled to the front of the small hall, anorak slung over his shoulders, trousers brutally tapered, ending short of his ankles. Eyeing the audience with something almost like hatred, he tried to smile.

'Here in the Volcano Show,' he began, making a grandiose circle with his fingers, 'we patiently await the next disaster . . . We began showing films here twenty-eight years ago. The last time we had a big explosion here in Iceland was during the three o'clock show, on 17 June 2000. At 3:45 P.M. there was a 6.5 Richter scale earthquake in Hekla, the biggest for eighty years. It was so very violent we felt it in Reykjavík, the seats started going up and down, nobody ran out, people thought it was part of the show.'

Everyone laughed. The Volcano Man stared balefully at the crowd, waiting for them to subside. 'My father began filming after the war. In 1963 he filmed the island of Surtsey coming out of the sea. On 8 September 1977 we had an eruption of a pipe by Lake Mývatn, the volcanic lake in the far north of Iceland. This was my project for the next sixteen years. There was a very big magma chamber under the ground, and when the magma chamber erupted, the ground went down. The main problem was when the crater was open, it was never more than for four hours, so I had to wait there. All my money disappeared into Lake Mývatn, I hope to be able to fish it out some day.'

Fainter laughter. Fidgeting from the party of English school-girls. A stifled yawn from the Volcano Man. 'In one day the whole town was raised by thirty centimetres. A bathing cave near Mývatn that day became too warm for bathing. It still is. Another one used to be too cold for bathing. That day, it became perfect.'

A last laugh from the audience and the Volcano Man stumbled away, shaking his head. I imagined him muttering in the projector room while he started the film. The film further defied the audience: there was no plot, no drama, it was a doleful account of the Volcano Man trailing around, trying to reach volcanic explosions in time, chartering aeroplanes, seeking death-defying experiences. Though the Volcano Man was clearly hoping some violent disaster would save him from any further appearances at the Volcano Show, real physical harm evaded him: the magma moved too slowly to threaten him; his helicopter always worked, despite his predictions that it would crash horribly on the rocks.

'Once,' his voice narrated, over the flickering blurred shots of magma explosions far in the distance, 'we got some four-wheel drives, and drove across the ice cap. We had heard scientists say there were fractures in the rocks. Our four-wheel drive ran out of gas in front of the lava flow.'

On the film, there was an explosion from a piece of ice far away; the camera panned, the picture coming gradually into focus.

A remote image of fire spluttering onto the ice, cracking the surface. The voice-over came again, steeped in disappointment: 'Fortunately we managed to start the car again.'

The show ended in a shuddering anti-climax, and we all filed slowly out of the hall. 'Come again,' said the Volcano Man, indifferently.

The wind gusting the rain into my face, I walked around the lake. At the hotel, the rooms were painted pale shades; the furniture was pine, everything adapted to minimalism. The aeroplanes whined into the city airport. A group of teenagers in jeans and trainers ran along the street pushing a stalled car, sweating in spite of the rain and wind. The crowds streamed into the bars, and I followed them to a place called Kaffibarinn. They sat in groups drinking in a steady progress, moving from reserved to riotous. They drank until they were ready to dance. Then they pushed the chairs back and started to sling themselves around. The barman said to me: 'See them, they want to kill themselves. It's amazing more don't die.' He laughed, showing a mouth without front teeth, and pulled everyone another pint. The thumping bars of Reykjavík were packed with the denizens of studied decadence, trying for total alcoholic collapse. The drinkers began ricocheting out of the bars in the small hours, filing towards the kebab shops. They lined up along the edges of the pavements, baying across the road at each other.

Abandoned to the soft evening, in the town that staged its own eternal return of rain and wind, I stayed on the streets as the colours of the sky shifted from rain-grey to deep blue. The small town resounded to a low beat from the bars and the clubs; the night was cold and dank. As the sun began to rise, the streets quietened. The wind died. Everything seemed to wait, for the collective hangover of the morning.

Reykjavík was the transition point between homely steamer and weird country, and the nineteenth-century travellers struggled against the feeling, but they had to admit to finding it less strange than they had hoped. Instead of a baroque cathedral, manufactured entirely from lava, or an enormous troll palace on a hill, they found a line of shabby buildings spread out on a sallow shore. 'Viewed from the sea, the capital of Iceland has a very mean appearance. It is situated in a narrow flat, between two low hills, having the sea on the north-east, and a small lake on the south-west side,' said Sir George Steuart Mackenzie. 'The little town of Reykjavík consists of a single broad street, with houses and cottages scattered around. The number of inhabitants does not amount to 500,' said Madame Ida Pfeiffer. 'There are but two streets, and these are hardly worthy of the name. Decayed fish, offal, filth of every description, is tossed anywhere for the rain to wash away, or for the passer-by to trample into the ground,' said Sabine Baring-Gould, M.A. Useful, was the best they could reach for. Quaint, a few rolled the word around in their mouths, trying it out, but somehow it didn't suit the cramped houses and the smell of putrescence. Must get better they decided, galloping off on their horses, to wax euphoric over some hot springs.

Brooding on the quayside, away from the groups, was Richard Burton, staring at the view. Burton was preparing to spend a summer in Ultima Thule. It was the custom to throw a Thule in at some stage in the travelogue, like Mrs. Alec Tweedie, modestly alluding to the ancient place, before moving onto the contemporary wonders of the lava plains. But Burton levelled an exacting gaze at the question of Thule. Burton was certain he could solve it, the millennia-old mystery. It was the sort of challenge he was likely to enjoy—an explorer in sinewy middle age, he had stamped a hundred firsts onto the unwitting sands of Arabia and the Middle East. He had sauntered to Mecca; he had been the first European to see Lake Tanganyika. He had played the part immaculately—the Victorian enthusiast, the autodidact of the Arabian sands, effortlessly fluent in an array of languages, writing up his travels in wilfully baroque prose.

Shortly before his arrival in Iceland, Burton had submitted his fire and impatience to the hands of a painter, Lord Leighton. The portrait now hangs in the National Portrait Gallery in London. Leighton could make beauty burn on the canvas, the luminescent folds of an orange dress spring to life, flicker and never fade, but with Burton he stuck to his darkest shades, mixing them into a sludge colour on his pallet. The explorer sits against a black backdrop, wearing a sombre suit, his arm resting on the deep red of a chair. His beard is full and impressively groomed, bunching from his chin onto his tie. He casts a haggard cheek towards the painter's brush, a cheek with a jagged scar from a spear wound, and turns his eyes towards an unknown point. The only light is the brilliance of his face, his glare.

Burton had been strangely worried about his appearance on the day of the sitting, concerned that he might be painted as a scarred maniac. Don't make me ugly, there's a good fellow, he had asked Leighton, flashing his vehement stare at the painter. Don't paint my necktie or my tiepin, he had added, capricious demands which Leighton nearly obeyed. The painter twisted the necktie into the shadows, leaving only a glint of metal. He gave Burton the eyes of a mesmerist; saving the viewer from the force of the look, he turned the eyes away.

It was a dark portrait and it made a strange man of Burton, like a supernatural visitation, looming out of the blackness. It suited the solitude and vehemence of Burton's style, his refusal to parrot prevailing opinions, as he prepared to solve the old question of Thule. Burton was painted by Leighton during the time he was preparing to travel to Thule. He wanted to clear up the darkness that had been 'heaped by a host of writers upon Thule,' he had decided. He recognized that Thule had been Britain to the Romans, Scandinavia to later scholars, and had done general service as synecdoche for the northern lands. But he was certain that Thule was applied to Iceland, and to Iceland only, from the earliest stages of its exploration. Iceland was the place Burton called Thule, the land he thought worthy of the old epithet.

Finding the arrival in Reykjavík slightly tepid, Burton slipped into fantasy, staging himself a joyful pageant. As his ship docked into a grey harbour he lined the Ancients up on the quayside, like a cross-temporal welcoming party. Guest of honour was Pytheas, who 'evidently referred to Iceland' in his account of Thule, thought Burton. And he recalled the words of Pomponius Mela, who described Thule as a land famous in Greek and Roman poems, where the winters were dark and the summers bright with constant sunshine. Mela had mentioned the Orkney and Shetland Isles, and the Scandinavian Isle elsewhere, so he couldn't have been thinking of them when he mentioned Thule, said Burton. From this, Burton claimed, Mela's Thule was Iceland, though his maps were uncertain.

Writing his *Natural History*, Pliny the Elder had named a host of islands near Britain before he turned to Thule. Ireland, Pliny wrote, lay beyond Britain, and other than that there were smaller islands: the Orkneys separated narrowly from one another, the Hebrides, and the seven 'Acmodae,' which might have been the Shetlands. The most remote of the recorded islands was Thule, and 'at one day's sail from Thule, there is the frozen ocean,' wrote Pliny. Burton marshalled Pliny into his welcoming party, though he had written about Thule in his section on Britain, but this, Burton decided, had been charming ignorance, and a sensitive interpretation would make Pliny an advocate for Iceland-Thule. And though Claudius Ptolemy had placed Thule further south, his measurements were bound to be wrong, wrote Burton, so it was best to ignore Ptolemy's longitudes and latitudes, and just assume he had meant Iceland too.

The Venerable Ancients—Burton dragged them to the quayside, forcing bunting into their hands, enlisting them in a ghostly procession of long-dead experts, waving banners: 'You are now in Thule.' Saxo Grammaticus, Cluverius, Harduin and Dalechamp, Bougainville, Hill, Penzel, Pontanus, Thilo, Mercator and Mannert, listed Burton, an incantation of names, as he stood in the harbour surveying the cracked lava plains of Iceland. All of them thought that Iceland was Thule. Burton could see no reason to doubt the reality of Thule. Iceland might have been discovered by Pytheas, or even by the Carthaginians before him. 'The old tradition of Thule, though different ages applied the word differently, was never completely lost,' Burton thought. Though the official rediscovery of Iceland dated from the Norse arrivals in the ninth century, there was evidence to suggest Irishmen had been going there in the century before, if not much earlier.

At least as early as the eighth century, wide-eyed clerics had been stepping onto this cracked land, casting themselves to the ground, seeing devils in the dark piles of lava. Seafaring Irish monks arrived on clerical outings, looking for an empty place to pray. They found pure white plains, dark hell pits; they scrambled around on the beaches, struck by visions of men dressed entirely in white, imagining Judas Iscariot chained to a rock, suffering eternal torment. Latin-muttering, margin-illuminating monks, trying to escape their blue-black cows, the wet pastures of Kerry. They found islands where tables were laid for dinner, covered with fish and grapes; they found themselves intoxicated by the smell of fruit on these opulent islands, but they would turn a corner, and find a devil urinating on their boat. They reported back from Iceland, which they called Thule, describing it as a place where the sun shone through the night in the summer, so bright that you could see the lice in your shirts, they reported. It was a confusing land the clerics found, full of mysteries, and they used it like a hermitage, sitting on the rocks, hearing the voice of God in the rumbling of the glaciers.

Burton drew in a later source, as further proof of his theory. There was Christopher Columbus, who might have sailed to Iceland, which he called Thule. From the dusty evidence, it seemed that Columbus might have sailed in February 1477, before his expedition to the New World. He knew Seneca, he knew the lines about the coming time when 'the immeasurable earth will lie open, when seafarers will discover new countries, and Thule will no longer be the extreme point among the islands.' Columbus found that Thule was as large as England, and the sea was not frozen, though the tides were rough, and the waves rose twenty-five fathoms twice a day. It was a place where the English went to trade. Columbus's claim to have reached Thule had been almost as controversial as Pytheas's original story. He was doubted because he had claimed the waves around Iceland were astonishingly high, because he placed the island too far north, and said that he sailed far beyond its coasts without being stopped by ice. Columbus was accused of being a braggart, who couldn't hear of a place without claiming to have reached it. Others suggested he had arrived in Iceland, but had exaggerated the details to make his journey more compelling.

Burton was part of another, later, list of names, brought in as an expert witness for an Icelandic Thule. Writing in the 1940s, the Canadian explorer Vilhjalmur Stefansson used Burton as part of his argument that Thule had been Iceland. Stefansson believed that the ancient Britons had heard of Iceland, or even reached it in their boats, and told Pytheas about it when he arrived in Britain. And Stefansson was convinced that Columbus had been to Iceland. Sailing through sluggish seas, Columbus might have been surprised by a sudden storm, and in the chaos of the swell, waves smashing onto the deck, might have overestimated the height of the waves. Stefansson had a handful of points to back his argument that Iceland was Thule, but his main proof was Richard Burton. Richard Burton, wrote Stefansson, had believed that Iceland was Thule, and Burton was 'known to some as a great figure in the history of nineteenth-century travel . . . admired as belonging with Caesar among those who can both do things and write about them.' The summing up for Iceland appeared conclusive, wrote Stefansson.

By the time he turned his attention to Thule, Stefansson had a long and controversial history of Arctic exploration behind him. He had proposed excitable theories about what might lie around the North Pole, imagining it as a region rich in minerals. In 1913 he had led a catastrophic expedition on the *Karluk* and had left his captain and crew when the ship became frozen in the ice. Many of those remaining on board died after the ship was sunk by the pressure of the ice. The survivors were forced to struggle towards Siberia. Stefansson returned safely, having spent years among the Inuit populations of the north. He needed the force of Burton's personality behind his theories, the icy glare of a convinced Victorian, surveying the sources.

———— ◦◦◦◦ ————

At midday, Johannes the poet was sitting with a beer, biding his time. We were in a bar around the corner from the Town Hall, where young Icelandic couples were spread across sofas, drinking coffee and reading the papers. Johannes was small and dark-haired, wearing a tattered blue suit, a grimy white shirt falling out of his trousers, a style of deliberately debased formality. Johannes wrote skittish verse about life in the north. His hands were stained with ink, as if he had recently tipped an inkpot across them.

'I write in the tradition of the Sagas,' he said, immediately, as I sat down. 'We all in Iceland write in the tradition of the Sagas. It wasn't so long ago, everyone knew all the Sagas; they sat around in the evenings reciting them. On the farms in the valleys, there wasn't much to do. They called it the Icelandic Library, the old men and woman reciting the Sagas to each other, to their children and grandchildren, and of course eventually they knew them off by heart. I write in this tradition; as an Icelander it is inherent to me,' he said.

'You asked me about Thule; I have even written a poem about it. I wrote one about Thule, because it is the most ancient reference to our nation, it shows that people knew about our country even before Christ. My poem is about the idea of a perfect land, and how that might be, and how Iceland has never really been a perfect land, because of the violence of the rocks, and because of the difficult history of the people. It's been a hard time, for the people. They lived well, though the Vikings were rough and vicious, until they were taken over by Denmark, and then after that the country slid into a decline for centuries, until the nineteenth century, when our poet Hallgrímsson took up literary arms for Iceland, and tried to stir his countrypeople up. He just wanted them to care, he was an amazing man. Jonas Hallgrímsson. I'll find you a poem by him too.'

That was how Johannes talked, a thick stream of words, with no real sign of stopping. It was perhaps the coffee; it was perhaps the overflowing bar, with the Icelanders draped scenically around; it was perhaps the length of the days, the awareness that the daylight would continue through the night that made Johannes so verbally energetic. Johannes opened his notebook, coughed into his ink-stained hand, and said, 'This is my poem about Thule:

A LAND THEY WEREN'T QUITE SURE ABOUT
UNCERTAIN AND DERANGED
LOST FLAMES OF FIRE COATING THE ABANDONED ROCK
AN UNKNOWN LAND, UNTIL THEY CAME.
A GREEK IN A WARSHIP WAS THE FIRST,
HE ADMIRED THE ICE AND THE SUN AND TURNED AROUND
THIS LAND WAS TOO MUCH FOR HIM.
THE VIKINGS DRAGGED THEIR BOATS ACROSS THE SEA
THEY WANTED ANOTHER LAND
FREEDOM THEY CRIED WHEN THEY SAW THE ROCKS
FREEDOM FREEDOM FREEDOM

FREEDOM.

'That's just the first verse; there are another fifty-two. One verse is just the word freedom, repeated thirty-four times. I like the word "freedom,"' he said. 'If you come to the café in November I am doing a poetry week. My subject is Liberty through Poetry. Sometimes, when I feel like it, I will organize a poetry evening, with a free salmon supper for anyone who can recite one of my poems from heart. This is no mean feat; I never write anything less than thirty stanzas long. I believe in the oral tradition. The Viking poems were originally recited—like your tradition, your Anglo-Saxon poems, with the scop—the poet. The scop was such a great thing to be, a poet sitting by the fire, with a beer, and then suddenly they'd call on him to make up a verse about anything—usually the same old things, of course—a battle or a dead warrior—and the scop would launch into something—I think that's a wonderful thing to do. At my recitals we try impro-poetry—where the audience decides the theme, and I jam with it, and I set a limit of forty-two stanzas to my improvisation. I like to improvise in iambic pentametres, but it's hard, you can imagine.' He laughed.

'You should try our beer, Thule beer, it's very good, brewed in the north, in our second city Akureyri,' said Johannes, handing me a bottle. 'I never write without having drunk half a crate of the stuff.'

There was something gently preposterous about Johannes. There was something gently preposterous about our encounter, as he sucked at his ink-stained fingers and spilt his beer on the table. His hands were shaking; I wasn't sure if it was nerves or an excess of frenetic energy. He was staring earnestly at his bottle of beer. 'Could you recite me a poem?' I asked.

He sucked pensively for a while on his beer bottle before saying: 'No, it's the summer. There's no time in the summer. It's in the winter I get really verbose. In the summer, haiku, maybe a sonnet. Only in the winter can we do epics. There's not much to do in the winter in Iceland. Perhaps people are glad of a chance to sit still for a while. We have a writer,' he added, 'called Halldór Laxness, who won the Nobel Prize for Literature, we are very proud of him. He was no poet, of course, our only poets are Hallgrímsson and me on my best days, but Laxness wrote all about the countryside, and he said that it's all very well thinking the countryside is full of the past, full of the memories of former Icelanders, and seeing the landscape as a great symbol of Iceland, but there are days when all we notice is the sun, the sun shining on the hills. On these days, the sun is stronger than the past. You can't always be banging on the drum, you know, some days you just sit and enjoy the warmth on your toes.'

Laxness loved the damp bogs where the farmers tended their sheep, the winds sweeping along the treeless hills, the sound of rain on stone. No Icelandic writer better evoked the vastness of the valleys, the broad winter skies, stained a deep blue, the simple lives of the people. His characters were disturbed, at times, by the strangeness of the land around them; in *Independent People* a farmstead seems to be haunted by an ill-favoured spirit, and the farmer finds his life slowly destroyed. They sometimes longed for escape, though when they stood on a quayside watching the ships being loaded, holding tickets to the USA, they found they couldn't leave; they turned their horses around, and galloped back to their cold valleys.

Later, Johannes rubbed my hand with his ink-stained palm, told me to read his poems, and then disappeared onto the street.

——— স988———

I left Reykjavík, under a cloud of rain. I drove out towards Thingvellir, the centre of the weird Icelandic Thule, once home to the Viking Parliament, the Thing. The road wound past scree mountains oppressed by mist, the valley floors scattered with shrubs and slender birch trees, the soil a vivid shade of orange. In a sudden sunny interval, the geothermal town of Hveragerði steamed under the scree. Small bakeries were selling dry cakes and salmon rolls, but the restaurants were shut, their blinds pulled down. The skies darkened and clouds hovered above the small town. The road ran across a plateau, as rain began falling in thick streams onto the dank grass. Across the farmland and the mud ridges I saw clouds of smoke rising slowly from Geysir ahead, mingling with the rain and the mist.

Geysir was a village engulfed in a geothermal haze. Through the mist the barrack-shapes of two hotels and the white concrete walls of a petrol station were dimly visible. At the field of the geysirs a few tourists stood in the rain, waiting for one of the boiling pools to erupt and blast a column of water out of the sand. Smoke was rising from the ground, drifting with the wind. The ground was multi-tone: red sulphur sand streaked with blue, brown and yellow, soft grey-white silica; coral-like rocks; rusty moulds, coated with water from the explosions and lashed by the driving rain. I stood over the steaming pools, watching the water bubble. The rain drowned out the soft gurgles and splutters from the steam pools. There was a rock kettle, with steam bursting out of a funnel, and a brilliant blue basin, with a puddle of water bubbling inside it.

At the Geysir Hotel they were serving up salmon in the restaurant, and when the rain started to fall harder everyone retreated there to watch the drifting clouds from a distance. The napkins were folded into towers on the tables. 'Like the geysir spout,' said the waitress, smiling, as I sat down. The food arrived, and no one much noticed it. Everyone was fixed on the view through the window, sitting at an angle to the tables.

We all waited patiently, and as we speared salmon onto our forks the smaller geysir rumbled up to an explosion, spraying the plain.

In the early nineteenth century they had lined up in tents on the geysir field, bedding down not far from the Great Geysir: 'We pitched our tent at a distance of about one hundred yards from the Geysir, and having arranged matters so that a regular watch might be kept during the night, I went to my station at 11 o'clock, and my companions lay down to sleep,' wrote Sir George Steuart Mackenzie. William Jackson Hooker, Fellow of the Wernerian Society of Edinburgh, had arrived in 1809, and was disturbed during the night by an explosion, followed by 'a most brilliant assemblage of all the colours of the rainbow, caused by the decomposition of the solar rays passing through the shower of drops that was falling between us and the crater.' Persistent, these travellers would stay for several days, camped by the geysirs, awaiting the subterranean rumbling, counting the minutes of the explosions, and noting them down in their immaculate pocketbooks. The geysirs, they wrote, danger of approaching them, rules to be observed, suspense while waiting, transparency and clearness of the waters, beautiful diversity of colours, eruption of the geysirs. They wrote poems, paeans to the red nostrils of the Great Geysir, imagining it like a dragon, its waters like fiery breath, a boiling deluge poured across the blasted heath.

Later Burton, Morris, Trollope, Mrs. Tweedie rode out, enticed by tales of water hurled two hundred feet high, accompanied by an immense rumbling under the earth. They trotted out from Reykjavík on horseback, jolting on the rocks. They had read the ecstatic reports of Hooker and Mackenzie and the other earlier travellers. They knew the place was renowned for weirdness, for the surprising effects of blasting water. So they stopped off at Geysir, expecting to be startled out of their wits.

No one camps on the geysir field any more, though a campsite further down the road was half full of sodden tents. The tourists lined their cars up outside the Geysir Hotel and the Great Geysir lurked, inactive. Centuries of pressure under the earth had created a large bunion of rock around the pool, but the waters were still. There was a smaller geysir, called Strokkur, still doing a regular turn as I stood under the drifting smoke clouds. On Independence Day, like an ancient primadonna, the geysir is dragged on stage to perform its former turn. In honour of the Icelandic nation, it is coaxed. A reluctant patriot, it lies sullen until tonnes of soap flakes have been hurled into its depths, and then, rumbling as if to say, oh, if you insist, it produces the spectacle: a thundering under the earth, a retching expulsion of steam and water, and a sputtering anticlimax as the waters dwindle to calmness again. The Icelanders used to spit into the geysir holes, thinking that way they spat at the devil, but now they work in the gift shop selling burgers and postcards, while the tourists peer cautiously into the geysir pools. I watched the bubbling of the water, gentle at first, then rising and falling with greater intensity, until the water formed into a viscous film, like an immense furious jellyfish, puffed out with the force of a powerful current. The water was suddenly sucked down, then with a belching groan the geysir exploded—a cloud of water and steam, sending everyone racing backwards clutching their video cameras.

Standing at the field, the practical Mrs. Alec Tweedie experienced a moment of dismay; the Great Geysir would not play, she wrote, as if it was a famous violinist struck by shyness. To our great mortification, she added, it failed to play at all throughout the visit. Strokkur, the more obliging soloist geysir, was filled with earth sods, which it duly vomited in a cloud of steam. Richard Burton was unimpressed, standing by the dank and unexploding pool of water. 'Throwing stones at it works, firing a gun stops it boiling,' wrote Burton. He failed to see much interest in the occasional explosions. 'I cannot but hold the geysirs to be gross humbugs,' he added. He had seen a shiver and a general bubble, half veiled in white vapour, which rose like a gigantic glass shade from the still surface, and then trickled down the basin sides. He gave it a long inspection, and wrote the details into his diary, sniffing the sulphur fumes, finding the smell like rotten eggs, and deciding it was just a poor beginning, and greater wonders would soon emerge.

Tweedie and Burton and Morris trotted off, in search of something still stranger, the women teetering side-saddle on their horses, in line with social decorum, the men shouting orders at their guides. Not bad, they all agreed, exploding water, rather interesting, rather strange. But they wanted wild weirdness, in the manner of the verse, in the manner of all the old dreams of the north, the 'other world' of Thule. Their horses bucked over the stones, nearly tipping the women off, in line with convention. Tweedie was astride her horse, defiantly trotting off with the men. Burton was riding ahead of the pack, finding their pace too slow, accustomed as he was to galloping across the desert. Things were sure to be slightly stranger in Thingvellir, they thought, and if they weren't, they had heard startling stories about the lava plains in the north and the spectral waters of Lake Mývatn.

As I stood there, the smaller geysir was firing well, regularly racing up to its climax, interspersing real explosions with a few feints—bubbles boiling in the pool, looking like they might explode then subsiding with a wheeze. I lingered at Geysir for an afternoon, watching a few more explosions. The four-wheel drives sat in the rain outside the Geysir Hotel, and the restaurant with a view of the plain was full. I stood for a while in the Geysir Museum, watching films of lava bursting through rocks. Then I drove out of the rain-drenched town.

I drove through dense shrubland across a mountain pass. The road wound along stubby fields, and the car bounced on rocks. I could see the plain of Thingvellir, the valley of the first Icelandic Parliament. A grey-green meadow in the distance, stretching towards a glassy lake with pointed islets. A pale white line of light illuminated the valley, showing the seamed face of the land, and the dusky foliage of the birch wood beyond the region of the rifts. The mountains stretched away—Armannsfell, looming against the dank clouds, Lagafell, the long jagged line of Tindaskagi, and lurking in the distance the white mass of Skjaldbreiður. The hills were gaudy in the spectral sunlight, set against the pale lake.

The Victorians walked through the chasm to reach the plain of Thingvellir, descending along a small, steep, dangerous path, across large fragments of lava. They walked beneath colossal blocks of stone, lofty walls, uncertain and slightly disturbed. Here, they hoped, was the centre of the weird land, the ancient land of Thule, the ghastly sublime they had sought—approached through a deep fissure called Almannagjá, fire rocks blasted by successive eruptions.

The early inhabitants of this cracked land were the Vikings, and the nineteenth-century travellers poured into the valley clutching

The Prose or Younger Edda, Popular Tales from the Norse, The Saga of Burnt Njal, translations from the Icelandic Sagas. The Vikings were arriving in Iceland from the 860s onwards. An early arrival was Naddod the Viking, who was driven onto the coast by winds. When he was sailing away he saw a snowstorm ripping across the mountains, so he called the island Snowland. Gardar the Swede arrived around the same time, modestly calling the island Gardarsholm. Floki came slightly later, with three ravens, which he hurled off the ship to show him the way towards land. He sailed along the coast of Iceland, and eventually landed at Vatnsfjord. The winter and spring were cold and when Floki climbed a mountain he saw the fjord full of sea ice. He called the country Iceland.

Iceland was an unclaimed, unregulated place, a place to start a new society in. Anything could be imagined, anything created, the Vikings thought, as they arrived from the western fjords of Norway: ships full of opportunists, the intrepid, the bored, the exiled, risking the journey to another place. Some fled the draconian attentions of King Harald Fairhair, who was whiling away the late ninth century trying to control the Norwegian landowners. By the thirteenth century, the *Historia Norvegiae* described the great island 'which by the Italians is called Ultima Tile,' inhabited by a multitude of people, 'while formerly it was wasteland, and unknown to men, until the time of Harald Fairhair.'

Ketil Flat-nose and family made a typical retreat, which was etched out in one of the Sagas. Ketil Flat-nose came from a prominent, powerful family in western Norway. When he learned that King Harald Fairhair was expecting him to submit absolutely to kingly authority, without receiving any compensation for kinsmen killed by the king's forces, he decided to leave the country. There was little honour to be gained by sitting at home waiting for King Harald's henchmen to chase him from his lands, Flat-nose decided. His sons had heard good things about Iceland: it was a country where land was available and there were always whales off the coast and salmon in the rivers, they said. The sons set out for Iceland the same summer, landing in the west, though Flat-nose, who did not want to spend his dotage on a fish-farm, set out for Scotland. After landing in Scotland, Flat-nose immediately set about plundering and pillaging, and then made peace with the Scots and, so the story goes, was given half the kingdom of Scotland. Some of his family went to the Orkney and Faroe Islands, and eventually his daughter Unn the Deep-minded set off to find her brothers in Iceland. The Saga about Flat-nose and his children ended with one of those lists of descendants the Vikings loved, running away through the generations: 'Alf's daughter was Thorgerd, the wife of Ari Masson. . . . His father, Mar, was the son of Atli, son of Ulf the Squinter and Bjorg Eyvindardottir. . . .' These Vikings had names to make legends of, names like Grimsson Red-cloak, son of Grim Ketilsson Hairy-cheeks, Asbjorn the Fleshy, Ragnar Shaggy-breeches, Asgeir Audunarson Scatter-brain, Audun the Uninspired (a poet), Thord Snorrason Horse-head, Eyvind the Plagiarist (a poet), Eyvind the Proud, Hrolf the Walker, Thorbjorg the Little Prophetess, Hall Styrsson, son of Killer-Styr, Sarcastic Halli (a poet), Sigtrygg Silk-beard, Finn the Squinter, Thorbjorg Gilsdottir Ship-breast, Hallfred the Troublesome (a poet), Ref Steinsson the Sly, Groa Dala-Kollsdottir, mother of Bersi the Dueller, Hallbjorn Half-troll, Ketil the Slayer, An Bow-bender, Thorhalla Chatterbox, Odd the Hermit, Eirik the All-wise, Thorbjorn the Pock-marked, Thorir Ingimundarson Goat-thigh.

At first there was no ruler of the Viking retreat, no administrative centre; the new arrivals stayed on their farms, among the vast flat plains. In 930 a legislative body of important men was created, and Thingvellir was where the settlers gathered, for the meetings of the Althing, the National Assembly. The word recurred across the Viking Empire: in the Tingvold of Norway, the Dingwall of Ross-shire, the Tingwall of Hjaltland and the Tynwald of Dumfries and the Isle of Man. Imagination amplified the uncanny sunsets, the shadows lengthening over the dark plains, and in the Sagas the nuances of legal process mingle with breathy tales of trolls, ghosts, berserks and enchantments. The Vikings had travelled far, they knew the Anglo-Saxon world; their writers knew the works of Bede, St. Augustine, Pope Gregory the Great, Alcuin. In the long winter nights, they told stories; they had many stories to tell. The silent grandeur of the plain at Thingvellir reproached later Icelanders, as the country turned to corruption, and they idealised the past, compiling Sagas and early stories, writing out the Norse myths.

The Icelandic painter Thorlaksson painted Thingvellir in 1900 as a place of rich greys and blues, the mountains reflected on the surface of the lake, a solitary horse in the foreground, staring beyond the frame. An iconic image: the bizarre semi-hostile nature, the semi-wild animals, and the empty silence, as the sky swirls over the dark mountains. In Iceland in 1900 there was no need to paint nature pink, or gold, as Man Ray would later paint forests. The emptiness of the Icelandic landscape hardly called for ironies of paint. There was no need for the blurred visions of Monet and the Impressionists, objects perceived through a haze of light and dust, the snapshot portraits of Toulouse-Lautrec, the fractured images of Picasso and Braque. Thingvellir in 1900 was stark and unrefined— a place of black rifts and pallid lakes, lit by a trembling sun.

It was the same as I stared across the plain. A plain driven through with a dark chasm, caused by the clash of tectonic plates. The plain was silent, except for the sound of cars leaving the car park, their tyres skimming on the wet road. There were a few tourists wandering the slippery trails, peering into the chasms, pausing on the wooden bridges to look at the silver river.

I stood on the plain flanked by deep rifts, gullies in the yielding turf. The river Öxará meandered across, spilling out muddy streams. The lake of Thingvallavatn glinted in the cold afternoon sunlight. It was a strange valley, there was something haughty about its windswept stretches, its indifference to the comfort of its visitors. The paths I walked were wet with fresh mud, and the rain fell harder, sending up a cloud of spray from the lake. The plain was spartan and mysterious; there were a few signs stuck into the mud, signalling the place where malefactors were drowned, or the place where the visitors built their booths, protecting themselves from the swift rain sweeping through the valley. I stood on a bridge over the glistening river watching the rain splash on the surface of the water. The scenery wore the dampness well, the dark rocks were slick with wetness and heavy clouds scudded across the sky.

There was Anthony Trollope, visiting Thingvellir on a tourist trip in the 1870s. With his hosts Mr. and Mrs. John Burns, and the other travellers—Admiral Ryder, Admiral Farquhar and Mrs. H. Blackburn—he rode on horseback across the plain. They had more horses in line behind them, carrying their provisions, which they had brought with them from Scotland, not trusting the local food. Down the rifts in the rock he and his group peered, seeing black deep water at the bottom, 'almost infernal to be looked upon,' Trollope shuddered. Mysterious and violent, he muttered. The blasted fields of Iceland were too much for his party; Mrs. Burns his hostess discovered at Thingvellir that she could hardly go any further, her horse had proved uncomfortable, the heat and labour too great, and the bother of riding side-saddle had quite finished her. She slipped from the pony, sweating, apologizing to the party, longing to go to sleep in a bed, she confessed. But they had to sleep in the church at Thingvellir, the women lying on the steps around the Communion table, walled off from the men by a little rail, and the men down the nave, like memorial tablets. They tried to be jovial, but everyone had a curious night, sleeping by the altar of the small wooden church. Waking to find the moon glinting on the Communion silver, casting an ethereal light across the pews. Subterranean heat, eruptions, an ill-omened look to the place, wrote Trollope, who enjoyed a blackened sky and a thick ominous sunset.

At Thingvellir, the nineteenth-century travellers stood, as the tourists stand today, at the Hill of Laws, Lögberg—'the heart of Iceland,' 'the greatest marvel,' wrote William Morris. It was Morris I was thinking of, as I walked towards the Hill of Laws, where the Speaker of Laws stood, his voice echoing off the rocks of Almannagjá, reverberating back into the valley from the sides of the chasm. For Morris, the landscape of Iceland was the last link to the world of the Icelandic Sagas. At Thingvellir he was quite ecstatic, writing in his rain-splashed diary as the storm dripped onto his hat, and refusing to go into the church because he was having a sudden and perfect vision of Ref the Sly. Morris wandered around, the rain soaking through his hat, thinking about the Vikings. Fantastically intrigued by the Vikings, seeing phantoms, his imagination transforming the plains. If he came to a patch of marshland, roughly in the right place, he thought that here Thorolf Dark-skin, who had been stealing livestock and offering up both men and animals, had sat down in the swamp and wept, because he saw his enemies were going to kill him. Jokul son of Ingimund had followed him there, to this piece of marshy ground Morris had just arrived at, and it was here or roughly hereabouts, he imagined, that Jokul said to Thorolf Dark-skin that he was a great monster and a villain without courage. Here, Morris suspected, Jokul dealt the death blow and Thorolf Dark-skin sank into the marsh. Here was the place where Njal the lawyer stood stoically awaiting his nemesis, and where Osvif lived, the son of Helgi son of Ottar son of Bjorn the Easterner son of Ketil Flat-nose son of Bjorn Buna, and this was where Gudrun did the washing, the most beautiful woman to have lived in Iceland.

Morris found a rough utopia: his bent was anti-modern; his tastes turned to lavish medieval scenes, knights on horseback, damsels with long tresses, and in Iceland he saluted a simple and archaic life. He savoured the small settlements, their low gabled sheds like grey tents, built on a rare patch of green in the desert, with sheep and cows grazing around. For Morris, it was an 'Isle of Refuge,' the home of those 'representatives, a little mingled with Irish blood, of the Gothic family of the great Germanic race.' A country very remarkable in aspect, he wrote, little more than a desert, yet the most romantic desert to look at: a huge volcanic mass still liable to eruptions of mud, ashes and lava. Anyone travelling there would be apt to hope, wrote Morris, if they knew nothing of Iceland's history, that its terrific and melancholy beauty might once have been illuminated by a history worthy of its strangeness; nor would they hope in vain. The bizarre contours of the lava fields, the exploding glaciers, the mountains dripping fire, had brought forth a race of bold warriors: 'the delightful freshness and independence of thought of the early settlers, the air of freedom which blows through them, their worship of courage, their utter unconventionality.' Their heritage, he added, had been sustained to the present day. The modern-day Icelanders, as Morris found them, spoke the language of the earlier Gothic tribes, 'almost intact,' and 'the shepherd on the hill-side, the fisherman in the firth still chant the songs that preserve the religion of the Germanic race. . . .'

Onto the blank resonance of the valley, the cold greyness of the lake, Morris conjured a cast of Saga warriors. Under the shadow of Almannagjá, he imagined immense crowd scenes, with thousands of extras, Viking warriors lurking in every rift. Morris worked himself into a thrilling frenzy, gasping at the cracked earth and the rivers of fire, remembering old stories of Viking warriors. He saw cold blue hills and blackened rocks, and patterned the scenery with imaginary spectres, spilling Vikings, wraiths and eidolons onto the empty mountainsides. He saw a land unlike his own, bringing the consolations of difference—the empty plains, the wide-eyed innocent inhabitants, as Morris found them, living in their simple land. The hills and stark valleys of this Saga-land, scarcely changed since the Saga age.

In 1874, shortly after Burton and Morris had gone home, the new Icelandic Constitution was signed, giving the Icelanders some domestic autonomy, after years as a Danish colony. 1874 marked a thousand years, probably, since the founding of Iceland by the Norse sailors. A host of journalists appeared in Iceland, observing the events, feeding their domestic audience of Saga-fans with news of the liberation of Saga-land. The Icelanders chanted a celebratory verse:

'Ages thou numberest ten, unconquered and long-biding Thule!
Hardy mother of men, Thor grant thee life through the ages,
After thy sad, sad past, may Happiness smile on thy future,
And Liberty, won so late, crown every blessing with glory.'

We were once Thule, the people chanted, and we will be great again. Just look outside, at our weird country, they might have added; how could we not be great, with this extraordinary auto-mutating landscape, constantly creative, a Protean reverie—stretching and pirouetting into lava statues as far as the eye can see?

The placid waters of the lake stretched beneath, a great sheet of water with an island lying in the middle looking like a broken-down crater, great pointed hills on two sides of it, the heavy grey mountain of Armannsfell behind, and the lava lining the slopes to Skjaldbreiður. The spiky hills stood dark against the sky; the deep water was green like the cold sea. A soft wind blew across the lake, and a long line of mist drifted across the plain. I took a cup of coffee in the Valhalla Hotel. A woman served me, blonde, pale-eyed, setting the coffee down with a watery smile and then disappearing, apparently for ever. I sat in the nearly empty room, with a fire dying in the grate. A German couple sat a few tables away, hidden in the semi-darkness, murmuring a low commentary on the plain. The wind shook the windows. Outside, a van moved slowly across the muddy car park, driving into the misty evening. I watched it cross the valley and the glinting river, until it disappeared into the receding contours of the mountains.

———— ∞ ————

The ring road in Iceland runs north towards the volcanic region of Mývatn, a place of blasted rocks and pastel plains, where the sun lingers through the night in the summer, shining a pale light across the scarred landscape. Through marshlands and craters the road runs, along the base of grey and purple mountains, past blue waterfalls cascading through gullies. Past the petrol stations and snack-bar villages, civilization pared down to essentials. The road turns to rubble at times; it passes through lush green valleys; it rises into grey mountains, past lunar slabs of rock in pastel shades. The mountains become multi-tone—the whiteness of the snow stark against the orange sand-cones and the dark ash slopes. At the coastal towns everything is coated in mist and the dull shapes of farms loom from the whiteness. The road runs past the silver waters of lakes, over the table mountains. When the mist falls away, there are rivers and a few slender firs, clinging to the rocks. There are hotels, surrounded by baroque basalt pillars. The mists swirl across the plains. When the light dwindles, patterns begin to emerge from the lava, the piles of rocks like stacked-up coals, the deep blue river carving a channel through the valley, the conical peaks jutting out of the uneven ground. The lowland plains are coated in grasses, scattered with boulders; the mountain slopes are delicate layers of ash rock, with snow dusting the higher peaks. All these cracked slopes stand with the clouds casting shadows across them, the empty road winding under them.

The landscape is transformed as the road reaches the north. The colours change from gentle greys and browns to the brilliant orange of the sulphur hills, the white of the snow on the peaks gleaming under the silver light. When the road reaches the volcanic centre of Mývatn—a lake blasted by past explosions, surrounded by thick fields of lava—the buses drop off their passengers, leaving them at the hotels and campsites. They are left in a volcanic plain, surrounded by enormous piles of ash and pools of water steaming in the twilight.

I arrive in Mývatn as the landscape fades under a star-swept sky. The bus grinds to a halt in Reykjahlíð, the main town at Mývatn, a tiny place of a few houses and hotels and campsites, deluged on all sides by greying lava rocks. Low mountains of sand and ash rise around the town, their colours dull in the twilight. The hotels are all full, so I walk to a campsite on a pile of lava, trying to escape the midges that hang around the edges of the lake. The clouds are thick and black by the time I have put the tent up, and the stars have been obscured. I sit for a while on the lower slopes of one of the hills, looking out at the green islands looming from the rain-spotted waters. There's a busload of French tourists setting up camp close by, and the smells of their cooking make me ravenously hungry as I sit in the tent, staring at the view. Mývatn is a fire-blasted place of black rocks and steaming sulphur pools, with the volcano of Krafla lurking to the east. At 3 A.M., I am woken by the wind lashing the sides of the tent and the persistent thrum of rain on canvas. I unzip the door of the tent and peer out. The skies are a pale grey; the lake shines under scudding clouds. The islands radiate a cold light. A long lion-shaped mountain sprawls to the west, a table mountain to the south, and another pile of black ash lurks in the distance. The rocks are shaped like creeping shadows. The air smells of rain and moss.

I start awake throughout the night, as if in response to a noise, but whenever I unzip the tent the pale skies swirl silently and the lake gleams under the moon. Nothing moves across the charred rocks, and the irregular mountains cast their baroque shadows on the valley. It's as if the lake is haunted by the ghosts of explosions, by the shocks and sounds of a rumbling volcano, or as if something in the atmosphere makes me uneasy, causing me to jolt upright at intervals. By morning I am tired and unkempt, mumbling greetings at the French campers, who have already packed up their breakfast things and put on their walking boots by the time I emerge from the tent. The lake is mesmerizing, the wind tousling its surface, the waves sluicing against the spectral moss islands. The whole valley is disorienting; everything is improbably coloured, every rock clashing violently with its neighbour, and the ground I walk upon is pitted and gashed.

Most of the Victorians never reached the north. Many of them turned back at Thingvellir, already satisfied. Slightly exhausted, variously impressed, saddle-sore, Trollope and party trotted back to Reykjavík, as did Mrs. Alec Tweedie, who had much enjoyed her trip in this far-off region of ice and snow, so full of natural curiosities, so abounding in ancient history, so isolated and so quaint. She had not made much use of her fishermen's boots, but that was for another time, and her serge dress had been most practical. But the stalwarts packed up their horses and travelled north. Muttering about the Sagas, longing to see something still stranger and emptier, something even more like Thule. William Morris trotted north, sounding sporadic eulogies to the simple contemporary Icelanders. Richard Burton galloped north, hardly thinking about the Vikings but fascinated by the exotic, hoping to find more of it. He galloped off, hurling polysyllables into empty space. Erminities of ice and snow, he muttered, twirling his words like batons. Jerking his head backwards, trying to keep a distance between himself and the other packs of tourists.

Mývatn was where the terrible burning mountain of Krafla lay. In the early years of the nineteenth century, the travellers couldn't persuade the locals to take them there. Widespread opinion was that Mývatn was so chilling and unearthly that only the word "hell-mouth" could be applied to this part of the trail. Hideous gulphs, the travellers noted, festering stagnant waters, craters like cauldrons, emitting thick black smoke. The last eruption of Krafla, they whispered, was terrible and impetuous; it vomited flames and matter in a state of fusion, which rolled down in torrents and inundated the neighbouring fields. There were stories of rivers of fire, rolling three leagues from the mountain, a league in breadth, propelling globes of fire into the air, brilliant red balls which could be seen from miles away.

The morning was windswept. I walked across moss and lava towards Hverfjall, a black decapitated cone looking like a charred sand dune. The route crossed a dust and shrub track, the ground crackling under my feet. I walked slowly towards the red mountains. The track was deserted, the wind blasted dust into my eyes. I walked towards the Leirhnjúkur crater, where the hot springs were drawn on the map like blue tadpoles, piled up around the volcano of Krafla. It was beautiful, but cold and pale, a place of shadows emerging from the hollows, stretching along the pitted surface of the valley.

I struck off on a track along an empty mountainside, into a lava forest—the lava like gnarled branches, twined together. There was a rock bridge between two valleys. On one side the approach to Krafla, where the geothermal power station was smoking and steaming, its pipes running in intricate silver lines across the valley. On the other side was the lava forest, a memorial to past explosions. It was a two-sided view: the pastel paleness of the Krafla range, with the orange and cream mountains bright under the sun and the black wreckage of the lava rocks.

I dropped down along the side of the lava fields and followed their edges to the south. I walked to a point where the lava came to a halt, and I could see across to an offshoot of dark shapes, blackening the floor of another valley. The pastel mountains rose above, and the steam drifted from the sulphur pools below. As the afternoon drew on, the landscape softened, and I began to leave the lava behind. I walked through dust and grass layered upon gentle slopes. Ahead loomed the block forms of low mountains, crouching on the horizon, and the smooth sides of the Hverfjall crater looked like a smudge against the white sky. I was thinking of the legions of past travellers, who had stood and gazed at the lava field, like a freeze-frame image of an ocean on a stormy night. It was a sci-fi desert, with the rust colours of the mountains and the sharp black forests of lava. Undulating plains, erupting into perfect cones, splayed ridges, crater rings, table mountains standing isolated in space, with nothing but blackened rocks and vibrant flowers at their bases. There were rocks coated with reddish paste, and hissing pools, and the blue and white shapes of the glaciers in the south.

The Victorians stumbled above bottomless crevasses and engorging ravines; they looked across the ragged horrors of the blackened lava fields, towards the unknown vastness of the glacial plains. Morris found the region full of brutal mountains, and his horse jolted over the old lava, grass-grown except where the rocks thrust up through the moss. He looked across the great burnt pyramid of Námafjall; he admired the lava and grey-green slopes climbing towards the drab waste of the sulphur fields. He gazed at a curious collection of small cinder hills and lava, grown about with sweet grass. He found the lava near Krafla 'terrible-looking enough,' all in dirty flakes at one end, or broken into rough fragments. He wandered through marshy tarns; finding islands of grass in the lava flow, he found huge clinker rocks of lava at the foot of the hills, steep sandheaps burned red and yellow by the sulphur. He passed through hills of sand and stone, a big green plain, a black ridge, mist and drizzle, 'so that our guide was at fault,' and then he reached a long lava valley with low walls.

Into the trance came Richard Burton, muttering on the rocks. Standing in the lava forest, Burton struck a different note. Burton was comically furious. He had reached the crater lands of Thule, and insisted that he found them beautiful and arresting, but hardly *unheimlich*, hardly weird. He had suspected this all along, he had doubted that reality could be in any way as bizarre and disconcerting as everyone had promised, and in Mývatn he was convinced. 'I imagine,' he wrote, irritably, 'that most of the *contes bleus* about this great and terrible wilderness take their rise in the legendary fancies of the people touching the outlaws who are supposed to haunt it.' The surface was uneven, but hardly mountainous as other travellers had reported. It was a pile of old lava, far from devilish, with long dust-lines and stripes tonguing out into ashes and cindery sand. Burton thought it was a case of general hyperbole. Too many travellers were returning to Britain, parroting the expected, the wild weird version of Thule; whole travel books were being published using only the words 'horror' and 'amazement.' These people, Burton was beginning to think, had either never been anywhere else before, or they thought their books would sell better if they crammed them with exaggerations.

They saw scenes of thrilling horror, of majestic grandeur, and of heavenly beauty, where a more critical, perhaps more cultivated, taste would find more humble features, Burton decided. The landscape was the same, but the people had changed. The inhabitants were wiser, less superstitious; they no longer believed that Satan lurked at the bottom of the volcanoes, and for a fair wage, would take a tourist to the summit of almost anything, however sulphurous. The tourists had changed; they knew what to expect. They came with a dozen accounts swirling in their minds, of exploding springs, the land cracking into fire, the volcanoes spewing flames. A civilization in its childhood might be awed by the look of a place, Burton said, but a civilization as world-weary as the Victorians should seek out the useful in any land it came to, and try to harness the power of the nature it found.

He was playing devil's advocate, commanding the landscape to impress him, and his disdain seemed staged to me, a contrarian's response. Mývatn was exotic, undeniably so. It was a landscape full of odd shapes and surprises, a landscape of anomaly, its every contour and gradation defying expectations. Nothing fitted, no line of hills seemed to lead to another, and the colours were always shifting. Covered with geothermal power stations and the signs of tourists, the landscape was not entirely wild as I walked back to the campsite, but it was certainly haunting in its variegated rocks and jarring colours. But there was something that interested me in Burton's fury. It suggested a clash between expectation and reality. Burton expected travel to supply the exotic, the constantly arresting and extraordinary. When he lacked a superlative view, he lashed the landscape for its failure to astonish. When the weather was like domestic weather, wet and windy, Burton was enraged. Into the fantasy of a wild weird land came recalcitrant guides, thieving hosts, and the insistent fall of the rain, the mud splashing their legs.

I knew that despite their best efforts, the Victorians had sometimes felt like this, as they struggled to keep a grip on their horses, finding their serge stuck to their legs, the rain soaking their bags, drenching their lunch, which was anyway a pile of mouldering cheese begged from a farmer in the previous valley. Trying to retreat back to a wild weird land, the Victorians found themselves sometimes cross and tired, tetchy with their guides. Even Morris occasionally rebelled, damning his guide, refusing to camp on a patch of festering bogland, and complaining about the uncomfortable back of his horse. In search of an Arcadia, they found a real country. It surprised and sometimes disappointed them, the moments when it was just a small, struggling land, full of people trying to make a living. They had wanted the lava to enthral them; they were hoping their travels through Thule would supply pure escapism. I understood it, even as I walked through the lava forest. Into the holiday bizarre, the vision of a former world, came daily trivia, logistics, or the mechanics of travel. I found a beautiful land, a land of low shrubs and rioting piles of stone, terrible sheer mountains, coils of soft mist with the sun refracted like a halo. I found thick, engulfing silence, as I stood at Mývatn at the end of the day, looking across the barren plain. I found the relentlessness of the rain, the cold evenings huddled in ascetic hotels, the walls vibrating as lorries ground along the road, a view of discarded oil containers dumped in the yard outside.

Burton decided to leave the tattered old banner hanging above Iceland—keeping *Ultima Thule, A Summer in Iceland* as the title of his book. But he had removed the sense of exclamation to the phrase. Ultima Thule was something else to Burton: it was the real country of Iceland rather than a northern dreamworld.

SILENCE

⸻

He kept up his 'Ultima Thule' habits of refusing invitations, shirking introductions; and declined into this 'let me alone and don't bother me state. . . .'

Ultima Thule, being the third part of the chronicles of the fortunes of Richard Mahony, Henry Handel Richardson (pseudonym of Ethel Florence Lindesay Richardson, 1870–1946)

When I was a teenager my family spent holidays in the Lake District, travelling there each summer for two weeks in a stone cottage near Windermere. I pretended to hate it, sinking with feigned boredom into the car, complaining about the length of the journey. Secretly I was delighted; I swam in Lake Coniston, walked through Grisedale Forest and boated on Windermere. I watched the reflections of trees glistening on the clear waters of the lakes. I splashed into streams, swam against the cold current, drinking the water when it swilled into my mouth, clear cold water from the mountains. I camped in the garden of whatever small stone cottage we were renting that year, to listen to the sounds of the night stillness and the drum of rain on the roof of the tent. I would wake my brother early, and we would run across a field towards Windermere, to watch the wash from the speedboats slapping against the sand, to stand on the beaches staring out at the cloudy skies of summer.

As we returned each year to the lakes, the landscape came to act as an aide-mémoire, each mountain and lake conjuring memories of former years, and I wondered what would happen in a landscape stripped of personal associations. I was an irreligious child, finding it impossible to believe in any force beyond the human, but I longed for some sort of intense experience, some epiphanic moment. For purely touristic reasons, I wanted to be struck by a sudden sense of a vast transcendent force, something overwhelming. I wanted to understand the sensation that seemed to have gripped most of the writers I enjoyed at the time: Wordsworth, Coleridge, Blake and Clare. Finding nothing of the sort in churches or treatises, I wondered about pure pantheism, the rapturous contemplation of the creative spirit in nature—the spirit in the stones, divinity revealed in the breathing of the trees and so on. I wondered what would happen if I stood alone in empty space, looking at the vastness of the rocks. I remembered the fear instilled in me as a child by the shaking of trees in evening winds, as I stood ringing on the door of my parents' house, having been dropped off by a friend's parent in a car. I would glance along the street towards these forms, bowing and nodding in the wind, their branches seeming to reach towards me. Then the light of the doorway would extend towards me, I would be scooped into the warmth of the house, and the fear would fade.

Fairytales were played out in rustic places, dark forests, country villages, and Tolkien's *The Lord of the Rings*, which I loved as a child, was a mournful pastoral lament, creating an idealized Europe of green meadows and rushing mountain rivers, where small hobbits lived in holes in the ground, and tree herders spoke, and the enemy came as a technocrat, damming rivers and waging wars. There were dozens of gentle idylls in children's books: the Swallows and Amazons camping in the dales, their imaginations as rich as the view, naming the rocks after legendary mountains, finding treasure islands and pirates. Narnia was the unchanging forest, the Arcadia in the cupboard, or in the attic of the city house. There were darker Arcadias: the warped pastorals of the Susan Cooper books, which had been my favourites for a time, with their Arthurian world where pagan festivals bred surreal dreams—in one of the most febrile of the books a wicker figure thrown into the sea appears in a vision to one of the children.

In these books the fictional worlds were beyond the grasp of adults, except the occasional enlightened guardian, who understood the secret and turned out anyway to be a reincarnation of Merlin. They were gently didactic, adult writers trying to explain to children that later they might lose the ability to imagine themselves away from reality, or they would no longer have the time to. Later they would be forced to distinguish between the actual and the created; it would be a necessary part of their commitment to the world, distinguishing the plausible and rational from the insane, the eccentric, and the unfortunate. The rural Arcadias represented a state of innocence, a time when the individual could live free of the fetters of society, innocent of the realities of adulthood. The realm of experience—the world of adults, where rules were imposed on the imagination—was intertwined symbolically with the city. It was like the world of William Blake, in *Songs of Innocence and Experience*, which I read as a teenager—poems that pretended to be songs for children, but which spelt out the division between Arcadia and society in rustic images. Blake saw the country-city division less as a question of physical location and more as high symbolism, a supreme expression of the battle of the human spirit against the restrictions of society. For Blake, the countryside was less the place for a pleasing picnic and more a symbol of freedom from the fetters of convention, from the stultifying effects of orthodoxy, represented by 'mind-forg'd manacles' of the city. The *Songs of Innocence and Experience* divided the life of the spirit into states of freedom from social restrictions—states of innocence—and states of subjection—states of experience. London was where the individual was enslaved, 'bound with briars.' Emptiness and silence were freedom because they were devoid of the clamour of other voices telling you how to behave, what not to do, what to be.

After childhood, I moved only from city to city, moving

throughout my twenties from London to New York, to Paris, to Berlin, to Oslo, to London again. I was propelled by an obsessive urge to experience novelties: new places, new cities. For nearly a decade, I was unable to stay in any one place for more than a few months. I became addicted to the absolution of the aeroplane, the interim state of nothingness a mile above the sea, and the immediate immersion in a new environment at the other end of the flight, the mundane made interesting by virtue of its foreignness. I went from New York—stark skyscrapers, glass and concrete, the constant motion of cars beneath—to London, a riot of styles, representing a course of urban history, buildings built, ruined, burned, bombed, reconstructed; hills which had become estates; pastoral glades transformed into yuppie suburbs, the spirit of the place so Protean as to be crazed and schizophrenic. From London to Paris to Berlin to Oslo. The cities varied in endlessness—for relentless suburban sprawl London licked competitors; every sketchy parade of shops which seemed like the end of the city would be followed by another bank of interwar houses. Every year I was forced by a sense of pressure behind the forehead back to London, and then I would leave again shortly afterwards.

The city always drew me back, a city in one country or another. I was compelled by the show, the constant motion, the bizarre energies of colliding humans, crammed together in a lunatic experiment. Every sound represented a technology of the last century—the grinding of cars, the soprano whine of the plane engines, falling towards Heathrow, the bleeping of pedestrian crossings, the scream of burglar alarms, the sounds of stereos, pumping a bass-beat through car windows, through the walls of Victorian houses, never meant to withstand insistent thumping drum and bass. In a flat overlooking the Westway and the Hammersmith and City line, I watched the empty carriages, lit against the darkness, pulling into the station.

During a long humid summer in New York the whirr of the air conditioning unit had kept me awake for hours at night, and my thoughts had fluttered and twirled before resting on images of whiteness, vast plains of white ice, stretching limitlessly into the distance. I would doze, and the air conditioning unit would become a fresh Arctic breeze, blasting into my face, as I imagined a long, low plain of ice.

These were gaps in the old myth of Thule, the parts that remained uncertain through the centuries: just how far north Thule was, whether the sea had been frozen or sluggish, whether there had been midnight sun for months or just at the height of summer, whether the land was inhabited or empty, whether Thule was an island or not. These gaps meant that Thule could be formed and reformed, depending on your anxieties and predilections. Depending on what an Arcadia meant to you. It was a myth that could be made to fit, tailored and snipped at the edges, parts of it swept away, thrown in a cupboard, other parts cut in bright colours.

You could reinvent Thule whenever you felt a former Thule had faded, become tarnished. Even as Burton announced the loss of awe, kicking away the previous travellers, who were left fawning on the lava, his gaze turned towards the vast and ancient ice cap in the south. Despite his scepticism, he found he wasn't ready to leave Iceland. After Mývatn Burton carried on around the island, trotting on horseback across the lava deserts, staring ferociously at the view. He found there was something he liked, an element which compelled him: the silence of the plains, the ice spreading across the tops of the mountains, concealing ancient rocks. There was a silent glacier in the south of Iceland, a huge white blot not even mapped in 1872, an ice cap called Vatnajökull. A few years after Burton left, a determined man called William Watts crossed the glacier, travelling northwards from Núpstaður to Reykjahlið. Watts wrote later about 'the expanse of snow, losing itself in the northern distance; pure, silent, dazzling, beautiful, and spotless, save where a few black peaks and uncouth masses of dark rock protruded through the frozen covering.' It was a realistic sublime: the glacier was beautiful and spotless; the ice fields of Iceland, looming above the blistered plains and the curdled pools, supplied a sense of ancient space. It was a Thule of silence, a Thule of magnificent mountains and cold glaciers. A deep-time Thule, the indifferent ages revealed in nature, in the vast and implacable ice.

There's a ragged dust track leading to Vatnajökull which runs along the coast, weaving around the edges of the fjords. It passes cairns and stunted trees clinging to the dust, leaving the orange sand plains of Mývatn and passing into the monochrome mountains of the coast and the mist-shrouded plains. Cone mountains stand silhouetted against the darkening skies. In places the road is a rock track, hurling up pebbles as it passes through a lava field, the moss bright against the sand and the lava disappearing into a soft valley of low hills. The clouds are dark, hovering low above the mountains. A sign by the road says: DWELL IN A TURF COTTAGE LIKE THE OLD ICELANDIC VIKINGS DID!—but there is no trace of a cottage, or any directions to one. The sign stands, like a random lifestyle suggestion in the wilderness. The road runs across a river, into a terrain of rain-drenched hills and snow-capped mountains. The lava plains recede, and the mountainsides are green. A great plume of mist moves across the mountains ahead, drifting along the valley floor.

The white fog lies like wool on the ground, as I travel around the coast towards the south. The scree mountains disappear into the whiteness. The mountains tower above the concrete bunker houses. The road winds in an intricate pattern round the fjords, through green valleys, with birch trees and shrubs. The sea is white under a lingering mist; low rocky islands appear dimly off the shore. The basalt sides of the rocks have been carved into sharp columns and gullies by the pressure of ancient ice. The gradient sharpens, lifting the road into the cloud and rain; the bus passes into blankness.

Basalt chimneys disappear into the mist. At the coast, odd lonely rock formations emerge out of water, their sides rising steeply, speckled with moss. The mountains are divided into rugged shelves, which run horizontally along the rock faces. Everything is tinged with white mist shadow, thickening as it drifts up the sides of the mountains like smoke. In the south, around the town of Höfn, a junction for buses and four-wheel drives, the glacier tongues appear between the snow-covered mountains, lolling down the gorges, sending out a brilliant white glow.

In the languid summer evenings, Iceland is a nature church, with everyone bowing to the scenery. There's a cult of silence in contemporary Iceland, a cult of pure white plains and unpopulated mountains. Contemporary travellers turn to the astonishing emptiness of the interior, the riveting loveliness of the valleys, the peacefulness. Everyone is driving around Iceland in four-wheel drives, trying to get away from it all. Sometimes they drive towards the interior, bouncing their tyres on the rocks. But mostly they circle the island. The roads are never crowded. Only at the pit stops, the small towns, can you see the other tourists. And whenever we stop and talk to each other, we all say the same thing: the nature, the nature is so beautiful, so empty. We like the long shadows falling across the iridescent moss, the pewter lakes, the slow dying of the sun. Beautiful, we agree, and then we all climb back into our jeeps and continue on this quest for stillness. It is an anti-social impulse; the scenes we prefer are the mountains stripped of other people, the roads free of cars. This cult of silence understands purity as a plain white space, a space without the contaminating presence of other worshippers. A few we accept, a few hushed voices on the side of a glacier, a few demure trekkers nodding apologetically on a cliff face. But the hordes are antithetical to the stillness, so everyone is quick to leave the pit stops, filling up their four-wheel drives and taking off again into the silence.

In the phosphorescent morning sky, the cars move past the ice. The ice is piled high like a wall, stacked above the lava ground. At the base of the glaciers, the land is covered with pointed dunes of grey dust and moss. At the glacial lagoon of Jökulsárlón all the buses stop, and we all emerge into the frozen silence of the glacier pool. There are dozens of buses there, hundreds of tourists clutching cups of tea, but they fade into the background and the view is all ice—enormous chunks, patterned with dirt, like vast chunks of liquorice, striped black and white and blue. The bergs glisten as they move, slowly, towards the ocean. The sky is pale; everything seems blanched by the ice. The mountains stand behind; the glacier merges with the whiteness of the sky. Hundreds of terns circle around the river's edge. The bergs are stained with colours and reflected on the clear water, every berg ghosted by its mirror image. There are tour guides, saying that the view is transient; the glacier is retreating, causing the shoreline to erode, threatening the bridge. One day the road may pass this spot, and all the ice will have gone, they say. Everyone directs a camera at the ice, trying to preserve the place in holiday photographs.

I stand at the edge of the lagoon, sipping tea, watching the bergs twist slowly in the water.

After the glacial lagoon, the tourists seemed to vanish. The wilderness trekking centre at Vatnajökull was almost deserted. 'Besides,' said the manager, 'it has rained solidly for five days, so the tents have all been packed away, and the four-wheel drives have driven off.' He told me to camp anywhere. 'Everywhere is wet, it doesn't really matter where,' he added. Five days of torrential rain had swept across the valley, soaking the moraine sands, turning everything to mud. I picked a path through the lower valley, and dumped my bags on a patch of grass, where they sank slightly into the spongy sand. Delaying the moment when I would have to fumble with the tent poles, greasing my hands with mud, I left everything in a dirty pile and walked towards the glacier. The glacier was compelling: it had left debris across the plain, and it absorbed the sky, spreading across the whiteness. From the wilderness trekking centre I could see only a fraction of the mass of ice, and this fraction stretched for miles. I found no one on the paths as I passed a farm perched on the edge of a cliff and clambered over the sodden

ground towards a dirty glacial tongue and a long white river. The
mist was closing around the rocks. The rain began to fall again as I
descended along a long ridge, with the glacial tongue of Skaftafell-
sjökull visible below. There were vast ridges in the ice, coloured a
greasy grey, and grey lines like shadows beneath waves, successive
ice waves. I took a detour off the path and walked through wet
marshes until I was soaked, fording rivers, losing the way.

At the base of the mountain, I walked to the edge of the glacier,
where it declined onto the mud plains. The wind was whipping
across the valley. The stones and rocks on the wet sand were shattered; some had been smashed, others sliced into neat pieces, like a
cake. I crossed a fast-flowing stream and boarded the glacier at a
point at which the ice had reared up, showing a rough underbelly
coated in pebbles. The ice was like crystal buried under layers of
rubble; I rubbed off some of the upper dirt and rocks, revealing the
clearness of the ice beneath it. Clambering over a dirt pile I reached
the sliding surface of the glacier, which was streaked a slate-grey. I
felt a sense of a great gap—the white depths beneath the ice, and
the height of the white ice towering behind me. I heard a low
groaning sound from far within the ice. A river emerged from the
side of the glacier: a torrent which suddenly calmed and disappeared again further down. And it was not so much fear that I felt,
or any sense of pending danger, or any sense of the absolute; it was
more a sense of incongruity, the sensation which suddenly hits you
when you swim in deep-sea waters, and you imagine the bottomless depths far beneath your small, dangling legs. The glacier was
vast and ancient, moving slowly backwards, leaving a trail of shattered rocks behind. It emitted a chill, a force field of impenetrable
age. Beneath it were hidden lakes, torrents of water, and resting volcanoes.

Burton never arrived at the glacier; he only glimpsed the ice,
and the view alone caused him a moment of hushed reverence, a
significant volte-face. It was a dream landscape, he wrote. Beyond
the long white wave, ermine above and below spotted like a Danish

dog, two blue buttresses rose to the east, with a light-blue glacier spreading across the snowfields lying at the base. The sun was sinking as he watched the ice; the horizon rained light. He lurched into a last flourish, putting on his holiday baroque: 'the opaline play of the projections and prominences which catch the lights, the faint pink-azure of the shades, and the sky-larking of the cloud-hosts over the heads of the tallest peaks, set off by the umbreous black foreground, dull and sodden, by the beggarly features of the middle distance, and by the wash of deep damascene blue at the base, fall into glorious picture; and the presence of black spots suggest the haunts of some Troll-like race—I no longer wondered that there are superstitions about this mysterious realm of eternal snow.' Burton returned to the ship he had arrived on, steaming back to Britain, mollified by the glimpse of empty ice. At Vatnajökull, he had found something unusual, exotic in its stillness, worth the trip, worth the long crossing home. Because of this stretching silent ice, Iceland remained a Thule of sorts, thought Burton, a pure northern Arcadia, worthy of a few superstitions. The emptiness still allowed for pensive dreaming, moments of restful contemplation. It was a change of perspective: the wild weirdness of the land was less to be found in the exploding springs and the volcanoes and more in the properties of this silence, spreading across the mountains.

The ice haunted visitors, causing them to glance behind them, uncomfortable in the silence, in the empty ice-plains. The silence and the stones, the brilliant shades of the sand mountains, the swirling clouds of mist at the edges of the sea. There was grace and urgency, impressive force in the howl of gales, the rush of torrents, the roar of waterfalls, when the sea looked like cast iron, when the sky was charged with rolling clouds torn to shreds, when mists unfolded over the lowlands and when the tall peaks faded out of focus. I rested in the silence of the ice cap, loafing around at the edge for a few hours, watching a few straggling trekkers emerge along the path and stare at the ice-tongue for a while. As the evening rains began to fall onto the ice, I picked up my pack, and walked back towards the camp. Sheets of rain were slicing along the valley by the time I found my sodden bags. I stood under the canopy of the trekking centre, which had closed its doors for the evening, watching the moraine sands darken under the flood of rain.

W. H. Auden and Louis MacNeice came for the silence. They wanted nothing more, the exploding springs and volcanic eruptions hardly interested them. The poets travelled through Iceland in the 1930s, laughing quietly at the excesses of the Victorians, enjoying only the emptiness, refusing the rest. They were young—Auden was twenty-nine—kicking against the conservatism of their nation, but wary of world events, of the rise of Nazism in Germany, the biting political winds. A pair of poets, trotting delicately across the cracked plains: MacNeice in a long black raincoat and a peaked hat which he wore backwards, staring sullenly at the camera; Auden taking photographs. Auden had managed to persuade Faber to sponsor the trip, but he found himself suffering from writer's block. He had no idea at first what he would write or how he would write it. Fortunately, he had read Byron's *Don Juan* on the boat to Iceland, so he wrote letters to Byron in the style of *Don Juan*, his stanzas littered with hilarious rhymes. Auden and MacNeice found nothing but a thin unreal sun lighting the lava, simplicity like a spa cure. A consoling nothingness, devoid of great visions, or disconcerting signs from God, or moments of illumination.

Iceland supplied an escape from the noise of high society for Auden and MacNeice, mindful of the glare and hustle they had left. They called it 'over-emphasis'—the insistence of the city, the backchat and the self-pity, the constant noise, the radio and traffic lights. They spent a summer in Iceland, sissies on horseback, they joked, riding across the empty land. It was a place for contemplation, for those who had forgotten the 'necessity of the silence of the islands,' wrote MacNeice. 'In England one forgets—in each performing troupe/Forgets what one has lost, there is no room to stoop/And look along the ground, one cannot see the ground/For the feet of the crowd, and the lost is never found.'

They found themselves quiet in the country; MacNeice hardly spoke a word, he stood on the quay muttering Greek into his beard like a character out of Pound's *Cantos*, and after a long silence he said, 'God made the mice and the mice made the Scheiss,' and later he said, 'The dark lady of the Bonnets.' The accompaniment to their escape was the distant orchestral background, the news from Europe, the pleasant voice of the wireless announcer, like a consultant surgeon: 'Your case is hopeless. I give you six months.' War was coming, as they rode across the lava plains, as the 1930s turned to confusion, attempts at evasion, futile appeasement.

Byron was an unlikely correspondent for a voyage out of the city, far away from the smoky rooms, the gossip and the intrigues, the milieu he loved. But Auden agreed with Byron about Romantic ecstasies in nature; he mocked the devout response to landscape, the 'mountain snob,' the 'Wordsworthian fruit,' tearing his clothes and refusing to shave his chin, wearing a pretty little boot, choosing the least comfortable inn. It was a revolt against an earlier generation, a ridiculing of earlier intensities. 'I'm not a spoil-sport,' Auden protested,

I WOULD NEVER WISH
TO INTERFERE WITH ANYBODY'S PLEASURES;
BY ALL MEANS CLIMB, OR HUNT, OR EVEN FISH
ALL HUMAN HEARTS HAVE UGLY LITTLE TREASURES;
BUT THINK IT TIME TO TAKE REPRESSIVE MEASURES
WHEN SOMEONE SAYS, ADOPTING THE "I KNOW" LINE
THE GOOD LIFE IS CONFINED ABOVE THE SNOW-LINE.

He was very fond of mountains, Auden protested, he liked to travel through them in a car, and he liked green plains where cattle were, and trees and rivers. Auden thought the Romantic rot had to stop; it could hardly be seen as the greatest revelation known to humanity that the sun does not go round the earth, that man is no centre of the universe. He was particularly scornful about attempts to make friends with nature, nature humility which became simpering and laughable:

> FOR NOW WE'VE LEARNT WE MUSTN'T BE SO BUMPTIOUS
> WE FIND THE STARS ARE ONE BIG FAMILY,
> AND SEND OUT INVITATIONS FOR A SCRUMPTIOUS
> SIMPLE, OLD-FASHIONED, JOLLY ROMP WITH TEA
> TO ANY NATURAL OBJECTS WE CAN SEE . . .

The satanic rifts and belching devil pits were ancient and indifferent, and to keep doffing your hat and polishing off the best china for them was just as absurd as claiming to be master and lord over them, thought Auden. Mountains were pleasant in the dying sunlight, or under a rich red dawn: places to sit and watch a rustic scene or to set a camera on a tripod. The sublime was outmoded; when too many things were happening at home, Auden claimed that release lay not in intensity and passion, but in quietness and the non-event.

Auden and MacNeice came with all the phrases of the Victorians turning in their heads. Auden even produced a mock tapestry of quotes from earlier travellers, called 'Sheaves from Sagaland.' It was an array of bizarre sayings, compiled purely for the purposes of satire, full of profundities like 'Iceland is not a myth; it is a solid portion of the earth's surface' or random outbursts like 'Nowhere a single tree appears which might afford shelter to friendship and innocence,' or slurs on Burton's obsession with polysyllables, with one of his choicer phrases—'Ichthyophagy and idleness must do much to counter-balance the sun-clad power of chastity'— interpreted as 'Eat more fish.' They had dipped into everyone— Burton, Mackenzie, Ketil Flat-nose and his Saga friends—and they even found Shakespeare proving that nothing escaped him, using Iceland for an insult—'Thou prick-eared cur of Iceland'—in *Henry*

IV. They applauded William Morris, engaged in a dispute with his guide:

>—Let's go home. We can't camp in this beastly place.
>—What is he saying?
>—I'm not going to camp here.
>—You must. All Englishmen do.
>—Blast all Englishmen.

'Hear hear!' wrote Auden.

Auden piled all these former remarks into a single chapter, mocking them gently and pushing them aside, except one. One remark jarred, having nothing to do with the Victorians' Thule holidays: '*Für uns Island ist das Land*'—a phrase attributed to an unknown Nazi. For us Iceland is *the* Country. Auden laughed at it, adding a crack about Iceland's apparently being German, but the remark dogged him as he wandered around. It was an absurd statement, but he found himself in absurd times. It was the only one of the statements that he couldn't escape from. Unlike the others, which he could parody as the excessive remarks of a former age, this blank remark was part of the world Auden was trying to escape, the world of the stiff radio commentator, announcing the end of everything. It came from the suspense lurking under the dances and the parties, the febrile nerves of the 1930s.

During his visit, Auden was surprised by the quantities of German tourists travelling through Iceland on Aryan excursions. Auden found them on the bus to Mývatn, talking incessantly about *die Schönheit*, the beauty, of Iceland. But they meant a different sort of beauty, a different kind of purity; their interests had switched from landscape ecstasy to Aryan worship. 'The children are so beautiful, lovely blond hair and blue eyes. A truly Germanic type,' Auden heard them saying. The Victorians had admired the heirs of the Sagas, but they hardly had the same ideas as these later travellers, who applauded blond babies as part of the attractive scenery. One night, Auden shared a hotel with Hermann Goering's brother and Alfred Rosenberg. He found himself exchanging small talk over breakfast with Goering's brother, who looked, thought Auden, nothing like Goering. The Nazis, he wrote, 'have a theory that Iceland is the cradle of the Germanic culture.' Auden and MacNeice's *Letters from Iceland* was published in 1937, as Europe prepared for war, as the last meaningless treaties were signed, and Hitler prepared to annex Austria. The poets wrote out their travels as a brief turn in a graver show: they had seen the devout Germans coming to worship at Saga sites. They observed the shift from the Victorians, trotting through Thingvellir, waxing about simplicity, to the Aryan tours of the 1930s.

The blankness of Thule could be enrolled in any schema of fantasies about the north. It was a blank white space, available for misuse, its silent ancient rocks hardly likely to protest. It was a story of a last land, which had been debated and embellished over thousands of years. In the interwar years, Thule, like so many other stories about the north, attracted German racists, brooding on the defeat of Germany in the First World War. They were compelled by Thule as a myth of a pure land, mixing it up with their own fantasies about a pure northern people, the Aryans. Their dogmatism went against the indeterminacy of Thule, which had always been a word which suggested the ends of the known world, the places beyond the power of humans to conquer and influence. The brutal ideas of the interwar period were scattered across the ice plains.

SAVAGES

⦿⦿⦿

. . . Anarchs, ye whose daily food
Are curses, groans, and gold, the fruit of death,
From Thule to the girdle of the world,
Come, feast! the board groans with the flesh of men;
The cup is foaming with a nation's blood,
Famine and Thirst await! eat, drink, and die!

"Hellas," Percy Bysshe Shelley (1792–1822)

The idea of a land called Thule was taken up by a group of people meeting in Munich in the years after World War One. To disguise their activities, which were anti-Communist and anti-Semitic, they called themselves the Thule Society, and met in secret. The accounts of the Thule Society were garbled, written out by hysterical partisans, trying to make a name for themselves long after they'd been doomed to obsolescence, even by their former allies. But for a few years after the end of World War One, the Thule Society was a meeting point for future National Socialists, its guests and members including Adolf Hitler, Rudolf Hess, Alfred Rosenberg and Dietrich Eckart. The Thule Society was an early expression of the Nazi fetish for 'Aryan' tribes and northern lands, an early elision of an idea of natural purity with a belief in the racial superiority of a people. The Thule Society played a peripheral part in the agitation fomented in beer halls, the clandestine militias, the street battles, the rising suspicion of foreigners and the loathing of Bolshevism, out of which came the National Socialist Party. The Nazi obsession with northern lands was later forced onto the northern countries themselves when the German Army rampaged through Europe during the Second World War. Germanic racism, focused on Hitler, moved from 'Aryan tours' to violent invasions and breeding programmes.

In 1918 Munich was a faction-riddled warring city, tearing itself apart after the war. A city crammed with marginal elements, shuffling towards the mainstream, fighting on the streets. It was a city full of ready recruits for extreme causes. Disappointed soldiers, returning to a Germany made poor by the conflict, wandering the streets of Munich, looking for something to do, looking for an explanation for the chaos they had returned to. Disappointed civilians, who had lost members of their family and seen it had all been for nothing. A generation felt betrayed by the establishment, as in Britain and France, but this German generation was denied even the slender consolation of victory. The elegant streets of Munich's centre were crowded with people chanting slogans, demanding nothing less than revolution. In November 1918, a Jewish journalist called Kurt Eisner led a march on Munich's city barracks and the existing order collapsed. Eisner established a Bavarian Republic and presided over sprawling partisan chaos. He couldn't grasp the city; he couldn't persuade the Bavarians to accept a socialist revolution, anti-democratic as it became, increasingly remote from any ideals Eisner might have begun with. Initial idealism was replaced by a grim struggle for political survival.

The revolution fell into acrimony and desperation; after a few months in power Eisner was assassinated by Count Anton von Arco-Valley, a disaffected aristocrat. Eisner had been preparing to offer his resignation; his party had recently suffered a decisive defeat. Arco-Valley had previously tried to enlist in the Thule Society, though they had turned him down because he was partly Jewish. There were rumours that he had assassinated Eisner to convince the Thule Society members of his commitment to their cause.

Watching from the sidelines, terrified and militant, were the members of the Thule Society. They were a coterie of pseudo-academics, feigning a scholarly interest in the Sagas, secretly agitating against the Communists, the 'foreign elements' they thought were controlling the city, the international conspiracy of Capital, by which they meant Judaism, the enemies they feared were taking over Germany. Their leader was a faux-aristocrat called Rudolf von Sebottendorff, a man with a long nose, an indeterminate neck, small eyes like shallow indentations on his flesh. Sebottendorff's father had been a train driver with the surname Glauer, but Sebottendorff travelled widely in his early years, and claimed to have been adopted in Turkey by an expatriate, Baron Heinrich von Sebottendorff. Acquiring an aristocratic "von" was a tactic practised by the Ariosophists Guido von List and Lanz von Liebenfels, bourgeois Austrians both, with nothing noble about their lineage, who concocted a racist variety of spiritualism in the early years of the twentieth century. Sebottendorff managed to acquire tenuous aristocratic relatives, and with this new status he took to wandering around the Middle East, looking for patrons, reading about occultism and crafting chaotic theories about threats to the integrity of the Aryan peoples.

The Thule Society had previously been a local branch of the Germanenorden, a society obsessed with what it thought was ancient Germanic heritage, its members wringing their hands about the dilution of the German 'spirit' through the addition of non-'Aryan' elements to the population. Sebottendorff was an eager member of this group, having been lured by an appeal for 'Aryan' recruits, but when revolutionary elements gained control of the city Sebottendorff wanted a more mysterious title for the branch. He chose Thule, and claimed his group was dedicated to the study of the Sagas. The name Thule was innocuous enough on the surface, said Sebottendorff, but to those who 'knew' it gave a clear impression of the hidden agenda of the society. A clear impression because the old myths of the north appealed to extremist nationalists at the time, groups of Germans and Austrians in love with the heroes of the Sagas, leafing through tales of Viking violence. The Thule Society could have been what it claimed to be—a few scholastic Bavarians sitting around talking about the Sagas, a German version of the Viking societies in London. But the interests of Thule Society members went beyond the Sagas; their fantasy was a Germany stripped of all those elements they regarded as 'alien.' Only Germans 'of homogeneous blood through generations' were allowed to join the Thule Society.

The Thule Society set itself against the atheism of Communism and the materialism of modernity, claiming allegiance to an ancient spiritual force, the ancient heritage of the Germanic race. The society mixed reactionary mysticism with political agitation, and the 'Thule *Leute*' (Thule People), as Sebottendorff liked to call them, played a role in the militant anti-Communist activities in Munich, in the activities of the Freikorps, a militia organization. Alfred Rosenberg, who went on to become Hitler's propaganda expert, spent the early 1920s editing the *Völkischer Beobachter*, the Thule Society's newspaper. In a gloomy gothic typeface bleeding across the page they flaunted their anti-Semitism, goading the city to a fight—'Only buy in German shops!' they cried—their anti-Semitism inseparable from their anti-Communism: 'Against the Republic!' The Communists were Jews; Eisner's movement was an attempt by foreign Bolshevism to take over Bavaria, claimed the *Völkischer Beobachter*, fervently.

In a long line of dreams about Thule, those of Sebottendorff and his fellow 'Thule People' were the most savage. Sebottendorff had read old Zoroastrian texts describing a lost Aryan homeland, *Airyana Vaejah*, which some thought had been in Siberia. Thule, Sebottendorff thought, was the place where the Aryans had originally lived. He imagined Thule as somewhere hardly *unheimlich* at all, far from uncanny and strange. It was, he thought, an 'Aryan' *Heimat*, homeland. He took the Thule of the classical poets, the philosophers and the fantasists, and used its ambiguity for his own purposes, as a code word between like-minded extremists. Thule was just one of many symbols and ideas they used; the Thule Society members were fascinated by alchemical and eastern symbols: rising suns, daggers and swastikas.

By early July I was in Munich, a significant change of scene, from the shattered rocks and purple plains of Iceland to the tranquil forests of Bavaria. The sun was beginning to fade when I arrived, drifting towards the turrets and towers of the city. I took a tram from the main station, which rattled through the streets, past the concrete of Karlsplatz in the city centre. Stepping off at Sendlinger Tor, an entrance to the old city, I dragged my suitcase along a paved main street, past designer shops and organic cafés. On a warm day the city seemed sedate, a place of elegant buildings, painted pale colours, with the towers of churches rising out of the lower lines of housing. I walked along the slow streets, arriving at Marienplatz where the crowds ebbed across the square, fumbling with cameras and hats. The green onion domes of the Frauenkirche loomed above, one of the central sights of the reconstructed Old Town. Munich was severely bombed during World War Two and carefully rebuilt in the post-war years. Leering over the square was the neo-Gothic Neues Rathaus, its façade covered in gargoyles. There were a few people standing beneath, waiting for the clock to chime, when a pair of copper figures would appear, dancing stiffly.

Evening was falling across the city, across the patched-up buildings, across the reconstructed rows, the seams hardly showing. The streetlights were flickering into life, shining against the fine stones of the Residenz, the former palace of the regional monarchs, the Wittelsbachs. The trams whirred along the streets, past the cafés closing their doors and the shops with their shutters down. Neon lights blazed along Sonnenstrasse, pointing out the sex shops and cheap takeaway joints. Bells echoed from tall churches and faded monuments. Footfalls, the soft sounds of the locals going home, punctuated the stillness, and there were other locals forming orderly lines for the trams. The forests stretched beyond the city, green hills, clear lakes, miles of quiet countryside, under the cover of dusk.

I found my hotel, an inn near a food market in the centre, run by a beaming woman who dragged my suitcase out of my hands and thrust it into the arms of her son. 'Take it now,' she exclaimed. The son, a broad-shouldered teenager, lugged it willingly up the stairs. The room was decked in Bavarian kitsch: a dozen 1930s calendars framed along the walls, a range of wine bottles along the window ledge, dried flowers, wooden animals dangling from the light shades and signed photographs of faded celebrities. The effect was like a storeroom, hastily tidied for an unexpected guest. I found a place to put my suitcase and pushed open the window. Beneath, people were sitting in outdoor cafés in the market, eating portions of chips and drinking beers. The clocks chimed the hour around Marienplatz.

The bar downstairs was a beacon of noise, spilling jeering crowds onto the pavement. It drew me from my room. The scene at the bottom of the stairs was like a piece of performance art, entitled 'conviviality.' The Bavarians were sitting around tables, while the hostess slammed glasses of beer into their hands. Silence was *verboten*; everyone screamed and cheered, laughter came in basso waves across the room. The tables were engulfed in noise, a sense of community so pronounced it seemed like collective madness.

I sat by the fire, and a table called towards me. 'Who are you?' 'Why are you here?' I mentioned Thule, and one of them interrupted, a man with a blond moustache, who told me his name was Martin. 'Thule? But why here? Thule was in the north!' he said. 'You should go to the north!' said another. 'Why are you here?' another consortium of Bavarians was asking, and then the hostess slammed a vast tankard of beer in front of me, and they all forgot the question and cried: 'Your health! Your health!'

The guttural sound of Bavarian German merged into a soft sound track—pleasantries, comments on the weather. It had rained; it would rain, everyone agreed, sounding like a lesson in the complexities of German grammar. After Martin turned back to his friends, I spent the evening reading Goethe, leafing through *Faust* to find his song about Thule:

> *Es war ein König in Thule*
> *Gar treu bis an das Grab*
> *Dem sterbend seine Buhle*
> *Einen goldnen Becher gab.* . . .

In English the lines mean something like: 'In Thule there lived a king, faithful to the grave, to whom his dying beloved gave a golden cup.' It all works out mournfully enough: the king prizes the golden cup above all his other possessions, and drinks from it at every meal, while crying for his departed loved one. And when he comes to die, he hands over his kingdom to his heirs but refuses to give anyone his golden cup. So, in his castle by the sea, he drinks for a last time from the cup and then throws it into the waves below. After seeing it disappear beneath the water, he closes his eyes and dies. It is a fairytale song, its location in Thule suggesting a faraway land, a forgotten royal house. Thule is just one among the many references Goethe toys with in his play: from inevitable reams of classical mythology to tales of northern witches, elves and gnomes. It is another cameo appearance for the idea of Thule in a tale of unmeasured human ambitions, the ambitions of Faust for knowledge, which lead him to his pact with Mephistopheles. The refusal to accept imposed limits, the interplay between fantasy and reality, compelled Goethe. He took up these themes in his first major work, *The Sorrows of Young Werther*, and Werther became an early romantic archetype, a man in love with the 'inexpressible beauty of Nature,' a man of impetuous energies and charisma. Werther walks through valleys teeming with vapour, warmed by the meridian sun, he throws himself down by trickling streams, lying close to the earth, sniffing at plants and little insects, muttering ecstatically about 'the breath of that universal love which bears and sustains us.' But though his nature love runs to pantheism, Werther's desires are focused firmly in the human world, and when his love is unreciprocated, he falls into despair. Thwarted, his dynamism turns to destructiveness. Refusing life on any terms except his own, he kills himself.

Romanticism bubbled into the nineteenth century, poured into the paints of Caspar David Friedrich, who painted silent shores clad in mist or russet sunlight glinting across forests. Friedrich added spiritual yearning to his landscapes, making the scenery allegorical. In his paintings, he contrasted dying nature, trees decaying on a darkened mountainside, with white clouds and rising fog offering a fleeting suggestion of an invisible world. In *Sumpfiger Strand* he painted figures with their backs to a darkened shore, turned towards a cloudy sky, with traces of sunshine behind the clouds. The figures seem to wait for the clouds to lift, for the brilliance of the sun to be revealed. Carl Rottman, Joseph Anton Koch and Ludwig Richter painted heroic landscapes of hardy rustic people living simple lives in the country, praying under the trees, struggling against harsh winds. They were sometimes sentimental, like Richter painting pretty peasants decked in garlands, but then Richter could rise to moments of pity and terror, standing his rustics on tenuous mountain ledges, blasting them with winds, showing the agony in their faces. They were ecumenical: they roamed from Italy to Greece to Scandinavia; they painted any landscape they found striking. Some, like Rottman, showed a penchant for still blue Mediterranean waters and ancient ruins under a shifting sky; others preferred northern greyness. They were humbled and inspired by the vastness of the mountains, the physical embodiment of the complex workings of God, or the Life Force, or the World Spirit, finding themselves transported from the concerns of the everyday. The strain of German Romanticism had its florid moments; the nineteenth-century Bavarian king Ludwig II created the fairytale palace Neuschwanstein to the south of Munich and decked it with opulent gothic carvings, tableaux representing warriors in armour on horseback, lances at the ready, damsels with long tresses clutching their skirts. Ludwig II spent the family fortune on tapestries of Tristan and a theatre full of Wagnerian stage sets, and then succumbed to madness. A predecessor, Ludwig I, had adorned the Residenz with scenes from the Nibelungen Saga, though he tempered them with neo-classicism.

In the early years of the twentieth century, something began to shift. Reactionaries, fearful of the changes happening in Germany, turned nostalgically towards a nobler age, they thought. Extreme nationalists recalled the time when Germans were as Tacitus described them, a tribe of strawberry-blond warriors, living in the forests. At the end of the First World War there were German writers who claimed that the Germans had lost the war because they had not been rooted firmly enough in the soil. To glorify the land was to draw on the strength of unchanging ages, the vast forests and mountains, the abundance of nature, offering solace to a weak and beaten nation. The Thule Society members were transfixed by this dream of a rugged people living in the north, using it to console themselves for recent humiliations. The Nazis later dipped into this store of national myth, claiming that they followed a Germanic tradition, eliding Saga tales with Romantic ideas about the virtuous life in nature. Nazi nature love was the will to racial cleansing masquerading as heritage studies, a riot of pseudo-mysticism, rune readings and false history. They aped the Romantic transports of delight in the mountains and forests, but Nazi nature love was a form of national chauvinism—the people came first, and then the land, as the further proof of the purity of the people. Only the mountains imagined to 'belong' in some way to the Aryan race were to be memorialized. In the hands of the Nazis the ideals of Romanticism became a partisan obsession, spawning a range of things, from Hitler youth groups to an iconography of the Führer and 'his mountains,' though Hitler hated to walk uphill.

In Munich Nazi history seeps out from under the reconstructed stones. Hitler's rise through local faction fighting is well documented: his arrival as one of the uncertain soldiers; his meteoric ascent as an orator, addressing seething beer halls; his attempted putsch of 1923, when he tried to seize the city by force, and was imprisoned outside Munich. In the cult of National Socialism, Munich was the home of the 'movement.' Once he became chancellor, Hitler built a vast complex of buildings in Munich, around Königsplatz, a neo-classical square created by Ludwig I. Hitler wanted Königsplatz because of the regal columns and the shapely symmetry of the buildings. The buildings Hitler added to the square were brutal copies of this earlier neoclassicism, their columns harsh and unadorned, rising into horizontal slabs. The Nazi complex spread across the streets around the square; Hitler operated a deliberate policy of expropriation, which meant that by 1939 more than fifty buildings in the area were being used for Nazi Party activities. It became a site for Nazi carnivals and demonstrations: Königsplatz was where books were burnt in 1933; two years later, the square was paved with granite slabs and turned into a parading ground for Nazi troops. The former showpiece of the Wittelsbachs became Hitler's 'Royal Square.' By 1940 thousands of people worked there. The area had its own power supplies, warehouses for storing food, vast kitchens to serve the employed masses, its own post and telegraph offices. Underneath the buildings was an intricate network of bunkers and underground passages.

One of the main Nazi buildings was the Führer Building, where the 1938 Munich Agreement was signed, a failed attempt by a nervous prime minister to avert war. And against the backdrop of Ludwig's classical square, Hitler ordered 'temples' to be built, to honour the Nazi cult. There were two 'temples' for mystical ceremonies, the dramas of smoke and lights favoured by the Nazis. With these 'temples' Hitler made Königsplatz a centre of the pseudo-religion of Nazism.

They are now ruins, these 'temples.' In the early morning, I was standing in Königsplatz, looking at the fine white columns of Ludwig's buildings, with alcoves housing statues and pediments covered with bas-relief figures. With the Nazi buildings behind me, out of view, the square was harmonious. Ludwig's neo-classicism rose on three sides of the square, most of it created by a single architect, Leo von Klenze. Flags fluttered in the breeze; cars moved across the cobblestones. The morning was quiet and warm; the sun was beginning to break through the clouds. Yet when I turned, there were the plinths of the 'temples,' walls about six feet high, with trees growing on the top. The Americans ordered the destruction of the 'temples' at the end of the war, leaving only these remnants. They left the monumental ugliness of the Führer Building, which had survived the Allied bombing raids almost intact. Needing space in a devastated city the American troops used the building as a headquarters. Next to the 'temples' there was a board, offering a brief history of the square. It had been put up in 2001. 'Until now,' the writing on the board said, 'there has been no permanent reference on the site to the history of the square and its surroundings, a place where thousands took part in mass rallies to pay their respects to the cult of a death-dealing regime of terror which had no respect for human life. For a long time there was no reference on buildings which had been the architectural expression of the "capital of the movement."' The board ended with a message to all who stood there, surveying the buildings: 'Exhortation and commemoration of the Nazi terror must also bear reference to the sites of the perpetrators. This is the only way to ensure that the sufferings of the victims remain permanently in the public awareness.'

By the placard, I could hear a guide talking to her tour group. 'This is Königsplatz,' she was saying. The hybrid creation of former kings and later Nazis. The opulent columns of the early kingly buildings and the gloating ugliness of the Nazi bricks, everything jarring, the Nazi buildings straining for effect, designed for corruption. 'Please don't crowd too much around the information poster. Everyone can get a look,' added the guide.

The tour group stared round at the square. 'In this building,' said the guide as the tour group cast a collective eye on the blank lump of stone, close to where I was standing, 'in this building,' said the guide again, 'the British prime minister of the time, Neville Chamberlain, signed an agreement with Hitler in 1938, the appeasement pact.' And everyone nodded slowly, staring at the bricks. Now there was a music college in the Nazi complex; it was incongruous, but from inside came the notes of a sonata, played on a piano, nearly drowned out by the roar of traffic.

'Later,' said the guide, 'we will walk to the Feldherrnhalle, around the corner, which was where Hitler marched in 1923, when he tried to take over Munich by force.'

It was an anti-tour, an unfortunate turn for a city tourist board to have to take. Here, the guide would say, Hitler plotted the appalling events which would embroil the country in destruction; here some political opponents were brutally killed; here a former Nazi loyalist, Ernst Röhm, was condemned to death. Here the Nazis made the complex and delicate into something monolithic and savage. There were memorials throughout Munich, and an army of these guides leading people round the streets on tours of Nazi architecture and significant Nazi sites. On the sides of Ludwig's vast art gallery, the Pinakothek, next to Königsplatz, the post-war repairs were starkly visible. The bomb damage had been filled in with plain red bricks, which stood out against Klenze's ornate pale stone. Windows had been bricked up, as if the building were awaiting more intricate repairs. It made for a mottled façade, showing how severely the Pinakothek had been bombed. The centre of the building had been devastated, and rebuilt in this chastened style, redolent of a large factory.

I walked into the Pinakothek, and found the galleries almost empty. I meandered through the cold rooms, relieved to be out of the sun. In the Rubens room, there was an art student quietly copying *The Rape of the Daughters of Leucippus*, painting the pink curves of the women and Castor and Pollux on their black and white horses. The student was standing in ripped jeans, his shirt picturesquely covered in paint, dabbing his brush on his canvas. Walking past the student I found Rubens's portrait of *The Death of Seneca*, a dramatic canvas showing the philosopher preparing to die. Seneca had been accused of participating in a conspiracy and was forced by his former pupil Nero to commit suicide. Tacitus wrote that he severed his arteries and stepped into a basin of hot water. When this failed to kill him, he had himself carried to a steam bath, where he suffocated. In Rubens's painting, Seneca—a perfect muscular classical hero—is being helped by a doctor, who seems to have cut an artery in his left arm. Seneca is the quintessential Stoic, dignified and resigned, while on his other side, a scribe is writing down his last words. "VIR" appears on the page, suggesting VIRTUS. Seneca lifts his head, trying to ignore the pain of death, talking to the last about courage and worth.

It made me recall the Chorus of Seneca's play, with their ambiguous talk about Thule. It was affecting to stand by this portrait in the museum bombed in the war, surrounded by the stark bricks of Nazi buildings. This mottled museum, pieced back together again, with this portrait of Seneca preserved through wars. There was something continuous about Seneca writing about Thule, Rubens painting Seneca, and Ludwig I building his neo-classical buildings and collecting ancient statues in the nineteenth century. They were part of the same tradition, a Western classical tradition. Then there were the Nazis crafting their brutal pillars, thinking they continued the line of influence and creation. They had tried to manufacture their own mysticism, a deathly religion. They had built amphitheatres in forests, enjoying a rustic setting for their sites. And outside stood Königsplatz, where the trees were now growing on the plinths of the Nazi 'temples.'

⚬

The Thule Society had been a part of the climate that engendered Hitler, rather than a dynamic force in his rise. By spring 1918, Sebottendorff claimed the Thule Society had 200 members, and by autumn there were 1,500 members in Bavaria, with 250 in Munich, he claimed. During 1918 the Thule Society began meeting in rooms at the Four Seasons Hotel, which still stands in central Munich, on an imperial boulevard called Maximilianstrasse.

The hotel has a fine façade, with flags fluttering from poles, and tall hooded windows. The hotel lobby is bright orange, the effect of a glass roof stained in bright colours. The walls are wood-panelled; the stairs are marble. There is a large silver tea urn and a collection of armchairs placed around antique tables. The gold trimmings glint in the brightness. When I arrive, the lobby is full of tourists taking tea: a blonde woman in designer sunglasses and the easy casual clothes of the truly rich; a group of Japanese people waiting at reception, with suitcases lined up behind them. There are bright orange flowers on the reception desk, and on the wall hangs a tapestry showing a hunting scene. It makes for a glowing lobby at the Four Seasons Hotel, though the bar in the next room is dark, with heavy tables, creaking old doors and a few waiters wiping glasses.

I sit in the hotel lobby for a while, drinking tea, until the reception clears. Then I walk over and ask the concierges if they know anything about the history of the hotel. A book is produced and handed over. It's a hardback, crammed with photographs of famous guests and adverts for luxury goods. The hotel was founded by Maximilian II, who established a competition in 1858 for a new boulevard, which was named after him. 'There are a whole array of readily appreciable reasons for the outstanding status of this establishment in the hotel landscape of the Bavarian capital,' says the book. 'They lie both in the present and the past.' They lie in the princely origins of the hotel, in the long list of guests, a list including Queen

Elizabeth II, Prince Charles, George Bush Senior, Jimmy Carter, quantities of media celebrities, pop stars, tennis players, film stars from Woody Allen to Elizabeth Taylor. A roll call of the rich and famous, listed with pride by the hotel in its official history. But there is no mention of the Thule Society.

I find a senior concierge, who is serious and polite. He has a wide smile, revealing gaps in his teeth. He's immaculately dressed. He's greeted queens and princes and presidents. He's been photographed handing them over to the head chef; he's waved them off in their limousines. He tells me he knows a little about the history of the hotel. 'But you have seen our book; our book tells you everything you need to know,' he says, smiling. He's polite, but I imagine he's thinking that he has a thousand things to do, that there will soon be another wave of guests. The book is meant as the hotel's corporate reply to questions about its history, its prominent status in the upper echelons of Munich society over more than a century and its fortunes during World War Two.

'It's a fine book,' I say. 'But, and of course there are very understandable reasons for this, it says nothing about the Thule Society.' He has been very serious, and suddenly he laughs. Embarrassed, perhaps, or reluctant. Perhaps he suspects me of an indecent enthusiasm. He says, 'Oh, them. Well you know they are perhaps not my kind of people. Let us say there are different religions, you know, different beliefs, and those people had a very different religion indeed. A religion thankfully no longer observed by many people today. You know there are all sorts of people, unpleasant people, and they were here once, in the past. It is for that reason we don't mention them,' he says.

'What reason?' I ask.

'The reason,' he says, laughing nervously again. 'You know. There is a country with the Star of David on its flag, and these people would not really have got along with the people of that country. You understand what I mean now? I don't want to say what they were, but you know they were not pleasant people.'

'So you feel it is best they are forgotten?'

He is silent for a few seconds, then he says: 'A few years ago a production company from America wanted to come here, to make a film which included scenes about those meetings of the Thule Society. They wanted to film in our hotel, in the place where the society met. There was some debate about it, whether it was a good thing; you know, there is always the argument for talking about these things, to make sure people know the things that happened. But we said no in the end.'

'Where were they going to film?'

'Well, this society met in the Old Bar. That's where they met,' he says. 'So I suppose they might have filmed there. But we decided it is not something we want the hotel to be associated with.' He is still laughing, in a slightly odd way, as if I have opened a conversation that is slightly unacceptable, made something of a faux pas, but he is trying to help me out of the embarrassment.

He's employed to help, to answer enquiries, and he knows a lot about the history of the hotel. But he is in a difficult position. He's eager that I shouldn't push the questions further. He is hardly going to take me off to the Old Bar and show me where the proto-Nazis sat. He smiles and laughs as I thank him for his help. We move on to other subjects—afternoon tea, the weather outside. He stands politely, attentively, while we discuss the tapestry behind the bar. Then, he says uneasily: 'You say you knew about the Thule Society, somehow, meeting here. How did you know?' he asks. When I explain, he laughs with something like relief, a full-throated laugh this time, no trace of nerves.

Hotels, bars, restaurants are neutral places, where anyone can eat or sleep without being asked whether they are a potent force for evil or an innocuous passer-by. The Thule Society had sat in the hotel, talking bitterly about the supremacy of the Germanic race, and then they had vanished, to be replaced by other guests. Munich was full of places where unsavoury figures had sat, eating, drinking and plotting national resurgence. Places still trading, still serving up food and drink without asking questions of their customers. Practical necessity had extended the lives of many of these buildings after the war. As well as the Führer Building, there was the Haus der Kunst, another Nazi complex of columns and slabs, which was still standing by the river and was used for exhibitions and theatre productions. Many of the restaurants and inns where Hitler ranted and hectored were still serving up beer and noodles to their customers. The Four Seasons was still standing in central Munich, available for use. The Thule Society members had faded into obscurity, and no one was more eager to forget them than the polite concierge.

The concierge smiles as I wander off. He knows where I'm going, but he doesn't try to stop me. I walk along an opulent corridor with mirrors on the ceiling and pillars at intervals. It runs through the older part of the hotel, behind the reception. There are Maximilian salons in pale cream and white, with teacups and wine glasses ready in the corner, the curtains drawn against the damp day. Everything is bright and well washed, cleanly painted in light shades, except for the Old Bar, which has wooden panels and dark leather armchairs, with glass cabinets full of antique plates and cups and sculptures of birds. There's a portrait on the far wall of a woman riding side-saddle in long skirts. There's a round table set with a white cloth, surrounded by red-backed chairs. With an effort of the imagination, I could summon a collection of anti-Semites to the place; I could imagine them finding the close confines a pleasant place to conspire, to worship the ancient heritage of the 'Aryan' tribes. I could imagine their absurd evenings of Nordic song and dance, the high ceremony of a self-appointed elite. But in the intervening years the place has been bombed and rebuilt, renovated and restored. The room has no eerie atmosphere, no trace of the polemical vileness of the Thule Society. It's just a neatly restored room, in a luxury hotel, with a table set for tea.

Outside, the bells chimed across the city, the cars queued at the lights. The crowds were pouring into the Pinakothek, drifting past the Altdorfers and the Cranachs, past the painted landscapes. The crowds were surging onto the trams, travelling through the reconstructed city, stopping for cakes and ices at the cafés. The tarmac gave off a wave of heat as I walked along Maximilianstrasse, and the cars sounded like industrial noise, their tyres clanging on the tram tracks. I walked along lethargic streets, past cafés with their outdoor tables packed with people. In a crowded beer garden I waited for Ursula to come to the table. I'd been sent to see her by a professor at the university, who told me she knew everything about the Thule Society. Ursula, the professor had told me, knew all about interwar Munich, about the faction wars and militias and the seedy conspiracies. The professor thought, though he wasn't sure, that a member of Ursula's family had been in the Thule Society. It was perhaps best, the professor had added, if I didn't ask Ursula too much about this. When I called Ursula, she said she would talk to me, on the condition that she was neither exposed nor named.

The restaurant was filling up, but as Ursula sauntered through the door of the restaurant she looked six feet tall, imposing as she moved in high heels, dropping her coat into the arms of a waiter.

'Hello.'

'Hello.'

We nodded, we sat down; there was a curious air to the encounter, as if we were meeting in secret. Without any preamble, without ordering anything to drink or eat, she started talking.

'Everything is in darkness,' she said. 'It remains in darkness, it will always remain in darkness,' she said. 'Sebottendorff was a dubious man. A much-travelled adventurer. He had affairs, he lived in Turkey; he dabbled in Sufism, alchemical and Rosicrucian texts, he took Turkish nationality, he was accused of bigamy and of marrying for money. He was obsessed with the esoteric. The Thule Society had all of his chaos and obscurity.

'Sebottendorff said Thule was found by Pytheas in around

400 B.C.; Thule was probably Iceland, Sebottendorff thought. He knew Thule had been discussed as a real place. He knew Iceland was where the Sagas were set. The Sagas, he said, had made possible the development of the Germanic religion.'

We were sitting in the Hofbrauhaus, another place where Hitler had delivered speeches. The ceilings were plastered with paintings of pigs and platters, knives and forks. Women in Bavarian costume were moving between the tables, delivering mugs of beer and plates of food. In the beer garden the checked tablecloths were flapping in the breeze and a fountain trickled water. The doors of the restaurant swung open, and the sound of a brass band drifted across the courtyard. Ursula seemed not to notice. She screwed her eyes up against the sun. She fumbled in her bag for sunglasses. Then she spent a long time trying to light a cigarette. Shaking the lighter and inhaling, she said: 'You said you knew something about Thule. But these Germans, these Thule Society members, they took this idea of a last land in the north and made it the cradle of German history.' She paused briefly, and a waiter approached. 'Coffee,' she said.

'The Aryans, they thought, had knowledge of the magical power of the runes. The old runes,' said Ursula. 'As well as Hitler, Hess and Rosenberg, the other members and associates included Johannes Hering, Hermann Pohl, Theodor Fritsch, all anti-Semites, members of the Münchener Hammer-Gemeinde, the Wotan Lodge; they were all obsessed with the Sagas. All were listed by Sebottendorff as members of the Thule Society,' she said. 'Hering called the Thule Society "*die Treffpunkt*"—the meeting place. It's even confusing who was a member and who wasn't. Sebottendorff lied about everything. The Nazis Wilhelm Frick and Julius Streicher were named as members, also the publisher Gottfried Feder. In some accounts the chief of police was mentioned, and the *Oberbürgermeister*. Aristocrats, top officials, political agitators, millionaires. But the Thule Society was perhaps one of many small, unpleasant groups they joined.' The coffee came and Ursula drank it down.

'And a member of your family was also a member?' I asked.

She tapped her fingers on the table, a gesture of irritation, perhaps. 'We don't know. I said the lists are not reliable. It is possible, unlikely but possible. I don't think it is worth talking too much about,' she said, quietly. 'An ancestor of mine saw the Thule Society crest among her husband's papers a few times. But after the death of her husband, she went through his effects and never found it. By then it was the late 1920s; he might of course have lost these papers, or burnt them. He might just have been approached by the Thule Society and never actually signed up. I really don't know. It was the sort of society he might have joined, from what we know about this man. You of course understand that if you start rummaging through family histories in Germany you often find compromised figures, figures who allied themselves with all of this.' She said "this" with a curl to her lips.

'Could someone have attended meetings without realizing what the Thule Society was really about?' I asked.

'Unlikely,' she said, briskly. 'Sebottendorff used to give lectures blaming the Jews for the revolution in Bavaria. He spoke like this: "Our order is a German order. . . . Our God is Walvater; his rune is the Ar-rune. The Ar-rune means Aryan, primal fire, the sun, the eagle." A few years later this was the sort of language used by the SS. And later there was an element of planning that went on at these meetings.'

After Eisner's death the elected government fled, replaced for a short time by a collection of anarchists and afterwards by Communists, who declared Bavaria a Soviet republic. There were skirmishes between Freikorps soldiers and the Bavarian Soviets, and the Thule Society had links with the Freikorps. Their offices were raided, and some Thule Society members were captured and shot by the Communists in April 1919. Sebottendorff hailed them as martyrs; he later claimed they were the first people to die in the cause of Nazism.

The Thule Society began to decline, even as its members prospered. One of the founders of the German Workers' Party, Karl

Harrer, was a Thule Society member, but once he created his own group he left the Sebottendorff circle. By the late 1920s Thule Society members were a mere handful, and by 1930 the society had disintegrated entirely. Sebottendorff lost influence over the Thule *Leute*, and was dropped by his own members. He disappeared in the 1920s, roaming around the world again, as he had done as a younger man. He was bitter about their betrayal even in 1933, when he published his autobiographical account, *Before Hitler Came,* long after the Thule Society had become irrelevant. I had read his autobiography in the Bavarian State Library, a book printed in a typescript so Gothic the words seem to be trying to contort themselves off the pages. Sebottendorff's writing style was littered with archaisms, sudden explosions into ranting and blatant exaggeration. 'The Thule People died as the first sacrifices for the Swastika,' he wrote. 'The Thule people were those to whom Hitler first came, and the Thule People were those with whom Hitler first allied himself.' Sebottendorff struggled to prove he had created Nazism, listing the key Nazis who had formerly been Thule *Leute*. In Sebottendorff's version of history the Thule Society had been cruelly cast aside as the German Workers' Party became more powerful. With his self-hagiography, Sebottendorff tried to airbrush himself into history.

Sebottendorff's insistence on the origin of all things Nazi in the Thule Society was an unwise political move by 1933. The second edition of his book was confiscated by the Nazis; he was arrested by the SS, and encouraged to leave Germany. He disappeared on another global tour, arriving in Turkey, where he stayed.

'Sebottendorff lived out the war in Istanbul,' said Ursula. 'At least that's what I think. He drowned in the Bosphorus on 9 May 1945, shortly after the end of the war. Most likely he had killed himself.' She stubbed out the cigarette. 'You would, I suppose, if you had supported the Nazis in everything, even after they cast you out. If you believed, really believed, that you had created the movement which had died in the dust of Berlin. And he knew there was nothing for him once Nazism was over. His life was over. Ironically, you might call him one of Hitler's most loyal supporters, though Hitler had discarded him.'

We shook hands in the beer garden, squinting at each other in the brightness. 'You could go to the Residenz,' said Ursula. 'The riches are amazing. You see what the Nazis coveted; you see their longing for castles and palaces.' She walked away. As she pushed through into the beer hall, the sound of cheers and roars echoed around the cloisters, then the door swung back again and the sound died.

The sun was fading when I reached the Residenz. As the sky became sallow I walked through the Hofgarten, a small palace park. There was a Diana temple in the centre, where a lone busker was playing the violin. I trod on gravel, passing low hedges and pruned trees. There was a fence, its posts shaped like treble clefs, running through the park. The steady sound of footsteps echoed around the cloisters. The Residenz complex was being built as early as the fourteenth century, and a long line of prince-electors and later kings contributed their designs to its shape. After Maximilian IV Joseph declared Bavaria an independent kingdom at the beginning of the seventeenth century, the palace became increasingly opulent. Much of it was the work of Leo von Klenze, working through the nineteenth century, taking his influences from neoclassicism. The Wittelsbachs left it all behind at the end of the First World War. The last Wittelsbach king left Munich even before Kaiser Wilhelm II abdicated from the German throne in Berlin. The Wittelsbachs tripped down the stairs of their stone palace, past the stylish trompe l'oeil designs, abandoning rooms of family treasure and luxurious suites furnished with classical statues, moving through their dark courtyards, the stonework casting grotesque shadows. They closed the doors and left the palace to the crowds.

The Residenz swiftly became a museum. The National Socialists left it alone even as they began the building of 'temples' and monuments throughout Munich. But the war destroyed the place; in 1944 the Residenz was gutted by fire after a bombing raid on the city.

Inside, the restored rooms were vast treasure chambers. The ceilings gaped. There was a grotto with thousands of seashells stuck into the stone and a bronze statue of Mercury at the centre. The vaulting of the hall showed faded paintings, traces of past finery, fragmented scenes from Ovid. The windows were scratched and ancient, twisting the light, warping the view of the courtyards. There was a lot of fine wood in the place: beautiful cabinets in rosewood with a dozen secret compartments and tables decorated with intricate carvings and enamel pictures of Venice. In the Antiquarium, a long tunnel-like room, looking like an underground station with arched windows, there were classical busts lining the walls. The colours on the ceiling were subdued, because of damage during the Second World War, said a guide. But there were grotesque pairs of putti cavorting on the ceiling, and sketchy portraits of Bavarian cities and castles. The busts were of old Romans—a chronological series of imperial families. There were the wives, daughters and ancestors of Augustus, Gaius Julius Caesar's women, Nero's wives, the wives of Galba, Otho, Vitellius and Vespasian. Then there were the emperors, from Julius Caesar to Valerian, some of them with the names mixed up, a few losses sustained to the series. It was a grandiose piece of cataloguing, a decorative triumph for ambitious regional rulers. Among the emperors were random classical statues—a Hellenistic torso, a head of Hermes, a Diana with a broken nose, and an Aphrodite. There was a wooden fireplace, with the date of completion of the room carved onto it— 1600—and the name of the man who finished it all, Duke Maximilian I.

There were rooms leading into further rooms, opulently decorated with trompe l'oeil ceilings, and pictures of Napoleonic battles. There was a portrait of Ludwig I, staring benevolently at his riches. There were rooms filled with plates, plates with Roman heads on them, plates with rustic scenes of girls under bowers and cherubs, plates with Bavarian views on them. Rooms full of gold and silver in cabinets, candlesticks and serving dishes, everything slightly tarnished. There were rooms decked in tapestries, showing hunting scenes in forests. There was an audience room, with its walls coated in portraits of worthy peasant labourers, scything crops and tending cattle like virtuous subjects. There were stone rooms, with their floors coated in marble and everything else in muted shades of grey and blue and dark red. There were painted allegories—of the four seasons, of the elements, of the universe, of the church. There had been a painted allegory showing man as the conqueror of nature, but it was destroyed in 1944. There were great empty tables, cold fireplaces, everything sealed off, guarded by figures in uniforms.

There were rooms kept in semi-darkness, covered with faded tapestries showing battles and high points in the history of the Wittelsbach family. There were rooms which were almost empty, their furniture lost, except for a single sumptuous object, like a table with carved lion paws and a bestiary of mythical winged creatures for decoration. There were suites full of tortoiseshell cabinets, there were rooms plastered with gold paint, their ceilings lavished with pictures of putti riding horses, putti riding lions, putti holding onto other putti, putti playing with hearts, putti gambolling in every florid way available. The quantity of treasure was hard to absorb; I found myself walking swiftly past jewel-encrusted cabinets and delicately restored furnishings, simply because it was impossible to stand solemnly in front of everything. In the family gallery the Wittelsbachs stared from their portraits, ringed around with gold paint. Straight-backed men in fur-lined robes, sporting hats and beards as fashions required, and their wives, staring out at the empty room.

I passed through these quiet rooms, past red and gold walls, thrones standing unoccupied, a royal bedroom with the bed sealed off by a golden fence, with a chandelier glinting in the centre, and a craven overload of gilt everywhere on the walls, around the mirrors, around the portraits, splashed across the ceiling. I passed into what had once been the royal apartments of Ludwig I and his queen. There were paintings on the walls of mythical creatures, sphinxes and griffins, and then monarchical battle paraphernalia. History and power, the message was clear from the faded walls of the royal apartments. The command of symbols and former myths. Ludwig I's throne room had been neatly restored, with red curtains suspended around the throne and the ceiling patterned in Greek motifs. The parquet floor was polished. The walls were coated with classical columns and stucco reliefs, showing figures from Homer and Hesiod and Pindaric athletes in competitions.

Ludwig I had established a collection of classical statues in Königsplatz, called the Glyptothek, one of the buildings Hitler took for his backdrop. I was thinking of the Glyptothek as I walked out of the Residenz, passing through a gallery of portraits of the royal house. The Glyptothek is crammed full of Greek and Roman sculptures, originals and copies. I had been there on an earlier trip to Munich, spending an afternoon in the rooms. Everything in the Glyptothek has been mutilated by the passage of time; the statues stand, compelling despite their cracks and broken limbs and the sense of creeping decay hanging over them. There's an almost complete statue of a sleeping faun from the third century B.C., with huge thighs and calves and a hand slung behind its head. One foot has gone, one arm has vanished, but the legs are perfect, delicately fashioned. There's a room filled with statues of headless women—an Aphrodite, an Athena, the folds of their robes still immaculate. In a room surrounded by heads and trunks there's a statue of the dead son of Niobe, from roughly the time Pytheas sailed. The figure lies on its back, footless and handless, frozen in a backwards arch of death.

They were the remnants, fragmented forms of an ancient version of beauty. I was thinking about these fragments as I walked back from the Residenz to my hotel. Shattered parts of the past, somehow preserved, even in this city where everything burned. In the Glyptothek there are the remains of a temple to Athena: the broken stones of a pediment, put back together again. Athena stands in the centre, determining the fate of men, surrounded by headless warriors, warriors sadly deprived of limbs, made up from bits and pieces, some of them nothing but a couple of shins and feet. It is a stark piece of symbolism: these warriors, represented by a few salvaged parts, reduced from portraits of physical perfection to synecdoche. The temple has been tacked together, left in a foreign museum, far from its original site.

In the kitsch inn by the marketplace, the bar was dark and empty when I arrived back. The cluttered bedroom seemed small and hot. I pushed the embroidered covers off the bed, and stood looking out of the window at the quiet streets. Bells chimed from the church towers. The stalls were packed up for the night, their flowers and fruit under plastic sheeting. I sat up in the hotel room. I was searching around on the Net, surfing through all the contemporary madness about Thule, madness of a Sebottendorff strain. There was a horde of contemporary racist societies lurking on the Internet, peddling a poisoned version of Thule. Typing in "Thule Society" released a wild array of lunatics in love with the past, the Nazi Age, as they saw it. A Thule Net had been set up, to foster cyber clusters of the rabid, struggling with the basics. The Thule Gesselschaft, they frothed on their sites, spelling everything wrong, was founded under the initiative of Baron Rudolf von Sebottendorf. The Thule Gessellschaft, they added, in the same article, beginning to grow more confused, was created by von Sebbotendorf in 1908 one site said, or 1910, said another, or 1919, said a further. The GREAT, the INVINCIBLE Von Sebetondof, they wrote—Sebettenduff was their hero, though they just couldn't quite remember his name—and in the name of the Thule Gessleschaft, they wrote, Sebetendorf bought the newspaper the *Vulkishcer Beabagger*. Thuel Gessollshlock was the mother of Nazism, they concluded, with learned authority. Then, casting aside even a failing attempt at the facts, they would lurch into the violence of desperate fantasy. Hitler could not be dead, they said, wiping their tears away; it was impossible. So, they imagined, at the end of the war, Hitler had escaped in an aeroplane to Thule, a place, they generally seemed to think, a few miles away from the North Pole. On this frozen island, Hitler had been living for fifty years, having evidently become immortal at some stage in his escape-flight, a gatecrasher, an intruder in the classical dreamland. Deprived of the audience he lived off—they seemed to have made a living hell for their hero, without intending it. In their legend, he became a lonely madman on an island, like the hermits the Irish clerics found in the far northern ocean. A tyrant standing on a rock, commanding the clouds.

There were other sites with a pseudo-mystical bent, where the self-appointed clerics of the vapid Thule cult castigated the 'ennemis de Thule,' as one Frenchman wrote, in his chaotic study of Thule, the enemies of Thule who had replaced 'ancient rituals' with a 'foreign rite,' he added. The French were the original Aryans, he claimed, and his was a masochistic Aryan-lust, because the Saga obsessives would hardly have hailed him as a Viking hero. There was a picture of him on his site: a small Mediterranean man with a shock of black hair and a black moustache. Hitler and his brown-haired friends would have cast him out, this Frenchman muttering about the eternal religion of Thule, misunderstanding ancient ambiguities.

For the Internet ranters, as for Sebottendorff in 1918, there was an innate correlation between Germanic and Norse mythology, Thule itself and Nazi history. These sites were full of runes and semi-pornographic pictures of Viking maidens and muscular Viking men. I was thinking of a man like William Morris, fascinated by the Vikings because he thought they had created an early form of democracy. He had romanticized them, ignoring the Viking tendency to brutish violence, dwelling instead on their simple villages and intricate rule of law. He had thought the Icelandic Vikings were escaping from a tyrant into a community they created themselves. In the early twentieth century these strains of Germanic history were entwined with nationalist independence movements in Scandinavian countries, in Norway and Iceland. In interwar Germany, they were corrupted into the 'Aryan' obsession of the Nazis. The Thule Society sites on the Internet plastered borrowed images across their Thule Society pages, claiming them as a historical justification for their hatred. For extremists, these associations still remained. They still thought Thule was a code word for their 'Aryan' cult.

There were tenuous dreams which survived centuries: the classical dream of a land at the ends of the world, the romantic dream of the perfect landscape, a pure land, unchanged from Saga times. These dreams fascinated the German extremists, the Saga worshippers on Aryan tours, and they entwined the northern lands with their myth of the pure Germanic race. The Thule Society was disbanded, but the obsession with an 'Aryan' Empire created a cult—the SS. Heinrich Himmler, the leader of the SS, believed that German blood, or Nordic blood, was the 'best blood on earth.' The SS, he explained in a decree, was 'an association of German men of Nordic determination selected on special criteria.' His goal was 'the hereditarily sound, valuable extended family of the German, Nordically determined type.' He was certain that in hundreds of thousands of years this Nordic blood would still be the best. After 1932, all SS marriages had to be approved by Himmler and his men, and were only permitted if prospective brides conformed to SS ideas about 'race and hereditary health.' The SS had its own variety of inclusiveness: Himmler threw its doors open to suitable blonds of any 'Germanic' nation. Himmler took 'Aryan' recruits to the SS from Yugoslavia, Belgium, Denmark, the Netherlands and Norway. Himmler wanted to 'reclaim' Germanic foreigners from other countries.

In 1935, Himmler founded the '*Lebensborn*' programme—*Lebensborn* meaning the "Fount of Life." Germany had committed itself under the Nazis to a programme of sterilization, by which those regarded by the Nazis as unsuitable—the mentally ill, the physically 'impaired,' the mendicant—would be prevented from having children. There were also the people who were being killed, imprisoned or forced to leave the nation—Jews, dissidents, homosexuals and Gypsies. Into the gap left by these deaths and disappearances Himmler planned to add more 'Aryan' babies. Not wanting to waste any 'Aryans,' Himmler aimed to reduce abortions among racially 'suitable' but unmarried women, by creating maternal care homes. The *Lebensborn* homes were open to women pregnant by SS officers or police officers, once all the racial checks had been made. Homes were established where suitable mothers would give birth to their suitable babies; one opened in 1936 at Steinhöring, near Munich. These children were then either adopted by childless SS families, or, if the father had been enticed back to the mother, went home with their parents. SS wives weren't averse to the *Lebensborn* homes, and sometimes used them for their own births. Himmler liked to involve himself in basic details of care in the homes, spending long hours considering the best sorts of foods for his mothers, wondering whether porridge would make their children more like Nordic gods. The *Lebensborn* programme would, Himmler hoped, further strengthen the Germanic race.

Though the Nazis had gone on 'Aryan' tours in Iceland during the 1930s, they never invaded the country. British troops arrived first, surging across the sea to Iceland in May 1940. But Norway was occupied by German soldiers from the summer of 1940, and regarded by the Nazis as a suitably 'Aryan' land, packed with people of useful 'stock.' The Norwegians were encouraged to collaborate; the Nazis were inclined to favour them, so long as they joined SS Norway, launched shortly after the Germans began their occupation, or supported the Germans. When the Germans occupied Norway the *Lebensborn* programme was supplied with a Norwegian branch. During the occupation, thousands of children of mixed parentage were born—their fathers German soldiers, their mothers

Norwegian locals. During the war they were the prized 'Aryan' progeny of the Third Reich, but after the war they were regarded as guilty remnants of the past in Norway, blamed and ignored.

In 1940, in Norway, the strains collided. The dream of a land called Thule had compelled Nansen. He had disappeared into the ice talking about Thule, and he had talked about the far north as Ginnungagap, the abyss at the end of the world in Norse legend. He had imagined the North Pole as a giant from a Viking Saga, wrapped in his white shroud, stretching his clammy ice-limbs abroad, dreaming his age-long dreams. He saw his own Arctic explorations as a process of filling in the blanks on the ancestral maps, charting the worlds that the Vikings had imagined—the abyss at the world's end, Niflheim, Helheim, Trollebotn. Then, years after his polar travels, Nansen drew a direct link between his nation and the land of Thule. He published an immense Arctic history in 1911, entitled *In Northern Mists*, which ranged from the earliest incursions into the ice, from Pytheas and the Vikings, to the sixteenth century when fleets of British merchant ships sailed towards the White Sea. He was fascinated by the north, by all the ideas encapsulated in the word Thule. In his book, Nansen advanced his own theory of Thule. He thought Thule had been Norway, resolving the ancient controversy in favour of his own nation. He called his country Thule because he felt it was a beautiful land, its fjords and mountains supplying inspiration to the inhabitants, though they were poor.

It resolved more than a classical mystery for Nansen. 1911 was the year that Roald Amundsen reached the South Pole, and Nansen had given Amundsen *Fram* to sail in, an act of generosity rich in symbolism. Nansen turned away from active exploration, and rolled up all his calculations of the breadth and distance of the ice around the North Pole, his studies of the salinity of the seas, all the scientific experiments he had conducted in the hope that they might bring him a mile or so closer to the Pole. He had originally said he would sail beyond Thule, into the unknown ice around the

Pole. But he came home from the ice, and changed his mind. He decided in the end that Thule was Norway, and he found that Thule wasn't such a bad place to stay. The Tweedies and Trollopes had hoped Thule would be a strange place. But for Nansen, Thule was the longed-for vistas of home, the beauties of his own land.

The ambiguities of the story had compelled him, its combined challenge and warning. Nansen had oscillated wildly, between realism and wild fantasy, between pragmatism and idealism. His interests were never stable; he had tried a variety of disciplines; his talents were wide-ranging. After being an explorer he became a diplomat, then an international statesman. As he accepted he would never reach the North Pole, he turned to memories of earlier travel. He had sailed along the western fjords of Norway in the summer of 1893, on *Fram*, moving out towards the Pole. He decided these western fjords must have been Thule. When Nansen called Norway Thule, he was a famous man, a recognizable national hero. Anything Nansen said about Norway was of great importance to his country, and six years after Norway had become fully independent, Norwegian history was an emotive subject. Nansen had been a diplomat for his nation; he had even been offered the title of King after independence. Nansen's Thule was a patriot's gift to his nation, an attractive piece of symbolism, claiming Norway as the ancient northerly land, the mystery idyll in the far north.

Nansen himself was part of the northern history that the Nazis fixed upon. They wanted to turn Nansen into an 'Aryan' hero; Hitler named him as an early inspiration. They offered him the title *Übermensch*, but Nansen refused it. He remained aloof, a monumental individualist, refusing to fall. He died before the worst began, succumbing to a heart attack in 1930. But his life was touched by the forces that gripped Norway in 1940: Nansen's assistant in Russia was a man called Vidkun Quisling, a young Norwegian who seemed innocuous enough in the 1920s but who degenerated through the 1930s, selling himself to the Nazis when they invaded his country and leading the collaborationist regime. Quisling took the patriot's repertoire—Nordic history, exploration, Vikings and Thule—and used it as the Nazis did, to argue for the supremacy of the Nordic race. Ten years after Nansen's death, Norway was under the control of Nazi forces, its inhabitants struggling under occupation. German boats occupied the northern ports of Norway, intercepting convoys from Russia to the USA. They polluted Nansen's Thule, his pure landscape, the mountains he loved, with war and violence.

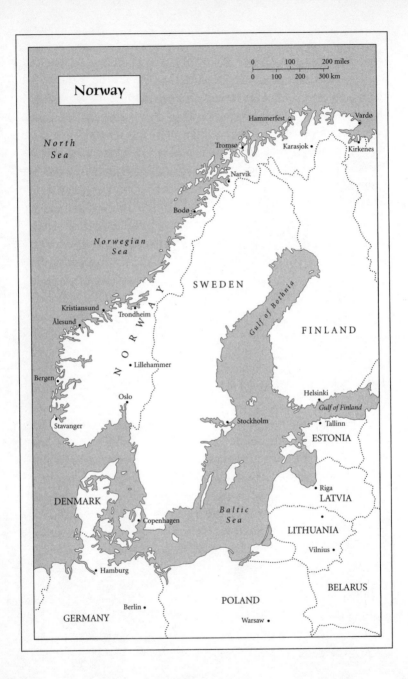

PURITY

〰〰〰

IN THAT UNDEFILED BRIGHT THULE,
THULE OF ETERNAL GAIN
THERE WHERE THE SOUL SEES NEWLY
FROM THE ISLES OF INATULA
TO THE GOLDEN BOWERED BEULA. . . .

IN THAT UNDEFILED BRIGHT THULE

"THRENODY. COMPOSED ON THE DEATH OF MY LITTLE BOY," THOMAS HOLLEY
CHIVERS (1809–1858)

The rain is soaking the bow of the ship and lashing the sides of the fjord. The rocks stand ancient and immeasurable on either side, plunging into the water, their granite faces reflected in the clear waters. I have been standing on the deck for hours now, looking out across the ocean. As light fades, the rain subsides, and the wind strengthens. It forces the water into irregular shapes: curves and taut lines, deep rifts. As the semi-dusk falls, the shapes begin to resemble faces—a sea of faces, grimacing and smiling in the twilight, twitching as the wind blisters the water.

The ship is an old coastal steamer, the fjords are the pride of Norway: the western fjords, stuff of a thousand holiday tours, a thousand tourist brochures. 'The most beautiful journey in the world,' the posters announce, 'the journey of a lifetime.' The sun is sinking slowly beneath the horizon. The ship moves sluggishly past the vast, high rocks, ploughing a furrow through the shape-shifting ocean. The deck is quiet; the waters are empty, the only motion the occasional blink from a lighthouse, orange flashes against the deep blue of the dusk sky.

The wind is wheezing through the gullies and fissures of the rocks; rustling through the leaves of the light birch trees, darting over the fine satin trails of slender waterfalls, tumbling from unseen heights. We are in a vibrant world of rock and trees, dulled to monochrome for the night: layer upon layer of tumbling mountains and dense green foliage, with crag mountains in the distance and thin rock spits sliding out into the fjord towards the boat. Across the water, there are the faint shadows of small houses, scattered at the base of the immense rock walls. They lie on stubby beaches, where the rocks soften into a horizontal plain, before being swallowed by the sea.

The night is cold. Everyone is below deck, except a lean old Norwegian sailor, in blue overalls, sitting further along the deck. He stares at the water, coughing and rolling a cigarette. He sits out here whenever he can, he says, in dusk shadow or bright sunlight, his hands curled around his cigarette papers, his eyes fixed on the rocks. Earlier, I thrust a map into his hands: *'Unnskyld, hvor er vi?'* Where are we? Pointing at the map, he coughed: *'Vi er her.'* We are here. We are in the continuously shifting 'here' of the voyage north. We are on the way to Thule, as Nansen saw it, as the Nazis colonized and burned it, as the contemporary tours slide past it on slow-moving ships. In Norway the twentieth century unfurls a series of layers. Nansen's sense of his country as a beautiful land. The Nazi fantasy about a pure Aryan race, and the northern lands they thought had formed it. The war and its destruction of the quiet towns along the coast. Then there's the vastness of the mountains, the contours of the fjords as holiday consolation for contemporary travellers.

Nansen imagined that Pytheas left the coast of Scotland and sailed to an island that might have been Shetland, where the longest day was nineteen hours. Then he sailed on for six days, in a northerly direction, until he reached Thule. An assortment of ancient experts had agreed that Pytheas described Thule as a land where the sun shone through the night in the summer. The nocturnal summer sun made Thule unlikely to be Shetland, Nansen decided. Geminus of Rhodes described Thule as a land inhabited by barbarians, who had shown Pytheas where the sun set. These helpful barbarians were crucial evidence for Nansen. If Thule was inhabited it could hardly have been Iceland, empty and silent at the time. And anyway, he added, Iceland was so far away that Pytheas could not have arrived there in six days. Neither the currents nor the prevailing winds bear in that direction, wrote Nansen, remembering his own experiences in the fierce storms in the northern oceans. This driving ocean would, Nansen decided, have carried Pytheas relentlessly towards Norway.

So, wrote Nansen, with a certain briskness to his tone, even if it seemed a pretty bold idea to claim that Pytheas was the first non-native to land on the western coast of Norway, this was how it had happened. The evidence, arrayed haphazardly but with conviction, was enough for Nansen. 'All the statements about Thule which have been preserved answer to Norway, but to no other country,' he wrote.

Pytheas had sailed, thought Nansen, from Shetland with a south-westerly wind and a favourable current towards the northeast, and had arrived off the coast of Norway in the Romsdal or Nordmøre district, where the longest day of the year lasted for twenty-one hours. There the barbarians showed him where the sun went to rest, thought Nansen. From here Pytheas might have sailed northwards along the coast of Helgeland, perhaps far enough to see the midnight sun somewhere north of Dønna or Bodø—among the jagged rocks of the north. 'After one day's sail from Thule,' wrote Pliny, 'the frozen sea is reached.' This finished it for Norway, but Nansen squirmed around the sources, arguing that Pytheas never saw the frozen sea for himself, but heard about it from the inhabitants. Hearsay might have been enough, the awed reports of local barbarians, of the sea that thickened to a paste. Pytheas might have puffed up his tale, combining rumours with his own experiences. Or, he might have mixed in the old idea of Ocean, the mythical paste, the vast river.

The ship left Bergen earlier, in gentle drizzle, passing the town to starboard, the white houses with orange roofs ranging up the mountainsides, disappearing under a low mist. The tall slant-roofed buildings lining the waterfront, painted red and yellow and white, their dates of construction ornately represented: 1729, 1709. The deep red-and-yellow painted walls and solid timbers summoning a past epoch of merchant seafaring, when Bergen formed the western edge of the Hanseatic trade area. Before the journey I had spent a week in Bergen, staying in a small wooden house above the old harbour. Every morning I would walk down the hillside to the harbour and buy some bread and a coffee from Baker Brun. I would sit outside the Hanseatic houses, looking across to the sea. The air was always full of the pungent smell of fish, as boats arrived with the morning catch, the market sellers loading up their tables with piles of salmon and mussels. All around me, Bergen lay, spreading up the seven mountains surrounding the town—yellow, red, white houses, red and brown roofs, made of wood. Sometimes in the mornings I walked into an old Hanseatic church before the tourists arrived for the day, to look at the floral-patterned ceiling, the gaudy baroque pulpit, the walls lined with dark paintings of illustrious Germans— Dr. Martin Luther taking his place.

The Norwegian coastal steamer is a common sight in these parts, running a constant route from Bergen to Kirkenes by the Russian border, then turning around and heading south again. It stops at isolated harbours, towns of thirty houses spreading up the sides of the mountains, fishing boats moored along the quayside. At each port, the steamers take on board a kleptomaniac's collection of cargo—tables, sofas, canisters, doors—future furnishings for a junkyard, ladled into the ship by a fleet of forklift trucks. And they carry tourists from Bergen to the north, and back again: a nonstop circle, if they like—from the lushness of fjordland to the dense greyness of the land in the far north, by the Russian border. There is nothing to do on this boat except watch the view, as the mountains slide slowly away, replaced by another range of rocks. The scenery is so beautiful that the hours pass swiftly, filled with the rocks and the sea. The sunsets are rich and bloody, spreading across the sea. The seabirds cry above the deck, and the wind rises through the night, causing the bow to plunge deeply, slamming against the waves.

⸙

Even as the chains rattled along the deck, I was feeling a sense of déjà vu. I had been here before; this was the Arctic country I had travelled most in, when my love of coldness and snow started to send me north, on brief holidays and later periods of residence. I had a tenuous link to Norway; my family had failed to present a cogent genealogical history, but there were rumours, long buried, that our ancestors had mingled with Norwegian Vikings at some stage, most likely in Pembrokeshire, and that this was the reason for various incidences of unusual height which occurred randomly through generations, including my great-great-aunts who had all been six feet tall. It was a family fable, impossible to prove, but it seemed to fit with my feelings, and from the age of ten I tried to persuade my parents to take me to Norway. They were reluctant: my mother suggested Scotland for trees and mountains and water, closer and half the price. Scotland didn't require a ferry crossing, argued my mother, because she loathed the sea. My father quite favoured the ferry; when we had lived in Suffolk we had often gone sailing on the North Sea, and he had never been entirely happy in the landlocked Midlands. My mother said she wouldn't mind walking in the mountains if we flew to Bergen but my father wasn't so keen on walking. Each year I asked, each year the sea versus air dispute continued. By the time I was fourteen, they were just glad I seemed to have a harmless fixation, so we went to Norway.

We took the ferry from Newcastle to Bergen, a crossing of a day and a night. The weather was stormy, the bow smashed into the ocean. My father walked along the deck and my mother stayed below in the cabin, silent, unable to eat. The ferry was the largest boat I had been on; at Bergen the cars filed out of its hold, emerging into a vista of mountains and trees. My parents rented a small chalet in a pine forest; everything became coated in pine needles, and I remember waking in a small bunk bed, my brother asleep in the bunk below, to the smell of bark and the sound of birds screeching through the trees. Some nights we couldn't sleep at all, because the sun shone through the night hours, and I remember a night when my brother and I had been whispering in our bunks for hours, giggling quietly at child humour, when my mother finally burst into the bedroom. Assuming we were in trouble, we fell silent, but we saw our mother was smiling. She had golf clubs in her hand. It was so bright, she said, that we were going to go and play mini-golf. Yes, it was late, or even early, but there was a golf course somewhere in the forest and she couldn't sleep either.

Each day my father and I sailed in a small boat, under a bridge across a great fjord. Squinting against the sun, gripping the tiller, though the water was smooth, because the vastness of the mountains made me uneasy. We walked to the glaciers, posing for photos against a background of deep blue ice, my brother flapping his arms in the cold. We ate stale bread sandwiches with thin strips of cheese; it seemed to be all we could find in the small cafés along the coast. I was never bored, though I was quiet during the weeks, trying to commit the view to memory, taking pictures with a small camera, thinking I would never travel there again. At that time, it seemed impossible I would return.

Though my parents cried off from further excursions, I plotted darkly for a few years, waiting until I could travel north again. At the age of eighteen I travelled along the coast with a friend in a borrowed car. On the ferry from Britain to Bergen we were ill, the sea churned around the bows, we slept on the deck. We drove from Bergen. Determined to get as far north as possible, we ate on our laps, taking turns at the wheel. Then, from land, the sea was the constant unknowable of the journey, stretching beyond reach. We spent every day driving, moving through the fishing villages and oil towns, the ancient car sluggish around the mountain passes, speeding up in the long tunnels filled with orange headlights.

We camped by the fjords, stewing tins on a campfire each evening, as the sun lingered long in the sky. We woke to the sounds of water crashing down the valley and the cries of birds echoing round the mountains. The roads were almost empty; we stopped occasionally in the oil towns along the way, visiting shabby museums cluttered with fishing nets, admiring the stillness of the twilight. We hiked up mountains, slipping on the scree, scrambling along rock ridges. We camped by the sea; the rock beaches were our daily home, where we struggled to find a place to pitch a tent. The rain fell hard on the roof of the car, punctuating the stillness; the sky was a stolid grey and the clouds formed rain-heavy clumps. The ground lay rigid and sparsely covered, a few tendrils of grass, patches of moss.

The sea was visible in the gaps in the low hills; by the end we were in the ragged northern mountains, where the coastline of Norway turns east towards Russia. The lights flickering on the blackness of the fjords. Sheer mountainsides, as we wound up and down the passes, through tunnels blasted into the rocks. The small wooden houses were reflected in the clear waters of the fjords.

<hr />

The beauty was unchanged. The first morning onboard, I looked out of my cabin at dawn and saw the fjord sides rising above the boat. The sun was glinting onto the water; through dark clouds the light fell in fine rays across the stacked-up mountains, which receded endlessly into the distance, like the eternal reflections of a hall of mirrors. Ahead there were hundreds more miles of mountains in rows, trembling under the heat haze. The colours stayed the same—the blue sky reflected in the still waters of the fjord, the dark shadows of the mountains in the distance. But the geometry was constantly shifting—curved mountain crags, sharp points, even plateaux, smooth mounds, rugged lumps. The mountains in the foreground stood bold and sharp-featured; as they receded they faded into intimations. One range dispensed with revealed another, looming in the distance; we were steaming towards it, our progress slow against the vastness of the gradients, the immensity of the sky. Even smallness revealed itself as enormity—small mounds in the distance grew gradually as we approached, until we reached them, and found they were imposing peaks.

The fjord sides were scattered with painted wooden houses, in bright colours, to offset the bleak grey of the winter. The boat was moving towards Ålesund, which looked from a distance like a town conjured from a Meccano kit, spray-painted white. Closer in, the white blocks were art nouveau terraces, their stark lines refined by murals and painted façades. A regional anomaly in the land of wooden chalets, it had the feel of an architectural experiment, a crazy scheme, realized out of sight of civilization. As the Germans built Bergen, so they designed the frontages of Ålesund. In January 1904, Ålesund burnt to the ground. Kaiser Wilhelm of Germany sent supplies and provisions to the town, and art nouveau Ålesund was born. The aesthetic has been subdued for the coast—the Jugendstil warriors and maidens with twined tresses replaced with anchors and flowers. The white and grey lines of the buildings slide out towards the jagged Alps of Sunnmøre.

The ship was passing the Romsdal district, where Pytheas first landed, according to Nansen, and was taken on the sunset tour by the barbarians. It was a beautiful place, worthy of a mystery myth or two. The shadow layers of the mountains surrounded the boat, serried peaks adorned with fine feathery waterfalls. The sunlight fell across the trees, flickering through the branches, turning the leaves purple. Low islands loomed out of the water, scattered with scrawny bushes. I sat on the deck, bewildered by the peaks and plateaux, staring at the sharp summits emerging from the dense layers of the rocks. The snow was stacked in thick piles on the tops of the mountains, filling in the hollows in the rocks. The boat moved down Geiranger Fjord, a narrow, steep-sided fjord, the mountains coated with thick firs. The region was, Nansen thought, the best of Norway: 'A glorious land—I wonder if another fairway like this is to be found the whole world over? Those never-to-be-forgotten mornings, when nature wakens to life, wreaths of mist glittering like silver over the mountains, their tops soaring above the mist-like islands of the sea! Then the day gleaming over the dazzling white snow-peaks! You may shrug your shoulders as much as you like at the beauties of nature, but it is a fine thing for a people to have a fair land.'

Today, the shores would have struck Nansen as positively over-populated, but he would have been surprised by their indifference—by the soundless small towns sheltering under the crags, with names like Brattvåg and Midsund, the windows of the houses blank. Nothing moved along the shore, as the ship steamed slowly north. The light hit the mountains, harsh and persistent, the trees were slender and parched on the barren islands, and still, nothing moved along the shore.

Molde, where the ship shook to a standstill, was a small place of low concrete houses, ranging up the tree-coated mountainside. Like so many fishing villages along the western coast, it was bombed to the ground during World War Two. Molde's nemesis came in 1940, as German bombers tried to flush out the king, who was hiding there. There's an old picture taken during the bombing, of the king and crown prince standing under a birch tree. It's a poignant image: the royal family, fugitives from Oslo, sheltering from the screaming of the planes as if taking cover from a hailstorm. When the ship docked the lights were on in the town; people were sitting on benches by the quayside, outside the waterside bars, looking up and down at the steamer. It had taken out their view—a relentless succession of stacked-up spikes and crags. The sun faded across a wine-red sea. Lights from the low-rise town were reflected on the water, and boats lined the docks, moored for the night, the wake from the steamer slapping against their hulls. The shadows of the mountains loomed across the water. Drenched in a deep blue dusk, their white tips glinting, and at their base, the sea.

Nansen imagined Pytheas sailing up the coast, finding natives who showed him where the sun went to rest, and experiencing the long days of the summer months. Galvanized by their hospitality, by the strange sights they showed him, he sailed on. A thousand years before the great Norse era, Pytheas sailed through what would become the Viking heritage trail, a source of pride to Nansen. This was one of the regions King Harald Fairhair concentrated his force on, when he unified Norway and sent the rebellious and independent across the seas to Iceland. The ninth-century farmers left their lands, and set sail across the ocean, a trans-European migration of the ruined and hopeful. King Harald stayed, glowering in the west, sending out messages to the remaining landholders, asking why they had not come to see him. The Norwegians of the nineteenth century, examining this great Viking past, felt, a little like the Icelanders in the west, that things had been in perpetual decay since the early medieval era. Since the decline of the Viking Empire, Norway had been constantly under the control of foreign powers—joined with Denmark for centuries, and then with Sweden since 1815. Between Nansen's first voyage and his account of Norway as Thule the union between Norway and Sweden was dissolved, and Norway became an autonomous country. Northern myths became fodder for independence talk. Nansen proposed the antiquity of his nation, its claim to an old tale about the north. Pytheas might have sailed past the idyllic fjordland north of Bergen, the rocks piled in layers. A fertile land, covered now with farms and dense tree growth—horse chestnuts, maples, holly, linden and copper beech. Pytheas might have passed northwards through the long, serene day of Nordmøre and Romsdal, the mountains by night a retreating pattern of dark blue shadows.

The small wooden houses were reflected in the clear waters of the fjords; the rain fell softly onto the verdant plains.

————— ✖ —————

And during the next day the boat moved slowly along the coast of Nordmøre, through archipelagoes of rocks coated with moss, layered with trees, everything shimmering under the heat haze. The boat passed into the clear waters of Trondheimsleia, with the rocks a brilliant blue under the fine silvery light. There were cornfields to starboard, bright against the deep green of the woodland. Stretching beyond were miles and miles of green and grey coastline: slender trees on stark rocks, brilliant patches of sunlight falling onto the dusty mountains. Pytheas, Nansen thought, would have sailed along the coast to the gentle plains of Trøndelag, the area around Trondheim, and towards the pallid clenched claws of the mountains further along the coast.

I was lulled by the motion of the ship. The landscape was grandiose, but its shifts were subtle and regular; changes in terrain were gradually realized, signalled from the south, as the trees dwindled on the slopes, and the forests gave way to rocks. The sky swelled, the sea darkened, the sun sank towards the horizon, and failed to disappear. A burnt glow fell across the waves; the long lines of the mountains receded into shadows.

In my early twenties, I had lived outside Trondheim for a few months, and I knew Nansen's Thule well. It was a place where I had watched the summer fall into a rust-coloured autumn, the trees slowly shedding their leaves. The trees lost their leaves to the slow creep towards winter, the light started to weaken, declining into a mid-afternoon dusk. The sun couldn't cling to the skies. I lived in a hut by a fjord and walked through the twilight mornings, across fields dusted with a light coating of snow, a coating which thickened as the winter became darker. The stillness was what most affected my mood; I had thought the long nights would drag me into inertia, but I found waking to a silent field of ice, the only motion the snow gliding onto the windowsill, created a mood of exhilaration. The snow shone, a white plain sharply distinguished from the darkness of the sky; everything was bold and uncomplicated. My hut was two miles from a small village, so some mornings I would walk there, across untouched snow, my feet denting the crisp surface, pushing through to the ground beneath. Everyone was quiet and friendly in this snow world; they waved from a distance, farmers walking in their fields, and people who by summer might try to fish in the fjords, waiting through the cold months. They waved and turned away, retreating from the ice-winds back to their houses. It was beautiful but it was impossible to walk for more than an hour in the cold air; it made my lungs ache, and my abiding memory of the time I spent outside Trondheim was the yearning for warmth in any form, an addiction to hot baths, saunas and open fires. I walked through the fields, thinking of where and how I would next become warm.

By the end I was almost acclimatized, I could walk through the winds as they blasted snow in my eyes, and in England for a while I was never cold.

The crisp coldness of the air made me think quickly; I wrote letters to everyone I knew, generating reams of paper which I stacked in a pile and tried not to use as firelighters. I read Knut Hamsun, the Norwegian Nobel laureate, who had loved the Nordland summer's endless day, the long light evenings, the rustling of the leaves in the forest, the darting of the light across the fjord. The skies of pale fire, the drift of the season into winter. Hamsun had started out in the 1890s as a crazy brilliant modernist, writing out the madness of the city and the desperation of the starving writer, in the reeling prose of *Hunger*. He had come from a small town north of Trondheim; he was from a poor family, and no one encouraged him to write; he passed his twenties as a mendicant, struggling to survive, emigrating to the States in search of something else, declining into a dozen piecemeal jobs. *Hunger* was the product of a raging and desperate frustration, his ravenous urge to succeed. Success began to ruin Hamsun; he became obsessed with his own rise from obscurity, his novels started to talk of nothing else. He became nostalgic and impatient; he lurched away from the city, writing nothing but rustic romances laced with sentimentality, tales of robust hunting men of few words, clumsy in elegant company, chasing the daughters of local merchants through the vibrant forests. They lived in huts like mine, they wore big boots, they knew nothing of manners and conventions; they were tormented brutes, aware that society judged them. They were good at whittling wood, and occasionally sheer frustration at their failure to ensnare a local beauty led them to a melodramatic act. One of the rustic hut-dwellers shot himself in the foot one morning because the beautiful daughter of the local businessman wouldn't talk to him.

I had sat in the hut, the snow stacked up outside the door, reading Hamsun's odes to rustic simplicity.

⸺∞⸺

When the ship slips past the Arctic Circle, there is no fanfare, no signal from the shore. There is a terse announcement from the bridge at 7 A.M. The landscape stays the same; the same stark crags and tree-coated rocks lounging low in the fjord. Streaks of ice and snow glint on the tops of the mountains. There's an island ahead, coated in red firs. In the small Arctic town of Ørnes, the sound of the ship's horn echoes around the mountains. We have reached another defiant, isolated place: a few elegant old buildings by the quayside, smaller houses stretching up the hillside. A sand beach slides down to the ocean; it is deserted, though the sun shines across it. Anywhere here, I imagine Nansen muttering to himself, as he saw these sun-drenched rocks. Pytheas might have arrived anywhere around here, and called it Thule. Here, where a lone crag casts a long shadow over the water, or here, on this barren islet, a thin coating of moss clinging to the rock. Thule as Nansen saw it is a place of wooden houses, in red, yellow and green, topped with slanted roofs. Lines of *rorbuer*—fishermen's huts—along the water's edge. The crushed peaks of the mountains, severe slices of granite colliding into irregular shapes, perverse dodecahedrons, drawn by a hyperactive hand. Then there are places where the mountains lurk like squat rock beasts, behind the long flat islands. It's a staggering land, constantly inventive and showy, producing new wonders of scenery. It's a place where the people are silenced by the immensity of the rocks, left staring quietly at the sea. Purple mountains rise in the distance, and the only sounds are the cries of gulls, twirling in the boat's wake, and the relentless sluicing of water under the hull. The fjord absorbs the colours of the sky; the sun casts a low haze across the mountains; the mountains reflect their shapes across the fjord.

It's a hot afternoon; the sun is shining onto the waves. The ship stops at Bodø, a small Arctic outpost. The mountains are beautiful. The sea is serene and glitters in the sun. The town is a collapsed street, diggers slamming into the cracked concrete, military aircraft screaming across the skies. There's a shopping centre in a state of destruction, with wire fences everywhere. The area was ruined at the end of the Second World War, when the Germans retreated from the Russian forces moving from the east. Bodø is a town of concrete blocks, interspersed with neat wooden buildings, rebuilt when the inhabitants returned home after the war. A memorial stands outside Bodø Cathedral: 'To the Memory of those from Bodø who gave their lives for Norway during the War and the Occupation 1940–45.' Cast adrift in Nansen's Thule, startled by the sun, I dive into the regional museum, and find a sketchy collection of junk and fishing tackle, distributed randomly across a couple of rooms. There's a large photograph of the town in 1939, before the destruction—rows of wooden houses, quaint and nondescript. And there's a shot of the town after the war—piled-up ash and debris, silence and thick smoke.

We passed slowly through a stretching shambles of islets and inlets, with the sun spreading across the sky. The light was gleaming across the pastel mountains, turning them purple. The sun shone like fire on the rock pillars. Small villages emerged out of the rock desert, and receded again, as the boat moved onwards into further miles of slab rocks lurking above the sea. There was the constant background hum of the engines and the gentle slap of water swirling around the bows. I sat on the deck watching the deckhands coil the ropes, and then I dozed for a few hours, curled in a sleeping bag, under the shelter of the ship's bridge.

After Thule, as Nansen defined it, the stark crags of the Lofoten Islands emerged ahead—an archipelago of barren crinkled rocks, emerging violently from the sea. Lashed by storms in winter, serene and mist-scaped in summer. An immense wall of rocks loomed ahead, a line of mountains in the ocean. Rocks in the gathering dusk, looking like a vast island. Before the sun set, the boat made a detour into Trollfjord—the gathering shadows playing across the blackened crags, snow glinting like mist in patches on the rocks. I was woken by the shuddering of the boat as it turned around at the end of the fjord. The enormous sheer sides had been crushed close together, leaving a gap barely wide enough for the ship between them. In the half-light, it seemed to me that the rock formations of Trollfjord resembled nothing so much as anguished faces, encased in stone: great simian ridges, deep sockets, gaping mouths, severe and strange.

In his Arctic history *In Northern Mists*, Nansen had written about a mythical ancient tribe of the far north, the Hyperboreans. The Hyperboreans were a people who knew neither war nor injustice, neither age nor disease; they supped with divinities, they invited Apollo over for a dance and dinner, they entertained heroes, Perseus among them. Only the divine and semi-divine knew where the Hyperboreans lived; the poet Pindar gave elusive descriptions: 'travelling neither by ships nor on foot could you find/ the way to the assembly of the Hyperboreans.' They were an immortal race, living beyond the fierce north wind, in farthest northern Ocean, where the tired stars sank to rest, where the moon was so near that it was possible to see the imperfections on its surface. Some sources said there was a marvellous temple, shaped like a sphere, which floated freely in the air, borne by the winds. There were three giant brothers there, twelve feet high, who performed the service of priests to the sanctuary. When they offered the sacrifice and sang hymns to the sound of the cithara, whole clouds of swans surrounded the temple and settled upon it.

Though they lived in the northern zone, their land seemed to be quiet and perfect, a place free of the harshness of the north wind, of the sleet and snow, the driving rain. They were the only race living in the north-east who did not encroach continually on their neighbours, unlike the Scythians, Issedones and Arimaspians, who were cramped together in the north, and oppressed constantly by griffins and other bizarre creatures. The Hyperboreans were a musical tribe, passing the days playing the lyre and the pipes, listening to choirs. They had escaped Nemesis, and when they grew tired of life—of this song-filled, flower-strewn life—they threw themselves, with wreaths in their hair, from a cliff into the sea.

The myth of the Hyperboreans was gradually entwined with Thule, so the poets sometimes wrote about the Hyperborean waves crashing on the shores of Thule, or the Hyperborean peoples of Thule. They seemed the right sort of inhabitants for a mystery isle; their origins as uncertain as those of the land of Thule, any lurking truth clouded by anecdote and poetry. Nansen was a scholar of precision; he dismissed suggestions that the Hyperboreans might actually have been an early Germanic tribe. But when Nansen named Norway as Thule he knew the Hyperboreans were part of the mythical package. It flattered the people, the notion that their nation might have been visited by Pytheas, that it might have been the source of the idea of Thule. And it also flattered the people to link them imaginatively with the Hyperboreans, the grand old immortals of the north. It was a useful piece of national symbolism, for a nation finding its feet, struggling to emerge from centuries under the overall control of its neighbours, Denmark and Sweden. Nansen had a strong sense of ancestral pride; the Viking exploration of the far north received extensive coverage in *In Northern Mists*. His Thule bound the Norwegians up with the discovery of the far north, making them an ancient nation of Arctic people: first the local population welcoming the explorer Pytheas, and later the explorers themselves, pushing towards the North and South Poles.

Nansen's patriotism was of a robust sort; he had been a key negotiator during the Norwegian independence talks with Sweden, a key representative of Norway abroad, a key candidate for president. Yet Nansen was never blindly partisan; he was never obsessed with his own country, to the exclusion of all others. He ceded the Arctic quest to Amundsen, a relentless, obsessively driven explorer, who cared less about international geopolitics and more about simple adventure. Nansen turned to the epic disaster of Russia in the post-Revolution era. During the 1920s, he became involved with the League of Nations, working as high commissioner for the repatriation of prisoners of war, helping to return Russian prisoners held in Germany and German prisoners held in Russia. He worked to alleviate the famine that hit Russia in 1921; when he was awarded the Nobel Peace Prize in 1922 he used the money to establish farms in the Volga region and the Ukraine. The Nobel Prize particularly recognized his part in devising the Nansen passport, which supplied stateless refugees with identity and travel papers; beneficiaries included Vladimir Nabokov's family. He was accused of naivety, by his peers and by later writers, of being manipulated equally by the Americans and the Russians. He might have been aware of the tactics around him, but was too fixed on his goal to care.

And in the 1920s, as Norse mythology was bound into nationalism in the northern countries, Nansen was linked to a folksy domestic party called the Fatherland League. The Fatherland League wanted a strong Norway, a nation that could protect itself from the creeping threat of Communism, as they saw it. Nansen lent his powerful jowls, his sonorous charisma-drenched presence, to its calls for the Norwegians to fulfil their potential. Even in this, he couldn't stay with empty phrases, with rhetoric stripped away from action. He was increasingly a reluctant figurehead, too diverse for the shriller forms of nationalism. It was a fortunate reluctance, prescient in the circumstances: after Nansen's death, the Fatherland League was drawn towards extremism, hijacked by Nazi sympathizers.

The boat passed crags to starboard, with tree-coated rocks low in the fjord, and I thought of Nansen's house outside Oslo, which I had visited on the way to Bergen. I had arrived on a bus out of Oslo, which had stopped on a major road. Nansen's house lay up a narrow lane; when he lived there it had stood beyond the limits of the city. Most of the house was being used as a research institute, but the director of the institute took me up to an unheated room, at the top of the house. The room was usually kept locked, and the researchers stayed away, but the director had a key; his office, he told me, was just opposite, and a sense of the past must have permeated his days, as he walked past the locked door. He twisted the key and we entered a neat study, with a view of rust-coloured ivy clambering on the walls outside. On the desk there were hundreds of handwritten sheets of paper in neat piles. There were shelves stacked with leather-bound books, and cloying pre-Raphaelite paintings on the walls. More austere were the black-and-white photographs, scattered around, of an explorer, diplomat, statesman and his family. As I stood by the desk, my hand on the chair Nansen had sat in, I felt the sense of a gap. The trappings remained, preserved in their places, but the unifying consciousness had vanished. A few Nansen flasks were stacked in a corner, for taking samples from the ocean, just one of Nansen's inventions, which had included the tailored runners of his Nansen sledge, and his own recipe for pemmican. There were files of correspondence from Russians, stacks of fountain pens, knives to sharpen pencils. Nansen had laboured in the room, struggling to solve the problems of another nation, writing letters, preparing his notes, petitioning governments and the League of Nations. Nansen had overworked in the small cluttered study throughout the 1920s. He saw the carnage of the First World War, and he kept thinking that hard work might solve it. Yet he couldn't gather all the parts together.

Had he lived into the 1930s, Nansen would have been surprised at what happened to his former assistant Vidkun Quisling. Nansen had met Quisling through Russia, where Quisling had worked as a military attaché in St. Petersburg. Nansen employed Quisling throughout the 1920s in famine-relief enterprises and in the attempted repatriation of Armenians from Turkey. When Nansen wrote *Russia & Peace* during 1923, Quisling helped him. Nansen found Quisling a competent administrator, and recommended him for a series of jobs in Russia, the Balkans, and the Ukraine. Asked once to recommend someone to speak about Russia, Nansen recommended Quisling. After Nansen and Quisling stopped working together, they exchanged letters; Nansen sent Quisling New Year's greetings shortly before his death. They were hardly friends; Quisling was much younger, much less senior, and Nansen by the end was a regal and fixated man, concerned more with causes than with individuals. Like any other budding opportunist, Quisling struggled to link himself with Nansen; after

Nansen's death, Quisling supplied commentary and reaction in the press, trying to bind himself to Nansen's reputation. It was a game he was still playing at his trial for treason, after the end of the Second World War, when he claimed Nansen had been like a protector and a father to him. But Nansen had been like a protector and father to Norway, in the popular imagination; it was a feeling many shared.

During the 1930s, after Nansen's death, Quisling began to work on his 'philosophical' ideas. Quisling developed a fantasy about the north: he thought Norway was the homeland of the Nordic race, and believed the nation should play a leading part in the Greater Nordic Peace Union. The Nordic race, he believed, was a force for global civilization, and by working together, Quisling believed, the Nordic or Nordic-friendly countries would create world unity. He wanted the Scandinavian countries and Germany and Britain to form a 'Nordic League.' Quisling maintained that materialist creeds would collapse, and be superseded by a return to spiritualism.

I imagined, as the boat moved along the coast, that Nansen would have dismissed Quisling's world-changing scheme as utopian adolescence. Nansen's enthusiasms and passions were undercut by a brooding sense of melancholy, bordering on despair. It was a state of sensitive paralysis that had come to him during the Arctic night, even as he marvelled at the beauties of the ice floes. It was a form of humility, a reluctant acceptance of the insignificance of human desires and doctrines in the face of the vast emptiness of the northern regions. A writer of vivid imagination, a myth collator of eclectic tastes, Nansen was also precise and realistic, qualities fashioned by the trial of theory during Arctic travel. When Quisling began to entwine his variety of nationalism with the schemes of the German National Socialists, Nansen would have despised the presumption and barbarism of the Nazis, their belief that world orders could be created through violence and destruction. As he had recoiled from the totalitarian force of the Communist state, Nansen would have been repulsed by the curtailing of individual freedoms inherent to the Nazi order.

Quisling was a minor political figure, in a small country, but he craved political power and philosophical influence. He had a brief stint as a cabinet minister in the early 1930s for the Agrarian Party. His strangeness, his introversion, his extremism combined to make him unpopular. There was a bizarre moment during his time as a minister when he was apparently attacked in his office at knife-point. Instead of sounding the alarm, Quisling sneaked out of the building and went home, and only called the police later. It made everyone uneasy; something was unclear about the story, and it contributed to a sense that Quisling was bizarre and untrustworthy. The gulf between desire and attainment fell like a shadow across Quisling's career, as he struggled to emerge from insignificance. He founded a group called the Nordic Folk Uprising, based on the 'fact' that 'Norwegians along with other Scandinavian peoples form the core of the large folk family which represents the most valuable racial contribution to humanity, the great Nordic race,' said Quisling. During the 1930s, Quisling became increasingly concerned with racial 'purity' and anti-Semitism. He talked about 'blood consciousness,' marching his men through working-class districts, trying to gain support from the disaffected. Quisling wanted the regeneration of the Nordic race as much as the Nazis—he hoped the Norwegian population would swell to 10 million by the year 2000. He would have been disappointed: Norway's population in 2000 was less than half this number. In 1933 he founded the National Union, but his party failed to attract popular support. In elections leading up to the war, it was always scrabbling around at 2 or 3 per cent of the overall vote. By slavish imitation of the Nazis, Quisling hoped for a similar coup: he dressed his militia in brown shirts; he insisted on being addressed as the *Fører*, the leader. He was in contact with the German fascists during the 1930s; he sent off a telegram to Hitler thanking him for all his work for the 'Germanic and Nordic *Brüdervolk*.' He went to visit Hitler and Rosenberg in Berlin in the winter of 1939; he tried to negotiate for the leadership of the new Nazi Norway during 1940.

When Hitler invaded Norway in 1940, Quisling announced that he was the leader of Norway, and ordered the Norwegians not to resist the German forces. While the Norwegian king refused to acknowledge him, Quisling kept addressing the nation on the radio, in the newspapers, announcing himself as the prime minister, telling the Norwegians to collaborate. As a tactic it failed; Quisling was largely disobeyed and once the lack of popular support trickled back to Berlin, Hitler withdrew his support for Quisling's coup. Quisling was humiliated, and ordered to go to Germany. Around this time the word "quisling" came into use across Europe, meaning a traitor, a man who tried to sell his country to an invading army. 'A vile race of quislings—to use the new word, which will carry the scorn of mankind down the centuries—is hired to fawn upon the conqueror, to "collaborate" in his designs and to enforce his rule upon their fellow countrymen while grovelling low themselves,' said Churchill in 1941. George Orwell took it up, describing treacherous *quislingisms*—meaning devious manoeuvring and lies. In the summer of 1940, the Norwegian king and members of the pre-war government fled to London, where they remained as government-in-exile throughout the war. Quisling wheedled his way back to Norway in the autumn, and took command of the collaborationist government. He spent the war railing against the Jews, the Freemasons, capitalism, Marxism, democracy, Bolshevism, England, the U.S., Churchill, Roosevelt, Wall Street and the London Stock Exchange. All these evils, Quisling kept saying, were attacks on the Germanic peoples.

Quisling thought the British had begun well, as stern Anglo-Saxons, with *Beowulf* a respectable early Saga, and then they had been receptive to the Viking conquests. But he thought the French had ruined it for the British, invading them, mixing them up with all sorts of un-Germanic elements, softening their language, drawing them away from the true brotherhood of Nordic nations. This was why Britain was being so disappointing about Nazism, Quisling had argued, because of this Romance strain in the national character, which had caused the British to lose their way. There were collaborators throughout Norway: there were the members of the council of commissioners who governed the country under the leadership of the German *Reichskommissar,* the thousands punished at the end of the war for treason, the dozens who were condemned to death. There were the tens of thousands who joined the Nasjonal Samling, supporters of Quisling's movement for Nordic supremacy. Several thousand Norwegians fought with the German forces, choosing to enlist in the Nazi cause. Yet there was the other side: the thousands of resistance fighters in Norway, the thousands of Norwegians who died fighting with the Allied forces, who were imprisoned in camps in Norway and Germany during the war years. There were savage reprisals from the Germans against those Norwegians who worked on the clandestine ferry route from western Norway to the Shetland Isles, shipping refugees from the occupied country. Nearly a hundred thousand Norwegians went abroad, half of them to Sweden, where they lived out the war. The king and the Norwegian government worked in London, trying to gather forces together.

After the war, Quisling was tried in a Norwegian court. He was charged with treason and with trying to bring Norway under foreign control. To the end, he repeated his claim that the coup of April 1940 and his position as minister president in occupied Norway had been in Norway's interests. He went to his death protesting his benevolence, clinging to a misguided notion that he was making the consummate sacrifice for his ideals. 'My work, our effort, has never really come to light,' he claimed in his address to the Norwegian Supreme Court, in October 1945. 'I have come to understand that there is a divine power in the universe, and that this power is connected to the development of those who live on this earth, and that what is happening here on earth during this important time is a watershed marking the beginning of God's kingdom here on earth.' Perhaps, he said, his benevolent intentions had 'turned out negatively' on this occasion. He passed his last days writing frantically, imagining he might leave a meaningful philosophical legacy. He was condemned, and shot.

This fantasy of a pure northern race propelled Quisling towards vicious collaboration. Quisling imagined the racial superiority of the Nordic race as proven by, entwined with the grandeur of their rocks. It was a ragged mess of foolish pride, racism and a personal quest for power. The fantasy compelled others, who never went so far as Quisling, Norwegians who stopped at ideas, though their ideas were brutal enough. Knut Hamsun was ruined by the war, and by his own sense of the superiority of the Nordic people. Hamsun became an antithesis to Nansen, falling into the mire Nansen avoided. They were contemporaries; Hamsun had written his seminal works as Nansen waited in the ice for *Fram* to move further north. They won Nobel Prizes within two years of each other. They were both fiercely determined, fiercely independent, and convinced of their rightness in most things. Nansen died with his reputation intact, but Hamsun's was ruined by the Nazi occupation of Norway, and by the choices he made in response to the occupation. Earlier a rebellious peasant, furious with literary cliques, Hamsun recast himself in a more sinister role, as a deluded nationalist, bellowing about the superiority of his country. Hamsun mistook the *völkisch* slogans of the Nazi Party for a robust defence of the ancient grandeur of the Nordic lands. He wanted Norway to be brought into the Germanic age. He wrote in support of the Nazis, entreating the Norwegians to help the occupying armies. He met Goebbels, and later gave his Nobel medal to the German as a present. He was introduced to Hitler; Hamsun was deaf at the time and spoke no German, so spent the interview shouting in Norwegian at the Führer. He wanted Hitler to agree to give Norway autonomy at the end of the war in the case of a Nazi victory, which Hamsun seemed to think was certain. Hitler was irritated by the interview, and, according to eye witnesses, stormed away, the exchange unfinished.

Hamsun later claimed he had been blind to the realities of the German occupation, that he had not fully understood what was happening in his country and in Europe. At best he was ignorant and self-deluding. But his fulsome support for the notion of Nordic supremacy was hard to explain away. He had hammered his colours to the Nazi mast, however much he later quibbled about whether he had joined Quisling's party or not. As the Third Reich unravelled, he wrote an elegy to Hitler.

In May 1945, when the war ended, Knut Hamsun was placed under house arrest by the police chief of Arendal, a town south of Oslo. Shortly after that, he was put in a hospital in a town called Grimstad. Hamsun never fully apologized; in a later account of his arrest, *On Overgrown Paths*, he claimed, 'I knew I was innocent, deaf and innocent; I would have done very well in an examination by the public prosecutor just by telling most of the truth.' There was a painful moment in Hamsun's trial for treason, when he defended himself on the grounds that he had been led to believe that Norway would have a high, prominent position in the great Germanic community which was now coming into being. 'We all believed it—to a greater or lesser degree,' Hamsun had said, 'everyone believed in it. I believed in it, that's why I wrote as I did.' He tried to implicate his nation, saying they had been as blind as him, but by then the war was over, and Hamsun was being tried by his countrypeople. Hamsun was judged to have 'permanently impaired mental facilities.' The Norwegian authorities evaded the issue, for their foolish Nobel laureate. Hamsun, before the war, was the laureate of northern Europe, of all these quiet, semi-deserted countries, with their long summers and their chill light-bereft winters. He lingered over the high clear skies of winter, the trees stripped of their leaves, the hills green and peaceful on every side, smoke from the cottage chimneys rising into the air. Hamsun botched it, to use the idiom of another writer who tarnished his reputation during the war, Ezra Pound. Hamsun took the savage route out of modernism, the savage route out of the romantic attachment to the Sagas. His was the route which led to violent retrogression, unbridled nostalgia for the tribal allegiances of the past. He ended at a wild extreme: misanthropy because men interfered with his view of the endless hills, a belief in Nordic supremacy because the people who lived in the endless hills were the Norwegians.

There was a commotion on the deck; the boat was stopping at Tromsø, the largest town in the north of Norway, a wind-lashed port, standing precariously on a barren island. We were nearly 70° N, and the landscape was beautiful and severe—vast grey slabs of rock slamming into the ocean, decorated with swirls of mist and dustings of snow. The fjord was overcast, and the mountains rose above. On the shore, a brass band was playing "I Do Like to Be Beside the Seaside." The music drifted across the water towards the boat.

In Tromsø the strains of the past hung in the cold air. Tromsø was a Mecca for polar history. It was a contemporary centre for wilderness tours. Its concrete housing reminded the casual onlooker that the town had been burnt during the war, and there was a rusting relic of the war, the *Tirpitz*, a German battleship sunk in the fjord, which gave up drowned artefacts to divers from time to time. We were in Arctic Norway, where the towns were subdued by the severity of the winters, and Tromsø was a practical place. The brass band was incongruous, like a luxury the town could hardly afford, piping us off the ship. I was beyond Nansen's Thule, further north than he had thought Pytheas sailed, in his imaginative reconstruction. But Tromsø had elements of a last land; for the Norwegian polar explorers of Nansen's era, Tromsø was the departure lounge, the last substantial settlement, before the North Pole. When Amundsen flew across the North Pole, in 1926, he flew from

Tromsø. When he flew out in June 1928 to meet an icy death, he left from Tromsø. He set off in a seaplane to hunt for an airship called *Italia*, which had been lost with Umberto Nobile on board. It was Nobile who had captained Amundsen's airship flight across the North Pole. Amundsen never returned from his rescue mission. Wreckage from his plane was later found, drifting on the ice floes. There were those who said he threw his life away, reckless to the last; others said that he was terminally ill and preferred to die in the ice.

The noise of the brass band faded as I walked along the harbour. There was a sign offering trips in an 'authentic fishing boat.' The Russian trawlers rusted slowly along the quayside. On the decks, Russian voices gave commands through loudspeakers. The sail lofts had been converted into hotels and apartments. There were shops offering quantities of Arctic tat, though no one seemed to be buying: fur gloves and hats, keyrings with pictures of mountains on them, postcards with the Arctic Circle drawn across a map of Norway. There was a fine bridge slung between the island and the mainland, linking Tromsø to its Arctic cathedral, a building mocked up to look like a pile of ice. There was a polar centre where seals performed slithering circles of a water tank, and an Arctic café filled with posters for poetry readings.

I jostled determinedly with a few local drunks for possession of a bench by the harbour, under a statue of Amundsen in oilskins, facing the ocean. Amundsen had flown out from Tromsø, to go to the rescue of a former friend, a former colleague on his flight above the North Pole. There were rumours that Nobile had infuriated Amundsen on the flight. Nobile had told Amundsen that the airship could only hold a single national flag from each party, a small pennant, nothing heavier. Amundsen had obliged, packing a small flag, the sort of flag a child might hold on a special occasion. Above the Pole, Amundsen had thrown the small pennant from the airship, watching it flutter towards the ice. Nobile had produced a vast box, containing an enormous Italian flag, and hurled its vastness onto the ice, trumping Amundsen's efforts entirely. It was a comic story Amundsen told, possibly apocryphal. It was hardly enough to prevent him from flying out to save Nobile. He balanced all, brought all to mind, and disappeared in a small plane, into the mist. The people of Tromsø had commemorated him with a solitary statue, now stranded on a traffic island, staring indignantly at the coast, trying not to look into the windows of the Comfort Hotel directly behind him. The statue was weatherworn and faded, but it was a clear rendering of the man, his unmistakable profile, his staggering nose, a nose like a challenge. I sat on the bench beneath him, looking up at his silhouette. There were rows of NATO soldiers walking along the quayside, waiting for a lift further north. The pale sun warmed the wind, which gusted through the streets, through the main street, which was dotted with wooden houses and dull concrete high-rise hotels. I passed along the quayside and crossed a scenic stretch of the harbour, past low wooden sail lofts, and a collection of antiquated fishing boats, a mass of polished planks and intricate rigging.

There was another Amundsen in Tromsø, a bust rather than a statue, staring out across another patch of water from the car park of the Polar Museum. The Polar Museum was full of compelling Arctic junk, all the rusting teaspoons and polished ski-runners and blurred photographs of explorers standing by boats and aeroplanes, preparing to launch themselves northwards. Row upon row of blurred portraits of nineteenth-century fur trappers, standing sombrely in front of a grotesque array of seal pelts. Away from the skis and sledges and navigation equipment, I stopped at a glass cabinet, containing a pocket-sized, brown leather copy of *Frithjof's Saga*, a tale of chivalric courage and frostbitten love, adapted from an Icelandic Saga by Esaias Tegnér. The book was opened at the frontispiece, which had an inscription in it, written by Amundsen, dated 1926: 'This book came with me on all my expeditions, Roald Amundsen.' Nansen, a Frithjof by name, could recite long passages by heart.

Nansen was there in the museum, among the skis and sledges and navigation equipment, in the newspaper clippings, celebrating his farthest north, celebrating the return of *Fram* to Norway, full of civic excitement. There were dour photographs of Nansen's later life in the museum, when he stared mournfully at the camera, and there was a large shabby waxwork, a puppet rendering of the man. This Nansen mannequin had a comically huge moustache, ruddy features, and an emaciated frame. The waxwork was falling apart; on one hand the fingers were sellotaped to the wrist. It was a bizarre tribute to the explorer, surveying the room with large blue eyes, staring at the torn newspaper cuttings and the maps of the north.

The sun slid slowly across the sky, its colours reflected in the clear waters of the fjord. Everything was very quiet in Tromsø, even as the bars began to fill. The cars moved slowly along the cobbled streets. On Storgata, the main street, the shops were beginning to close, shutters drawn against the long Arctic evening.

After a hundred more rocks, sullen in the cold afternoon, we had turned east and were heading towards the Russian coast. The ship was passing along the scrawny last rags of Norway, a country that shrinks from the swollen girth of its southern regions to the emaciation of the north. The mountains had lost their trees, and the towns were hard and functional. Hammerfest slipped past at 3 A.M., a place calling itself the world's most northerly town, its lights shimmering on the waves. Cold on the deck, huddled in a sleeping bag because I had fallen asleep while watching the sunset, I woke to the sound of the ship docking, and fell asleep again before we had left the harbour.

When I woke again in the rich dawn, the ship was sliding towards another old rock, this one with significance daubed upon it by earlier travellers. The atmosphere on deck was expectant. We were approaching North Cape, formerly the last point of Europe. I arrived in a strange mood. North Cape was a tourist magnet, a formerly significant goal, once a place embedded among thousands of miles of hostile nature, now easy enough for the tourists to find, as they reclined in the buses, clicking cameras at the rocks and tundra. North Cape was a significant rock, named by Richard Chancellor, a sixteenth-century English captain, who sailed past the lump of rock on the way to the White Sea. Chancellor landed at Archangel and set out for Moscow, where he and his crew were received at the court of Ivan the Terrible. Chancellor returned triumphantly to England, preparing to make a fortune in fur trading, the fashionable commodity from the north, but he was lost at sea the next year, on another profit-making expedition. North Cape stayed in the minds of sailors and explorers; the horn pointing out to sea was a landmark visible from the ocean as the boats sailed along the storm coasts.

I drifted through the glass-fronted building, built like a hi-tech physics department, called the North Cape Centre, a tourist hypermarket at the formerly most mysterious place. The Norwegian attendants suggested I might like to buy some North Cape merchandise, and nudged me towards a supermarket full of North Cape tankards, North Cape cuddly toys, North Cape postcards, North Cape pennants. A first wave of tourists moved into the supermarket, towards the videos of circling seabirds, through the aisles of trinkets, but I moved slowly onwards, down a corridor. Pushed along in a grand flow of tourists, I walked through an exhibition in glass cases, with plastic figures posed into tableaux, representing past visitors. There was a plastic figurine of the Italian explorer Francesco Negri, who emerged onto the rocks in 1664 and wrote: 'I am now at North Cape, on the exterior coast of Finnmark and at the roof of the world . . . My curiosity is now satisfied, and I wish to return to Denmark, and if God is willing, to my own country.' There was a description of the arrival of Louis-Philippe d'Orléans, who came in 1795, in exile from France. He visited Oslo, Trondheim and Bodø, and continued to North Cape. North Cape was the sort of destination that might attract a man like Louis-

Philippe, who later travelled on horseback around America. There was a portrait of the rocks, showing Louis-Philippe and his party on the shores below North Cape, preparing to clamber up the cliff. It was sentimental—the prince and his cohorts were standing above a swollen ocean, staring reverently at the great rock, while sailors struggled to lash the sail to the mast. In the background stood the great grey escarpment, blanched by a pale sky. All this idealism, this passionate excitement, splashed across the rocks; centuries of over-whelmed travellers, arriving at an escarpment which an otherwise forgotten sailor had called North Cape, and sinking to their knees: princes, explorers, sailors, traders. A great line of satisfied people; in the nineteenth century they came reciting lines from Henry Wadsworth Longfellow: the 'huge and haggard shape/ of that un-known North Cape/ Whose form is like a wedge.' They all came, they unloaded their quotations, like a picnic rug and plates, they re-laxed into the created significance of the rocks, and then they packed everything up and went home.

I moved on, through the empty restaurant, where champagne buckets were laid out ready for the lunchtime rush. At the edge of the cliff the tourists massed like seagulls, peering down at the grey ocean, which lapped the base of the cliff. They took photographs of each other, standing in front of the view out to sea.

When I returned to the boat, I watched the sunlight flood across the rocks, as the boat eased past the isolated settlements of box houses, designed and constructed after the war, planted on the soil. Past the layers of sandstone and granite, the striped mountains of brown and grey. I stood on the deck, watching the light gleaming across the pastel mountains, turning them purple. The sun shone like fire on the rock pillars. Small villages emerged out of the rock desert, and receded again, as the boat moved onwards into further miles of slab rocks lurking above the sea. The lights flashed at the entrances to the harbours, the night was rich and bloodied, the sun disgorging its colours across the water.

The sky was blue in the early morning, though dark clouds

lined the tops of the mountains. The sun cast a pale light across the empty land. The sun flickered across the purple mountains, the trees lined the roads, the roads wound southwards, receding into points at the horizon, a distant horizon, the sun drifting towards it.

The German troops had sat up in the north, waiting to fight the Russians, oppressed by the cold. 'The Arctic is nothing,' they were told by their commanders, but the winter storms chased across the sea and the nights were long and bleak. The Germans and Russians fought across the border for the port of Murmansk. Thousands died on both sides, as the struggle of the summer of 1941 dragged into the winter. Even when spring came, the troops were lost in snow blizzards, scrambling across ice-hard rivers, their guns frozen. The campaigns were stalled by the frozen season.

The occupation had violently altered the view; along the shore of the northern coast, in every town I came to, the story was the same. In October 1944, after intense fighting, Russian troops entered Norway. The order came to the German forces from Hitler that a scorched earth tactic should be used, without compassion for the inhabitants. They were to be removed by force, as necessary. As the Russians advanced across the border, the Germans burned every home, and retreated to the west. The German troops chased backwards from the Russian border towards Tromsø, hounding the inhabitants of the towns and villages into overcrowded refugee ships. The dead zone encompassed an area larger than Denmark; sometimes all that remained of a vibrant fishing town was its church, spared through piety or superstition, standing on an empty coast. Most of the inhabitants lost everything; sometimes they buried their valuables, their family heirlooms, hoping to save them. In one of the museums along the coast, I had seen two plush and silk armchairs, which were found buried in the ground and never reclaimed by their owners. They remained in the museum, remnants of a vanished town.

Along the coast, I had seen the displays of grainy black-and-white postcards of towns torched by the retreating Germans, before and after shots, grim in their contrasts. In Bodø Museum I bought a postcard of the harbour, from 1897, a shot of a crowd gathering on a short pier made of wood, staring out to sea at a steamer. A great cloud of thick white smoke gushes up from the ship's chimney. A faded reminder of the northern towns as they had been, as Nansen passed them in *Fram*, as the Germans first found them: quiet, isolated settlements, clusters of wooden houses, a solitary church rising above the sloped roofs. The inhabitants of the western villages saw the smoke clouds in the distance and heard the Germans approaching.

After the burning, nothing remained except shadows of ash, lying where buildings once stood, and the outlines of roads. Beyond, the rock islands in the harbours loomed large above the dust. After the end of the war, rows of ready-made houses were brought over from Sweden, hammered up in a week. New wooden rows were planted on the blackened soil, sparsely furnished and hurriedly decorated. Later the towns took to concrete—concrete bunkers, a line of concrete shops, a concrete library, sometimes a concrete church.

Kirkenes had been burnt, transformed in a day into rows of piled-up ash and debris, the mountains scarred by soot. At Kirkenes, by the Russian border, the boat stopped for the last time. The wind blasted through the concrete town square and Russian trawlers sat in the harbour. The sounds of Finnish and Russian mingled with the long vowels of the Norwegians. In Kirkenes the day dawned into a white brilliance, and the sea glinted under the glare. The streets were full of teenagers in trainers, and the older inhabitants were sitting in the sunshine, though the wind was cold. Kirkenes was a place of multi-coloured wooden houses backed by green hills lined with silver birch trees, stark against the pallid horizon. An iron ore mine stood near the road out of town, the machinery left to rust. The silver Pasvik River flowed to the Barents Sea.

As the wind bent the trees, I took a bus to the border, which ran through streets of large wooden houses, post-war constructions, and past frozen lakes, and across a bridge. It was another bizarre ride for tourists, in the anti-Disneyland of the north, where the main attraction was the vastness of the mountains. If you missed a trip, to a frozen escarpment or to an empty glacier, you could come round again; the monumental rocks never changed. There were even bedraggled tourists here, looking jaded and cold, clutching their cameras like amulets against disaster. They were quiet on the bus, as if they had hoped for something else, but they resolutely lifted their cameras to the view, to the signs in Russian and Norwegian, to the silver river. The road began in Kirkenes and ran to the Russian town of Murmansk, through the empty borderlands.

But we stopped at the border, at a white gate flanked by stone pillars, where soldiers sat in huts, guns on their laps, their faces obscured. A kiosk sold Russian dolls and ice cream. For a few minutes everyone stood uncertainly, leafing through the postcards, looking at the Russian and Norwegian flags, dancing side by side as the wind tugged at their ropes. Then the bus turned around again.

Later, I sat in a modest wooden house, on one of the homogeneous streets of wooden houses in Kirkenes, which ended in a small park. I was drinking coffee with a middle-aged Norwegian woman. Her house was mostly pink, the walls were pink, and the frills on the cushions; the shelves were covered with ugly china, the sorts of ornaments that appeared at village fête stalls and would be packed into boxes at the end of the day again, unbought. But she had bought in bulk.

She was Gunvor, and she was wearing pink, with her grey-blond hair scraped into a bun. She had a firm handshake, but she had welcomed me with a veiled expression. I understood why. Gunvor was the leftover debris of World War Two, the leftover debris of the Aryan obsession, Quisling's regeneration of the

Nordic race, Himmler's blond-lust. Gunvor was called a *krigsbarn* by her countrypeople, a war child. She had been called worse; she was called names throughout her childhood—half-breed, misfit, outsider—and her mother was sometimes called a German whore. There were thousands of children like Gunvor, maybe as many as ten thousand in Norway, and thousands in other occupied countries, but this still didn't make the Norwegian authorities inclined to favour them after the war.

During the war, Himmler's *Lebensborn* homes were established in Norway, and Hitler issued an order for 'the advancement of racially valuable German inheritance' by supplying care and provision for the children of German soldiers born to Norwegian and Dutch women. SS men could sleep with local women, without the fear of having to provide for the child: if the union resulted in a pregnancy, then the services of the *Lebensborn* homes were available, or the child could be taken back to Germany and supplied with foster parents. Some said these homes were breeding centres; neighbours imagined rooms of 'Aryan' seductresses, waiting for their next soldier. More likely, they were kept in line with Nazi faux-morality, overseeing the births of 'Aryan' children.

Gunvor was born, she told me, in December 1943. Her Norwegian mother had been working as a waitress in the army barracks where the German soldiers lived. Her father was an officer; that was all Gunvor knew. Her mother, she thought, had entered a *Lebensborn* home and had given birth to Gunvor. But a year after she was born, her father had left Norway.

'I never knew him. My mother never spoke about him, except once, and briefly. She married shortly after the war ended, to a man who didn't mind me. He died when I was ten. They had two other children, who never liked me very much because I was so unpopular at school.' She tried to laugh. 'You know how children are, when someone is called names, they don't want to be their friend. But we made things up years later. My mother and my stepfather are now dead. I never tried to trace my father, probably now he is dead too,' Gunvor said. 'Even my generation is now old.' She paused, and she motioned towards a plate of dry Norwegian cakes and a pot of coffee.

'Some of the *krigsbarn* did try to trace their fathers,' she said. 'I heard such stories later, I was glad in a way that I never knew mine. Friends of mine, people I have met through the *krigsbarn* networks and societies, told me that they went to find their fathers in Germany, and when they tracked them down, their fathers were so horrified to see them. By then, they had wives, they had other children; they didn't want to remember. There was one woman, she is an amazing woman, she went to Germany and her father knew all about her, but he told her to go away; he said that he wanted nothing to do with her. She was so angry, and she had all the proof, from her mother, so she took him to court. He was old and weak, and in the end he tried to stop the court proceedings; he was embarrassed, most probably, and he offered her money, he tried to apologize to her. By then she didn't care. She proved in court that he was her father, and then she left Germany and never spoke to him again.'

It sounded like a hollow victory, but Gunvor was consoled by it.

'Mostly people don't want to remember us,' Gunvor said. 'There were many people after the war who wanted us sent out of Norway, to Germany, where they said we belonged or to Australia, just to get rid of us. We were a horrible memory of all the compromises people made with the Germans, of the ways people made such mistakes during the war.'

Gunvor's face creased when she spoke, and her fingers moved nervously on her coffee cup. I had found her through a *krigsbarn* support group. She had responded politely to my call. But still, she hardly enjoyed talking about the past. The past had made her shy and suspicious. Gunvor's house was immaculately pink, cluttered with ornaments, but there were absences. There were no family photographs on her mantelpiece. Her curtains were drawn, though it was mid-afternoon.

'I was wondering,' I said, 'if you wished you had found your father.'

'It's better this way,' she said. 'For years I was very unhappy about it, not knowing him, I longed just to know a little about him. But whenever I said something to my mother, her face just closed up, she wouldn't speak. And now, I think I am glad. This way, I can imagine my father was a reluctant soldier, that he never believed in the aims of the Nazis. I can imagine he was a nice man, a kind man. My mother never said so, and he never took any interest in her. He must have known there was a child, but I don't know for certain.'

She was wilfully incurious, trusting to her imagined reality, her consolatory reconstruction of events. It was hardly surprising; the *krigsbarn* had a terrible time after the war. In the Aryan Empire they had been the ideal racial group; under Himmler's schemes the children of the *Lebensborn* programme in Norway were central to the project of the Third Reich. But after the defeat of Germany, the ideal progeny of the Aryan Empire suffered an immediate change in status. In post-war Norway, a virulent Germanophobia spread, and the *krigsbarn* and their mothers supplied an uncomfortable reminder of a period the Norwegians hoped to forget.

'Thousands of the mothers were put in prison, and their children were taken away,' said Gunvor. 'In Norway the top psychiatrists, such as the head of the largest mental hospital, said that the mothers had been insane, mentally defective, because they had slept with the Germans. So the *krigsbarn* were thought of as insane too; they were thought to be mentally ill because of their background. So they were treated like lunatics.'

Spurious medical conclusions, founded on notions of genetic taint, led to decades of maltreatment and neglect. The *krigsbarn* stayed in Norway, but many of them were shunned, hidden in children's homes, or shut away in mental institutions.

'There were *Lebensborn* children in Germany, Holland, France, in the Channel Islands, in Belgium, Denmark, as well as in Norway. We have networks,' said Gunvor, sadly. 'We think the Norwegian authorities concealed the abuse, or turned away. They didn't care.'

'What would you like to happen?' I asked. 'What would make things better?'

'For many people, it is too late. Their lives have already been ruined. There have been cases fought, for compensation, against the Norwegian authorities. We feel that a lot of people were deprived of an education and therefore could not work to gain money. So really they lost potential earnings, because of this abuse, aside from all the other terrible things that happened that you can't put a price on. But even if we got compensation, well, I don't care. It wouldn't help me. You see my house'—and she cast a careless hand at her pink room—'I am not poor. It is something else that I feel I lost.'

Gunvor rarely paused; she spilled out the story, trying to race through it, so she could return to the soft pinkness of her room, the flowers in the vase, the china ornaments cluttering the shelves. On the street outside, I imagined, people were walking dogs, cycling along the quiet streets, children were tumbling around in the park. But Gunvor's curtains were drawn. She could only hear the muffled sounds of the afternoon, the faint voices and footsteps moving past her door.

'I was never put away,' said Gunvor, 'because my mother was so determined to keep me. She was unusual. We lived a poor life together, even after she married. I don't know . . .' She paused, and wiped her brow. She was clearly uncomfortable, even now, even talking about the events of fifty years ago, even with her network of *krigsbarn* around her. 'I don't know. Perhaps if she hadn't married, then things would have been much worse. She might have been bullied more; I might have been taken away. Certainly no one wanted to be her friend, for years, and my stepfather was brave to marry her. He really truly loved her. He saw she had been young, she had made a terrible mistake. There were young girls, hopelessly ignorant, who thought the German soldiers were dashing in their uniforms. I don't understand.'

She was fumbling in a drawer, and she produced a black-and-white photograph and pushed it towards me.

'This is me with my mother. Here I am three,' said Gunvor. 'It is after the war.'

The girl with the child was trying to smile for the camera. She was a pretty girl with blonde hair, dressed smartly. She looked extremely young. It was a posed photograph, an act of defiance perhaps, when the authorities were trying to pretend the war children didn't exist. But perhaps I was reading too much into the motives of a young mother. She had loved her child, and wanted to have a photograph of her taken. Perhaps it was that simple.

'It's a nice photograph,' I said, because I could think of nothing else to say, and Gunvor took the photograph back and put it carefully away again.

'My neighbours bring their children home from school round about now,' she said. 'And you know, they don't know about my past at all.'

'Surely now it would be OK to tell them?'

'Yes, perhaps,' she said. 'But I came here so long ago, and I never told anyone. It would seem strange to tell them now. They would feel I had hidden it from them for so long. To a close friend, I might tell it, but I have never come to know my neighbours very well,' she said.

I imagined the loneliness of concealing the past from your neighbours, after all these years. Yet Gunvor insisted that she had been one of the lucky ones. She had ended up in a pleasant house, in a quiet northern town. It wasn't where she came from, she said, but she didn't want to name her hometown. 'I would feel bad for the people who shunned us; I don't want to point a finger at them.

They were just doing what everyone did at the time. It's a pressure, to be the same. There were people much worse off than me, I could tell you terrible stories. A friend I now know, another *krigsbarn*, he was in children's homes for all his life, he was never taught to read properly, he can't speak a word of English. He was bullied and mal-treated. He worked as a janitor, and has lived in poverty. These people were failed by the system. They were innocent, they were only children, anyone should have pitied them, but the state hated them, thought they were tainted by their genes.'

For years after the war, the state failed to intervene in the guilty maltreatment of the *krigsbarn*, taking its lead from the medical es-tablishment. In the haggard world after the war, children were blamed for the actions of the Nazis, for the actions of their parents. The children were punished by a society that could hardly bear to remember.

Later, I said goodbye to Gunvor as we stood in her hallway. She was used to people not liking her, she said, and it was always odd to meet new people. I had found I liked her a great deal, with her ner-vous hospitality, her cakes and coffee and her accelerated speech. I admired her for her lack of self-pity, even as I suspected that her briskness might be a veneer.

She shut the door, quite sharply, as if she was glad it was over.

———— ∞ ————

At Kirkenes I had picked up a car, driving it out of the town through the green forests and silver lakes, along a silent road to the east. The rocks were stacked up along the road. Nothing moved on the ridges. I arrived without noticing it in Karasjok, a small village by the Finnish border. I stopped the car, slammed the door, and walked around, ducking into a supermarket where everyone was buying hats and gloves, because the wind was growing harsher and more persistent by the hour. When I walked, I noticed I was sway-ing slightly from the sea voyage. The wind was trying for an early winter, tugging the leaves from the trees, landing them in piles. The countryside lay ragged and beautiful around the village, with the sun shining in a pale sky. I arrived at a wooden building, like a pine palace. Planks of pine, drawn into a curved wall, with props of pine set between them. Everything smelt of pine; the palace seemed to be new.

I had arranged to meet Pal outside the palace, and he was waiting, a small man, wearing a bright red-and-blue tunic, with a multicoloured hat, like a jester's. He had a sword tied to his belt.

'We were never Aryans,' he was saying. 'But our ancestors were in these regions for thousands of years, even before the Nordic tribes came, we think. Tacitus wrote about Fenni, but we think it was us all right. For a while the Scandinavian governments pretended we didn't exist, but they were so ashamed after the war, things got better for us.'

He rattled his belt, and for a moment I thought he might draw his sword, but he was looking for something else. He took out a key, and moved towards the pine door of the pine palace.

'This,' he said, pushing the door open, with a flourish, 'is the Parliament of the Sámi. You are more likely to have heard us called the Lapps, but we decided we didn't like that name.'

The entrance hall was full of lights and splashy paintings in bright colours hanging down the wooden walls. In glass cases they had stored a significant piece of fish skin, a significant piece of reindeer hide. There were rows of books and papers, and a few Sámi in bright tunics, sitting behind desks.

Pal offered a quick tour of the Parliament, taking in the president and a few other sights in the place. He had worked in the Parliament for a few years, he told me, since it was opened. The Parliament was made up of corridor after corridor of perfect pine, leading into large light meeting rooms, painted vivid colours. The Sámi, Pal was saying, were a quiet non-Aryan people, blanched out by the Nazis in their Nordic fetish. Blanched out by the Scandinavian governments for years. The Sámi, or people a little like the Sámi, Pal wasn't quite sure which, had appeared in ancient ac-

counts, called the Wildlappmanni, Scrithifini, Scritobini, Screre-
finni. They hunted through the forests and across the mountains.
They appeared in early writings on the north, in Tacitus, in Procopius, later in the medieval clerics, who made up wild fantasies
and entwined them with contemporary knowledge. They ate nothing but the flesh of animals, they couldn't sew, tying skins together
with sinews. They slung their babies over the branches of trees, so
the women could go to the hunt. These early Sámi were a curiosity
for centuries, with their strange magic, something called gam, and
their cloudy history, mixed up with fables and fantasies. Close to
the land of the Scrithifini or the Scritobini, or the Finni, was an
abyss of water, claimed the fanciful writers, called Ocean's navel,
which twice a day sucked the waves down and spewed them out
again. There were crazier rumours still, trickling through clerical
pens, that the Scrithifini lived near to the women with beards, and
the Amazons, and the Cynocephali, and the Cyclopes.

They had been ignored, said Pal, and suppressed for a while, by
Scandinavian governments wound up on patriotic slogans. But they
had a good claim to being the most ancient people in the north. 'It's
not a claim we'd make,' Pal was saying, 'and anyway we don't believe in the ownership of land. Mother Earth cannot be owned by
humans,' he said devoutly.

The Sámi never had a certain land; they hardly recognized the
national borders of the countries they lived in. They had herded
reindeer through generations around the northern reaches of Scandinavia. Lapland was a region in the north of Finland, but there was
a larger region of Sámiland, real to the Sámi, stretching across the
north of the Scandinavian countries, but hardly represented by
lines and divisions on the maps. It was a land unacknowledged, an
informal homeland for them.

The President appeared, a small man with dark hair holding his
sword like a pen, and he said he had to rush to a meeting but he
knew that the Sámi were the earliest inhabitants of the north, he
was quite convinced, and though there was no such thing as mem-

bership of land it was unpleasant to be sitting in the Parliament with no power at all. They had no power, no money, said the President, they needed a lot more money, and significantly more power, and the pipelines and oil wells that everyone kept building in the northern regions were not his idea of a nature-friendly use of the land. In Western society, he said, everyone was always talking about development, about money, but the Sámi had a different sense of things.

'You know,' he added, after a pause, 'we are not bitter about the past.'

He looked frustrated, as he nodded sternly, bowing slightly, shuffling along the corridor to a meeting. He wouldn't say what it was about. 'Business, business,' he said, clinking his sword against his belt buckle.

In the *Kalevala*, the Finnish epic, Northland, or Lapland, was a place of darkness and magic, a perilous place. The heroes Lemminkäinen, Väinämöinen and Ilmarinen wander the north: god-heroes, reciting verses and having fights. They slide through the frost-covered lands in the far north; they move through the wilds, hearing the dogs barking and Lapland's children crying, and the women laughing. Lapland is a fabulous place in the poem—the barren lands, the unsown pastures, the battlefields, the rustling grasses, the vast oceans, the black mud of the seas, the smoking whirlpools, the rapids, the clouds and gales and wind-blasted lands. It is a place where there is no daylight through the winter, it is the dreary north, its shadows veiling the lives of the inhabitants.

In the *Kalevala*, Väinämöinen is taken on an eagle's back to the furthest north, to the dark lands of the Lapps. Troubled by the terrain, he lies by a stream crying, asking to go home. Louhi, the queen of the north, rows him to a strange cabin, where she says she will show him the way home if he makes something for Lapland, an object called the Sampo—a sort of grail. Väinämöinen promises to send Ilmarinen, the smith, to forge the Sampo.

Väinämöinen returns home, and asks the wind to carry Ilmarinen to the dark lands of the north. The smith lights his fire, makes his bellows, and sets up a forge. Ilmarinen produces the bizarre object, the Sampo, with a corn mill on one side, a salt mill on another, a money mill on another, and a gleaming bright lid. The queen of the north takes the Sampo into the rocky mountains of Lapland, and buries it. Meanwhile the rogue Lemminkäinen decides to travel to Lapland. He visits Kauppi the Lapp to get some skis, and goes sliding through the wilds, skiing across swamps and over the blackened hills. Trying to win the girl of the north, Louhi's daughter, Lemminkäinen is killed. His mother comes to find him, travelling through the swamps as a wolf, through the waters as an otter, pushing aside the rocks and the stumps, searching for her son. When she finds him, dead in the river, she sews him back together again.

The north has something in it of the Underworld; Tuoni's black river runs like the Styx. Louhi is an ancient hag of the north, controlling events with a malevolent will. But Lapland is also where the beautiful girl of the north lives, and after Lemminkäinen has failed, Väinämöinen and Ilmarinen join the suitors' fray. She chooses Ilmarinen and prepares to leave the north, regretting the loss of her simple life, spent growing strawberries and flowers, eating butter and pork, leaving cares to the fir trees, to the birches on the heath.

Lemminkäinen, restored to life, kills the master of Lapland, and Lapland prepares for war. Fleeing from the armies, Lemminkäinen sets out by sea towards the north-west, but Louhi sends the Frost to follow him, and Lemminkäinen is forced to leave the ship and walk across the ice. Ilmarinen's wife, the girl of the north, is killed by a serf, and though Ilmarinen tries to console himself by forging a wife from gold, he fails. So he returns to Lapland, to ask for the other daughter of the north. He is refused, but he sees that the land is prosperous because of the Sampo, because it grinds things to eat, and things to sell and things to store at home. So Väinämöinen and Ilmarinen, with Lemminkäinen, decide to return to Lapland, to take the Sampo. The *Kalevala* culminates in a great war between Lapland and the animistic forces of Väinämöinen and his men. When Väinämöinen and his band claim the Sampo, Lapland becomes poor.

'And the Lapps became poor,' said Pal, looking at his watch. 'We lived in an uncertain land through the century, invaded and invaded again, its borders changing hands, from Finland to Germany to Russia, from Russia to Finland. We sat the century out, waiting for the wars to end.'

There was a strange atmosphere in their lush pine palace, a palace without any real power, because the Sámi were the dependents of Scandinavian governments, given a sort of guilt money, reparations for years of neglect. When I shook Pal's hand, and he unlocked the pine gates, gently pushing me back out into the windy street, I left feeling that some deep-lying dissatisfaction haunted the Sámi, some sense of ancient pride subjected to a continued humiliation. They told me they were poor people, living in countries they did not govern. About the important things, they said, they had no choice.

⁂

The Hyperboreans had escaped Nemesis, the Greeks wrote, but it was impossible to maintain the ideal of a remote north that escaped the ravages of the twentieth century. The white wilderness of Siberia became a place of prison camps and death; the white lands were spotted with the dark shapes of prisoners, dragged in chains. Nuclear submarines ploughed through the Arctic Ocean, conducting clandestine operations during the Cold War. Secret military bases were set up in Alaska, in Greenland, in Siberia. The Sámi had watched the Second World War, the German soldiers torching the towns. They had seen the official borders—lines which meant nothing to them, cutting through the lands they lived in—shifting throughout the centuries, as the regions fell under the sway of the Scandinavian monarchs, or the Russian tsars, later the Soviet Army, stamping through the north during the Second World War.

For a few moments, as the wind blasted across the hills and the evening fell, I thought I could go south. I could end there: it was a neat decline from ideal to disaster, from innocence to experience. It supplied the resounding note, the cymbal crash, with the explorers and Victorians coming on for a curtain-bow—the dream of Thule, bound into the polar craze in the late nineteenth century, savaged by 1945. I was gathering the Victorians, Burton, Tweedie and Trollope, the explorers, Nansen and Amundsen, into a choir, imagining them singing a mournful elegy, a lament to the lost ideal of Thule. Poor Thule, they were singing, sotto voce, ruined by the century, the perfect place, dragged into a terrible war. I found myself thinking of London, wondering if I should get back to my life in the city. It was late summer in London. The parks would still be green, the trees still decked with leaves. I could go back to the flat overlooking the Westway, and watch cars passing over the bridge, moving above the trees and houses. I could watch the streetlights turning orange in the early evening, and the neon strips flickering in kitchens below the Westway, walls vibrating to the rhythm of the cars passing overhead. I could return to the honest complexity of the city, a place where the present was raucous and the past was omnipresent. The city didn't feign a peacefulness it would fail to surrender. The city flaunted its antiquity, its violence and tragedy.

But I quelled my impulse to go home. I had begun with a series of questions. I had wanted to know what happened after the war, why the US Military had called its air base Thule, why Thule still meant northern wilderness, why the Nazis had failed to taint the myth. The Nazi version of Thule said nothing about the original fragments; it was merely eloquent about the minds of those who had misconstrued them. The ancient debate across millennia had been viciously interrupted, but I knew that it continued beyond the war. The mysterious history of Thule attracted others, with different secrets to hide, different dreams, living through the post-war years. The northern rocks and lakes were still gaudy in the summer sunshine; the allure of emptiness retained its potency. I had seen the travellers on the boat, watching the scenery; I had watched with them, mesmerized by the glow of the midnight sun hovering above the waves. There were questions left unanswered, lingering in the northern dusk. Leaving the Sámi town, and heading back to the airport of Kirkenes, I wanted even more to know about the post-war fortunes of Thule. What happened to Thule after the quiet lands of the north had been devastated, drawn into the carnage of World War Two? Who had picked up the skein again, the ancient argument about Thule?

FINLAND

Estonia

Gulf of Finland

Baltic
Sea

HIIUMAA

• Haapsalu

Tallinn

Kohtla-Järve

ESTONIA

SAAREMAA

• Pärnu

Tartu •

Gulf of
Riga

Valga

LATVIA

RUSSIA

0   25   50 miles

0   40   80 km

• Riga

FIRE

RANDOM ROCK
AND THE STAIN OF THE RAIN,
SMELL OF BRACKEN,
THE WINDY MOOR
AND THE WILD CLOUD,

AND RISING BLURRED
IN THE SHOWERY GRAY
A NAMELESS MOUND
OF THE PERISHED PEOPLE
WHO BUILT NOTHING . . .

CONTENT I SAVOUR
MY NORTHERN EARTH
TILL MEMORY'S SHUTTLE
DARTS ACROSS IT
A FAR PICTURE

"THULE," LAURENCE BINYON (1869–1943)

In the old controversy of Thule, there was another strain. There was a renegade group that thought Pytheas had never gone towards the ice seas and the Arctic mountains, but had instead sailed to the east, along the Baltic coast. He had never supped with the Sámi; he had never watched the Arctic sun descend across the glaciers. He had never sailed into the western fjords, marvelling at the rocks. He had never been to the Arctic at all. Instead, he had sailed towards Russia, finding lands that were later Lithuania, Latvia and Estonia. It wasn't a popular theory. Burton and Nansen had never lined up to endorse it. It dragged Thule away from the frozen Arctic and landed it at the Gulf of Finland. I didn't really believe this idea at all, but I knew there was a president who had recently lined up to defend it. He had a vested interest in Thule's having been somewhere in the Baltic—he was Lennart Meri, the first post-independence president of Estonia after the collapse of the Soviet Union. Meri's Thule was a piece of post-war restoration.

In the years of Communist control, Meri had written books about northern places. He had read through the ancients and devised his own theory of Thule. His theory was about the history of Estonia, and the history of the German tribes, but he had changed the meaning of the myth altogether. He had written about Thule in a desperate land, in a country that had been bombed, invaded by the Germans and the Russians during World War Two, occupied by the Soviet Union until 1991. For Meri, the old idea of a pure northern place was something to hold on to, as the Estonians watched the Russians polluting their land with military camps and nuclear sites. He had said that Thule might not have been a place at all. It might have been an event; the word Thule might have represented a meteorite that crashed into Estonian soil, hundreds of years before Pytheas arrived in the region, and caused a raging fire that burned the forests. In Estonian *tuli* means "fire," and Meri thought it might have meant the violent flames from the meteorite, a conflagration so horrifying that the locals were still talking about the event when Pytheas arrived.

I had a few ideas about how to meet Lennart Meri, who was no longer president of Estonia. He had served the maximum two terms and had then stepped down. I'd been making calls from Norway, calling friends of friends, and finally alighted on a pair who claimed they knew Meri. With a few addresses in my pocket, I landed into Tallinn's mist-clad airport.

The taxi ride passed through the Soviet layers of the town, the dull concrete towers, the seething main roads, with the buses lined up at the lights. Under a slate sky Tallinn old town rose from a small hill, hemmed in by Soviet blocks, stacked in rows at the disintegrating outskirts. Chimneys disgorged swirls of black smoke into the whiteness of the sky. Leaving the taxi, I walked across tram tracks and along the road into the old town. The old centre of Tallinn is a piece of salvaged Hansa, which somehow survived through centuries of power struggles and the violence of World War Two. The cobbled streets were packed with tourists, staring up at the stern-fronted merchant houses, multi-storey mansions, recently sliced into flats by incoming opportunists, foreigners who were buying houses in bulk, or locals who had managed to profit from the transition. Large towers squatted at the edges of the old town, their gates flung open. I walked along a wide street, past a French restaurant flying the tricolour, where some of the buildings were newly painted and others retained an antique shabbiness. The main square had a chiming clock, haunting the cold evening with a medieval resonance. There were ruined patches of land beyond the square, a row of buildings bombed during the war, never reconstructed. The land had been sold.

The Soviet occupation of Estonia came out of World War Two. At the end of the war, the armies of the Soviet Union moved across the Baltic States, leering across the Gulf of Finland. The Estonians thought they had been betrayed. They had watched through World War Two, as the Germans and the Russians sparred over their lands; they had been drawn into the fighting. Stalin wanted the Baltic States after World War Two, and neither Churchill nor Roosevelt did much to stop him. For nearly fifty years, the countries along the Baltic coast sank into Soviet grey; the people kept within the confines of the Communist Empire, though a few thousand escaped to Sweden. Fifty years later, when the Soviet Union collapsed, the soldiers went back to Russia, but they left debris scattered across the country—hidden military bases, nuclear submarine training centres, the decaying vestiges of collective farms. They left the shabby medieval streets of Tallinn, semi-decayed rows of Hanseatic mansions, alleys covered in ferocious graffiti, wizened gardens of dying plants. They left a nation nervously enjoying its independence, looking over its shoulder at the eastern border, wondering how long the peace would last.

In the tourist idyll of the old town, the shops sold Estonian knits and amber beads. I walked past the tourist bars and the crowded patisseries, where old Estonians waited at tables for coffee and cream cakes. I passed up a series of cloistered passageways to Toompea, the second tier of the old town, at the top of a low hill. The Orthodox domes of the Alexander Nevsky Cathedral, a remnant of Russian control in the region, were surrounded by touts. As I walked along, a young Russian approached me and offered to take a photograph of me in front of the cathedral. When I shook my head, his face fell and he moved quickly away. A series of winding streets led towards the edge of the hill, where I stood on a viewing platform, looking out at the industrial sprawl of the harbour, the long dull rows of cheap housing, the intertwined railway tracks. A man was selling CDs of his own music—a tall lumbering man with a blond ponytail and a donkey jacket, talking in fast clipped English to tourists who moved steadily away from him, trying to look at the view. An Estonian TV station was filming, the presenter broadcasting with the city as a backdrop, talking loudly to the camera. Graffiti had been splashed across some of the darker passages in Toompea, in the areas away from the Parliament buildings. Yet the renovation was happening fast, the place was full of newly painted apartment blocks, and the old town looked as though its last rough edges, its few remaining shady corners, would soon be gentrified.

In Tallinn old town prices were so high that ordinary Estonians went out to the cheaper places beyond the city walls, to the shabby supermarkets with their semi-empty rows, to the cramped cafés smelling of mould. The old town was a bizarre playground for visitors and affluent locals, its architecture preserved because the Soviets never redeveloped the ageing Hanseatic squares. The buildings fell into squalor, but they survived, saved from reconstruction in Stalinist toilet tile. The cafés were opulent, full of young Estonians who had found a fast-track in the new system. In the renovated mansions they ate international cuisine and talked about the future. At an old town restaurant called the Bonaparte, they were flying the tricolour and serving fine French cuisine. The restaurant was in an imposing Hanseatic building which had been restored in recent years. A well-dressed crowd was reading papers, smoking and buying croissants to take home. There was a low hum of conversation.

Mart and Karin were angled self-consciously against the table, dressed in casual clothes. Karin had long blond hair, her skin had been smoked to leather, and her hands trembled when she grabbed her coffee. On the phone, they had told me they could introduce me to former President Meri, but when I arrived they seemed elusive, slightly nervous, shying away from my questions about him. Instead, Karin said: 'I am a part-owner of a bar. We model ourselves on Notting Hill. We have bare walls except for photos of heroin chic. It's what people want to see.' Mart was outlandish, talking about his yachts and his luxuries; he had been made a millionaire by the last decade, though he wore his wealth nervously. He spoke an arrestingly beautiful English, without any trace of an Estonian accent; it was so notable I kept asking him how he had learnt it, while he talked about ski trips and the stock exchange and all the money he had made.

He said: 'Why don't you come with me to a Russian bar? We will drink shots of vodka. I have a boat; we could all go sailing. It's moored close to here. I have a beautiful country house. Do you like to ski? We can organize the most extraordinary, the most superlative skiing trips, though generally such snowy activities require a significant tolerance of sub-zero temperatures, far worse than your lukewarm European winters.'

'But your English,' I said again, 'how did you learn such good English?'

He laughed and said: 'It is superfluous these days. Extraneous, you might say. So I may as well enlighten you. I was trained in what we shall call, for lack of a better term, spy school. The Russians plucked me from my local school, and sent me there. We were taught a variation on the ordinary syllabus, with a greater emphasis on language acquisition, colloquialisms, and international knowledge. I have a rather encyclopaedic knowledge of English and American institutions, for example. I know enormous amounts about Ivy League universities and the English "Old Boys' network." If you invited me to a black-tie dinner, I would of course know exactly the outfit required. I am losing some of the fineries of my speech. But we were made to blend in,' he said.

He said he was created to slide into the professional elite in the USA or the UK, made as an establishment figure, designed to meet the right people, to mingle at exclusive gatherings. I didn't entirely believe him, though later when he caught me looking thoughtful, he said: 'Don't be such a Byronic malcontent,' and the phrase was such an unlikely one that I doubted my own scepticism.

Karin was saying, 'There is so much happening in Tallinn, it's a great city. I would like to travel, to go to the USA. I present TV programmes in Estonia. I am still able to do that, though I am no longer young. The young people who didn't come through the system understand nothing. They are spoilt already. We, the older generation, are the people who really understand how lucky we all are now.'

Karin and Mart were both thirty-something, and had grown up in Soviet Estonia; they had still been students when Communism collapsed. The generation that had prospered during Communism seemed irrelevant to Karin, so her sense of age was foreshortened. In Karin's gleaming new world order, half the population had been cast out, as the weary dregs of the Soviet system. Thirty was a fine age to become prime minister; fifty was too old, she said.

'Come to the Russian drinking pit,' said Mart. 'I will buy us some vodka and blinis. We have to support our impoverished minority, the Russians, brought to a sorry state now their empire is over. We Estonians pity the individuals of course, but we find it rather appropriate that the Russians should now be marginalized in the town they tried to ruin.'

We crossed the main square, ducking into a bar called Troika, where the waiters were dripping vodka into glasses arranged in rows on the tables. The bar was already filling up for the evening, large tables of people toasting each other and emptying their glasses.

'Let me tell you about the history of my poor nation,' said Mart, clinking his glass against mine, while Karin lit a cigarette.

Tallinn was built by invading armies, bellicose knights and rapacious merchants. Crusaders began arriving in the country in the thirteenth century, baptizing the natives, declaring northern Estonia a Danish province. The Teutonic Knights made an early appearance, and then the Hanseatic merchants came, sailing their ships to Tallinn, building mansions. There were peasant revolts, but the German Knights hung on, until greedy neighbours arrived—the Swedes, the Russians. The Swedes pacified the peasantry by selective acts of strategic benevolence; Gustav Adolf founded a university south of Tallinn, in Tartu. For all the superficial altruism, Estonia was governed by an oligarchy of Swedish and German nobles, who used the people as serfs. Estonia became a seat of German barons, bishops and burghers, a Protestant nation. The Baltic barons remained locally powerful, even after Russia sent in armies in the early eighteenth century. Later, after a deal between these Balts and the Russians, the region became the property of the tsar, with the Balts remaining as administrators and owners of vast tracts of land. Tallinn became a place of vicious social divisions: the aristocracy, the bourgeoisie held entirely distinct, making their money from trade, and the Estonian serfs, wearing their ankle-length black coats, with sandals and long fair hair.

After the Russian Revolution of 1917, Estonia was recognized as a free state. The Soviet Union renounced all rights of sovereignty, only to decide twenty years later that the treaty had been far from binding.

'You can understand,' said Mart, finishing his drink, pouring himself another, pouring me another, though I tried to refuse, 'that we are still a little worried about our border with Russia. And you may also comprehend why we have a strange sense of history. We were occupied by both the Nazis and the Communists, our country was entirely obliterated by their wars. They are both equally evil, I think, both equally reprehensible. You should talk to our recent prime minister, he's a close personal friend of mine, I'll put you in touch. His wife's grandfather was killed by the Nazis; his own grandfather was killed by the Communists. It gives you a particular perspective on these dogmas.' And he started fumbling with his latest-model mobile phone.

'Awful times,' said Karin, puffing smoke everywhere. 'We all know Russian, but no one wants to speak it. We try to forget. Though it is useful sometimes for business.'

'I can give you a collection of numbers,' said Mart. 'I know every-one, everyone you need to know. If you meet someone, ask them if they are acquainted with me. If they're not, then ignore them.'

Finally Mart gave me a piece of paper. The address he had scrawled out, Meri's house, was a short distance outside the old town, on a peninsula with a view back to the capital.

'I'll arrange you an appointment,' he said, as they waved me into the night outside the hotel.

———— ∞ ————

The following day I drove beyond the city walls into new Tallinn, where the streets became grey and the Soviet housing blocks loomed above the dirty houses. The trolley buses juddered along rough tracks, jolting the inhabitants into the suburbs, where the buildings degenerated into cramped wooden rows. The streets were lined with architectural horrors, Stalinist attempts at a hybrid style, superfluous columns stranded halfway up the sides of barren blocks, a sense of mournful ugliness to the whole. There were fleets of dusty archaic cars parked in the gutters, and signs to cheap ho-tels hanging from grey façades. There were sullen buildings housing technical colleges, and schools. Smoke rose from brick chimneys.

The city lay under dim sunshine. The sea shone in the pale light.

I drove out of Tallinn, through the marshes into a countryside richly forested in places, and starkly devastated in others, littered with sunken debris, wreckage from the past. The land was a brilliant orange; the low shrubs and bracken shimmered in the afternoon sunshine, which poured across the flat lands. The branches of the juniper trees hung over the roadsides. The countryside threw out jarring but resonant objects—among the forests there appeared the ugly breezeblocks and decaying steel girders of an abandoned collective farm. After an hour I reached Keila-Joa, pausing briefly to look at a waterfall, which thundered down a sheer rock face. There was a café selling herring sandwiches, a suspension bridge which shuddered as I crossed it, and a path winding alongside the river. I walked through the empty forests, a thunderstorm erupted, the trees bucked in a sudden wind, and clouds of rain turned the path to mud. Soaked, I ran through the trees until the forest came to an end at a grey beach. A glassy white sea stretched away; there were swans bobbing incongruously on the waves.

In 1991, Keila-Joa had been covered with remnants from the Soviet occupation. It was the site of a Soviet Army missile base, a patch of polluted ground, with liquid rocket fuel in the soil and groundwater. It had all been cleaned, a woman in the café told me, as I sat by the fire trying to dry my clothes. The polluted soil had been taken away, the water purified. But the collapsing military bases and decaying industrial plants remained, spread across the marshlands, bleakly symbolic of the Communist appropriation of the countryside, the state of enforced inertia, the enforced ignorance of the Estonians. The Estonians had no knowledge of what was happening within the barriers and fences; they had no control over what happened outside them.

Later, I arrived at Viimsi Peninsula; an Estonian flag fluttered from a pole. There was a security gate, but a thickset guard waved me through. President Lennart Meri had a fine view of the sea. Everything was silent, except for the sound of a dog barking. His house was an elegant Scandinavian-style place, with white walls. I brought the car to a halt by the door, as the dog began a staccato symphony. The wind blustered along the beach. The windows were dark, reflecting the ragged beach and the fluttering flag.

I was expecting an assistant to meet me at the door, but there was a sturdy old man bowing towards me. For a bizarre moment I thought he was Nansen, and my speechless amazement was hardly the right way to open. The hall was dark, he came out of the gloom; on an icy plain he might have passed at a distance for the old explorer stumbling across the snow. But he was reminiscent of Nansen even when we moved into the light, with his height and his fixed, brilliant eyes. He was wearing an immaculate suit, smiling bleakly at the silence outside. He gripped my hand firmly, and then he beckoned me into the house.

'Take your coat and put it over there. I am Lennart Meri. This is my assistant,' he said, pointing towards a young man with a clipboard. 'He'll be with us today.' And the man followed us as we walked, politely keeping a distance behind the former president.

Meri gently pushed away his dog and threw open a door into a library. He was supremely smart and upright and his library was equally meticulous, arranged into taut rows. We paused for a moment in the library, looking across the bay, out to sea.

'Here I remember my travels,' he said.

'It's a fine view,' I said.

We passed into a quiet study, books covering the walls, and he sat down heavily in a chair and then hoisted himself straight. He spoke slowly, sonorously. 'These shelves are filled with all the books I have to read, before I start my book. I hope I have time.' He nodded, at his shelves. He seemed to be joking; there was a trace of a smile on his lips. 'Yes, we can talk about Thule,' said Meri. 'I can even tell you where Thule is, as I understand it. But first I have to tell you a few things. This is a small country; no one knows much about it. You should understand a little of our country, if you want to hear what I mean about Thule. You should know that here, in this land, we are very much aware of our stones. We are very much aware of our marshes and beautiful lakes, and our islands and our lovely coast. We have been living here for around five hundred centuries. It has an effect on the way of thinking. You have the same feeling as being married for five hundred centuries.

'There are trees in this country which have been here for thousands of years,' the old president said, looking through the window, at the flag drooping on the pole outside, at the white glare from the sun.

'I remember before the Germans and Soviets came,' he said. 'I remember my childhood in the 1930s very vividly, my very elementary feelings. I remember that we did not have to lock our doors. I remember the very simple things which were so common. We had been away on holiday to France and we returned in our car—it was not very usual—on a hot day, and we asked to drink something in a village in Estonia, and I still remember that we were given milk, and nobody wanted milk. And I remember the feelings, that the farmer's wife was furious that we preferred water to her milk—that we would not take her hospitality. Everyone was very proud of their work. World War Two destroyed everything—it brought a tragic sense of understanding about history. Despite everything, events materialized in a way we did not expect.'

The Germans and the Russians fought in Estonia, and with the collapse of Hitler's armies the USSR gained control. The Estonian writer Jaan Kross saw it as consummate betrayal; he said it felt like a blow to the head with a club, a blow which made the Estonians feel that all resistance was futile. The scene was grotesque for the Estonians to imagine, Kross had written: Stalin and Roosevelt talking together in 1945, with Stalin smiling, speaking in sing-song Georgian tones, and the interpreter presenting the case—there was really no need for international observers in the Baltic States, no need between old war allies—as Roosevelt sat, wheelchair-bound, taking painkillers. Kross had imagined that Roosevelt had a terrible headache, he was in constant agony and he couldn't apply his mind to the problem. So he told Stalin to go ahead with elections.

Thousands of Estonians fled; by 1945 there were thousands of

Estonian refugees in Sweden. They hid on boats crossing the Baltic Sea; they rowed themselves across the sea. The purges soon began—most of those who had served in the Home Guard during the war or had been conscripted into the German Army were arrested and deported.

'The Soviet soldiers appeared with their bayonets, and the KGB men in plain clothes,' said Meri, casting a side-glance towards me. 'There had been a certain very primitive hope that the Germans would restore Estonian independence. This did not happen, and things became worse still after the Soviets returned. The Estonians lost more people during the first years of the Soviet occupation than during the German occupation. The Estonians lost more Jews during the Soviet times than during the German occupation. The Jews were lawyers, doctors, teachers; the Soviets thought they were class enemies and so they were deported,' he said, slowly.

Apart from his low, slow voice, the house was silent. During the hours we spoke, the silence was occasionally broken: by the jarring ring of the phone, by the grind of a car's tyres on the gravel outside. Mostly it lay heavily upon the room, a thick blanket of silence, threatening to overwhelm the place. He tried to talk against it, but it fell thickly into his pauses, and he often paused, as if exhausted by the effort of speaking into the dense silence. Into the silence Meri spoke, and before each word came a pause, a brief moment of surrender. When the word came it was perfectly placed, his voice strong and deep, his English studiously accurate, littered with unusual words, collected like curios. He held his head in his hands and stared onto the table.

'I went to the university in the south of Estonia,' Meri said. He straightened his tie, stood, and walked to the window. 'And I had to look after myself, so I went to the market. And I remember the marketplace with all the apples, and sausages, and fishes and meats and autumn flowers. Smelling in different ways. And the people were selling their products, the women offering small pieces of the sausages, to taste—it was all quite wonderful to me,' he said, smiling. 'A year later, nothing was left. When the collectivisation began, the village people were deported to Siberia, and soon after almost all of the villages were forced into the collectivized farms. All the profits went to Russia. This increased the resistance movement considerably. There were those who did not want to become collectivized and they went into the forests and joined up with others who felt the same. There was real hunger, only a year after the forcible collectivization of the farms. There was not enough bread,' he said, shaking his head in the twilight of the room.

'You know,' said the president, 'there were different periods of Soviet terror. A person could make a good political career in Stalin's time if he sent as many people as possible to Siberia, if he shot them in closed rooms. But in the 1960s, there was something of a break, and the Soviets realized that if you wanted sausages or fresh fish, then you had to have good relations with the local people. From this time on, they made more effort with the local people. Some local people were quite happy with this armistice. Others tried to push at the restrictions, to see what would shift.'

'It must have been difficult,' I said, blandly, and Meri nodded politely.

'I am very happy that I was born when I was born,' he said. 'In the last decade of the twentieth century I was able to see what a national movement could do, even under Soviet terror. We hated the Soviet way of command economy, the pollution, the destruction of our soil. Fighting for a pure Estonia became more the beginning of a fight against Soviet occupation. It had quite a lot of political aftereffects. Speaking about the use of the land, about who had the power to decide how it was used, this meant speaking about independence. And we gained independence.'

Meri had been one of the survivors; he had always been a writer, but his work was too scholarly for the Soviets, he said. They never read it; they thought it was obscure and pedantic. During the Soviet era, he had written on ancient tribes, on the small settlements scattered across the Siberian wilderness, he had written novels and plays; he had made documentaries. He did anything, he said, so that he could carry on. There were subtle hints which could be inserted into scholarship, small nods to the Estonian people, and Thule was part of this insinuation. Like a code word. It was the gaps contained in the word "Thule," the silences which had intrigued the Victorians, which had seemed like a challenge to the explorers, which had been corrupted by the Thule Society members. The gaps and ambiguities allowed Meri to think of writing about Thule.

'I have so many books on the theme, so many books still to read, and there is not so much time. What I know already is this: Pytheas is regarded as the first professional explorer,' said Meri, into the gloom, 'and Pytheas wanted to explore the northern part of Europe. There is no doubt that he was in England, because Cornwall was the main source of tin, at this time, so he was certain to have gone there. But my interest is a little different. Let me start like this: we know that some meteorites reach the earth from time to time. There is a huge and beautiful lake in North Finland, from such a landing we believe. All those huge craters were made long before human life began. Thanks to some Soviet researchers, I became aware a while ago that the island of Saaremaa was an exception.'

A meteorite landed on the island of Saaremaa, which lies off the Estonian coast. For a long time nobody knew when it had hit the ground. There was a great crater left in the earth, which had filled up with water.

'Saaremaa,' Meri added, 'is a very beautiful place, you should visit if you can. The Soviet researchers were not interested in giving an exact date for the landing of the meteorite; they were much more interested in trying to evaluate what traces an explosion of such force might have left on the soil. But when they got the results, they seemed to show that the explosion happened seven hundred years before Christ. I was forced to ask myself whether there are any symptoms in the collective consciousness of Estonians from the event still living on into our time. In the Bronze Age, something which fell with the force of the Hiroshima bomb, well you would think this would have a deep abiding effect on the way of thinking or the way of understanding the world. A meteorite approaching the earth would be moving like a super sound wave, and this would mean that on its way it would be first heard after it had passed. It was something very bright—let's say, like sunshine, and you could see this from a very far distance away—as far even as seven hundred kilometres, let's say.'

A blinding light which looked like the sun, and then a great boom, as the meteorite carved out a great hole in the earth. The president was staring carefully at me. He stretched out his hands, to suggest distance. He said:

'The very simple thought crossed my mind. When the meteorite landed on Saaremaa, it was something that could be compared by the Germans to the setting down of the sun. Seen from certain areas, from the Swedish coast maybe, it was the sun setting in the east. That is so very unnatural that it must have had a very strong influence on the ancient Swedish and German myths about the end of the world—the end of the gods. In thinking about these old times, one always has a small political spark in one's mind, and the thought that *Götterdämmerung*, the myth about the death of the gods, had its origin here on this small Estonian island gave me a lot to laugh about, when I thought of those bombastic last days in Berlin, after Hitler had shot himself and they played Wagner on all the radio stations.'

He was speeding up; the silence was retreating, wafted back through the door, into the neat library. Meri lifted his head. He was declaiming this last part, making an effort, trying to push his theory out. 'This was something that consoled me,' he said. 'I thought about Pytheas, the first great explorer, moving towards the east, perhaps arriving in the region where the tradition of the meteorite was known. It was interesting,' he said, smiling, 'in the descriptions of Pytheas's voyage there was a phrase, "the barbarians showed him the place where the sun went to rest." And people had always thought this meant the sun, that the barbarians showed Pytheas where the sun set.

'But I suddenly thought it might be the terrifying event, the sun falling to the earth, the meteorite, a burning disc like the sun, crashing into the island of Saaremaa. According to your Oxford dictionary, the words "Ultima Thule" can be explained only partly. Ultima is understandable, but Thule—your dictionary says it is a word of unknown origin. But *tuli* in Estonian means "fire." '

He smiled in the semi-light.

'You may be shocked,' he said, 'because I know that Tacitus said that Britain was Thule. The very idea that Ultima Thule might be Estonia would be appalling to every English person, I fear, and it will be more appalling to every Norwegian. It was, I believe, Nansen who placed Thule not far from Bergen.'

In the dark room, the president smiled at his small victory against the elusiveness of the sources, the strangeness of the history of his country. Outside, the land stretched to the dark sea, and everything was cloaked in dusk. The dog was barking loudly at the quietness, and there was a shuffling sound by the door, as a man stuck his head into the room.

'If I could perhaps . . .' he was muttering.

'Yes, of course,' said Meri, raising his head. He was polite to everyone, deliberately so, it seemed. The new arrival moved across to Meri and said something quietly in Estonian. I shifted in my seat, aware of a slight headache from the coffee. The room was cold; I reached for a coat and dragged it across my shoulders.

There was a short exchange in Estonian; then the man shuffled out.

I stood to leave, and Meri smoothed down his tie, smoothed his hands across his jacket.

'So you have the story of Thule,' he said, bringing everything to a final point, rubbing his hand across his forehead.

He stood and stared around the room.

I admired the man; his canvas was vivid and broad-brushed. It had a sense of drama: the blinding light, the flushed red sky, the darkness spreading across the land. The Germanic tribes saw the sun falling to the earth in the east; dust rose and clouded across the skies.

The explosion was immense and the effects could be seen for hundreds of miles around. The cataclysmic event passed into folklore—the burning island, the setting of the sun. When Pytheas came along the coast, the natives, speaking an early Baltic language, said, 'Tuli! Tuli!,' pronouncing it *Tooley, Tooley,* and pointed to the east. Fire, fire, this was where the fire had fallen, where the sun had crashed to the earth. This was where Saaremaa burned.

He thought it was true, like Nansen, like Burton, like the long line of explorers and writers, solving the ancient mystery of the north. Meri believed his own words, believed them passionately. But there was something more to Meri's Thule. Thule had become a story about purity, about an ideal land. Meri had said himself that the movement towards independence had burgeoned from environmental beginnings. At the end of the 1980s, purging the land became bound up with purging Estonia of influences from Moscow. Meri had been an environmentalist, a nature writer; he had argued against the Soviet exploitation of Estonian soil. As president, Meri had often defined Estonia as an environmentally friendly Scandinavian country, trying to lift the land out of the years of occupation. Thule was part of this reserve of symbolism, part of this sense of the Nordic allegiances of Estonia. It was another politicised Thule, another Thule for independence. Thule for regeneration, deployed to draw a small country out of the dark aftermath of World War Two.

The sky outside was dark. Meri moved slowly through his rooms, lined with books, to the entrance hall. I shook his hand, and he bowed.

'Thank you for coming,' he said, smiling. 'I hope you enjoy your stay in our beautiful land.'

The tall man stood in the doorway of his house, as the peninsula stretched away under the cold evening. His study was full of books he had to read. There was not so much time, he had said, perhaps there would not be time to do everything. But he had added his voice to the argument, the ancient debate about Thule.

He waved at the car, as I drove away. The night was cold as I drove along the Viimsi Peninsula, back towards Tallinn, where the lights of Toompea shone up the hillside.

The meteorite fell on the island of Saaremaa, so I drove towards the south.

I drove through the juniper glades and the evergreen forests, the twisted ruins of Communism scattered among the trees. The route ran along a deserted single-lane road, dwindling at the edges into rubble. The view scarcely changed: the long level roads, the forests stretching away, the red trees shining in the rain. The road was covered in rainwater and the car slid past the collective farms, their blue tiles and Soviet functional outhouses left to decay, grass growing through the shattered windows. At the town of Paldiski I was trying to find something to eat, but there was nowhere to buy anything in the town except a barren supermarket, its shelves bare. The town was a bleak place to pause at: a cluster of crumbling high-rise apartment blocks, some of them standing empty, awaiting demolition. The shops were plastered with dull signs; the men and the women stood on the street talking and staring. The buildings were streaked with fading blue paint. Smoke was rising from the chimneys of the main boiler house, a block of dirty bricks, surrounded by patches of grass and dirty puddles. Around the boiler house stood the ruins of functional offices, jagged iron skeletons, standing neglected on sodden waste ground.

There had been Russians here since Peter I built Paldiski into a port, intending to fortify it, though the work was never finished. The scrubland stretched to the cold blue sea. The earthworks for Peter I's fortification remained along the windblown coast, where the trees had been bent by successive lashings from the sea. The town was used and smashed and burned during World War Two; it was a naval base for the Soviet forces, and the civilians were bundled off, sent elsewhere, sent away into the juniper forests. It was filled with Russian sailors, and then the Germans arrived and made it a prisoner-of-war camp. When the war turned and the Soviet Army marched back towards the town, the German soldiers torched it as they retreated. During the Soviet era Paldiski was a garrison, and the outskirts of the town were full of military relics, significant objects, ugly decrepit concrete bunkers, crumbling slowly. By the coast there was a gargantuan office complex, with rooms stacked like prison cells in tight columns. A line of trees stood before it, branches outstretched, failing to hide its decayed walls. Looking for somewhere to buy some food I drove around this ancient office relic, a route no Estonian could have taken during the Soviet occupation, because the area was sealed off and civilians were forbidden to go there. The windows were empty, the glass was shattered, the roof had fallen down. It was a concrete skeleton, brooding on a windblown stretch of coast.

I found two women talking on a street corner by the building, staring indifferently across the patchy grass towards the blank sides of the building. 'What was the building?' I asked, shouting above the noise of the sea and the tormented sounds of ancient cars moving along the road. They didn't understand, I had to repeat the question, pointing and smiling, and then one of them said, '*Akula*,' and turned away. Looking back at the concrete relic, it was surprising, but I saw that it was shaped like a submarine, with a central tower and two slab-like arms on either side, stretching across the orange scrubland. It would have housed a replica submarine, used for training, hidden inside one more piece of Soviet concrete.

The building had been fenced off, but now the fence was broken and easy to climb. There were fences throughout Paldiski, red fences with signs telling the inhabitants to keep out, some of them defunct, breached in places, others apparently functional, enforcing contemporary prohibitions. There was a ring of fences around the silent derelict buildings on the outskirts of the town. Faded fences, tottering on their posts.

There were dirty secrets, smuggled away after independence,

like the nuclear contents of a pile of cream bricks, on the edge of Paldiski, with a rusty red-and-white chimney rising above. The Russians had kept the contents to themselves—a reactor or two, a laboratory—speeding the spent fuel back to Russia on tracks built for the purpose, a decontamination express train, carrying nuclear litter across the Russian border. They buried the rest in concrete.

When the train had disappeared and the tracks had disintegrated, there were still Russians in Paldiski. Estonia was still full of Russians. In Tallinn the lucky ones ran restaurants and tipped vodka into the glasses of the newly rich like Karin and Mart, who called the Russian bars kitsch and ordered up blinis and caviar. But many of the leftover Russians were still living in bleak towns, coastal ruins, living in the shattered blocks left by the Soviet Union. They were joined by the Estonian poor: the unemployed, the single parents who were sent to cheap housing in towns no one wanted to live in. The Russians lined the streets of Paldiski, whiling away the hours. They talked in groups, their eyes on the ragged coastline and the concrete blocks. Maybe the men were drunk, maybe they were just moving slowly through the afternoon, because there was nothing to do with the evening.

At the end of the empty road was the muted town of Pärnu, where the pebbled beach stretched to the cold sea. There were lines of wooden houses, the paint falling off their walls, the bricks crumbling like parchment. There was a fairground with a Ferris wheel, the empty carriages rocking in the wind. On a cranky carousel which kept stopping, children were screaming and clapping their hands, and then the rain fell, swift and hard, across the beach, and they were all picked up and taken away.

In Pärnu I stopped at the former summer house of a German-Portuguese millionaire named Ammende. Ammende built the place at the turn of the century in a wilfully, buoyantly decadent style. From the outside the building was a modernist brick parody of a country house with a superfluous tower sticking out of the roof. It stood out; the rest of Pärnu was low and wooden, like a lost Swedish village stranded on a Baltic coast. But Villa Ammende was celebrating its facelift. The place had been picked out of the ruins, dusted and painted, reopened as a Jugendstil hotel.

I was hammering on the doors, which were like the gateway to a Gothic mansion. There was no answer, so I found a cord and tugged it and something like a bell echoed through the building, the sound more like a buffalo in pain. Another pause, while the rain fell harder, beating onto the muddy road, onto the grandiose steps to the villa. I was hunched into my coat, beginning to think I would have to run back to the car. But then there was the sound of bolts being drawn back, and a face peered through a crack. A patch of darkness opened up behind him, as if the door entered into a void.

He said: 'Yes?'

I said: 'Do you have a room?'

He looked startled and slightly appalled, as if it were still the summer house of millionaire Ammende and I were in breach of every code of conduct in the Baltic aristocrats' rulebook, and then he opened the door a little more, drawing me towards the darkness. He said: 'Come in here, please.'

We walked into a dark hall, a few glass eyes glinting in the dark, staring from the stuffed heads of animals positioned around the stairs. There was a vast fireplace, a bronze monstrosity, its opulent curls tapered to art nouveau points. Everything was art nouveau—every intricately curled pattern, every curved chair leg, every shimmering frieze. There was something elegant about the lines, but then there were all the animals, a bestiary of dead things, as if the owner had recently been for a massive shooting spree, and had picked off a game park. There was a stuffed lion, hammered to the first set of stairs; a moose or two, stuck to the wall; a huge brown bear lolling on the upper landing. The man, who was pale and nervous, was fumbling for a piece of paper. Among the clutter of the overdressed hallway there was a small wooden desk with an inkwell, and he sat behind it and put the piece of paper down. He tried to find a pen. He rummaged frantically in a drawer. He started to blush.

I handed him my pen.

'Yes, yes, quicker that way . . .' he said.

His hands were shaking as he took the pen.

He had suffered a terrible shock, it seemed. He had been rattling around this empty mansion, enjoying the silence, and then there had been a terrible hammering on the doors, the sound of the bell tolling through the corridors. He was still slightly startled; he eyed me with suspicion.

'Nationality?'

'Occupation?'

The answer made him jiggle the pen around.

'What do you write?'

'Reason for visit?'

'How did you hear about the place?'

I told him why I was in Estonia, and he had a brief nervous collapse. He tried to hide it, but he was sweating when he lifted his face again and his hands were knocking on the desk.

'Really?' he said. 'You have been speaking to our first president?'

After that everything changed and he practically bowed me into the billiard room.

It was all beautiful and empty and slightly absurd. The billiard room was set up for a rainy afternoon, for visitors who enjoyed languid games while they smoked elegantly, stubbing the cigarettes into ornate ashtrays. There was a bar for cocktails, prepared for these affable legions of vanished gentlemen. In the drawing room everything was green—the ceilings were painted into luscious spirals; the tables stood on finely curved legs. Everything was abundant, defying the dour streets outside. It was like a set for an Evelyn Waugh novel, a perfect backdrop for decadent aristo-bohemia, slurred vowels over tea, indolent intrigues to the slow winding of the gramophone. Villa Ammende had been empty for years before it was restored into a hotel. I stayed a night, the only guest, eating alone in an echoing dining room designed in recovered opulence, opulence fanning itself, still remembering its nightmarish swoon, the years as a Soviet lunatic asylum, or prison, or training centre—the decadent corridors filled with the terseness of officialese. When a waiter came along the corridor, the footsteps echoed around the high ceilings. The bored concierge put me in the most lavish suite—perhaps in the name of Meri—a three-roomed luxury complex, with a sauna, a bedroom with engraved cupboards, art nouveau murals, and a living room with ornate oak shelves, full of German classics: Goethe, Thomas Mann, the Brothers Grimm.

It was beautiful, but there was an air of suspense to the rooms, as if Ammende had just gone off to the beach with a group of friends recently arrived from Vilnius, and would be returning for tea. Any moment, I thought, wandering through the empty corridors, disconcerted by the silence, a whole pile of aristo-Balts would appear—raffish, slightly tired after an energetic walk—and demand cocktails and ices. Any moment the gramophone would wind into action and a few women in furs would emerge to tap their fingers on the curved arms of the chairs. In the empty corridors, I kept turning around, expecting to find someone there with their hand outstretched, saying how do you do. There was no one there, just the glass eyes of a stuffed bear, peering from a balustrade.

This was the opulence which fled with the Balts. The Estonians never knew much about the champagne flutes and the delicate curved feet of the chairs in Villa Ammende. They said they were simple people, surviving through generations because of their affinity with the trees, their love for the swamp plains. It was a national story, a fable they told themselves, but they had been labourers for generations, living on farms, deprived of any access to wealth. Meri had been talking about it, the knowledge of the land, the attraction to simple things. It made them despise the Soviet system, he had said, because it polluted and exploited and never considered the corrosive effects of engine fuel or nuclear reactors on the countryside. There were Estonians who hid in the forests; some of them formed resistance groups, living for years out of society, away from Soviet repression.

It was a deep historical feeling, a memory of the stones, Lennart had said. Cleaning it up, cleaning up the wrecks of Soviet ships sunk in the harbours, the polluted lands, coated with fuel, the nuclear debris, the wreckage of the collective farms, meant a lot to the Estonians. They tried to clean away the past, the years of brown and grey, the suspense and dullness, the compromises they made, the collusion with the Soviets which allowed some to prosper. They tried to clean up the guilt, the regret, the ambivalence.

I slept strangely in Villa Ammende, waking to see the sun bright on the lawn, where aristo-Balts should already have been walking, perambulating under parasols. The house was silent as I walked down for breakfast. A waitress poured coffee, and the clinking of the spoon as I swirled in the milk echoed through the room.

When I left, the lonely man on the desk waved me down the steps. 'Come again,' he said. 'During the high season, we are very full. But other times of year, like now for example, you only need to give us a few days' notice.' I wondered if most of the time he and the waitress lived it up in Villa Ammende, twirling around the sitting room to music from the gramophone, leafing through the library of German classics, patting the stuffed lion on the head. The bacchanalia only stopped when the bell tolled through the corridors; then they put on their uniforms and became solemn and monosyllabic. As I drove off I imagined the man on the desk whipping off his grey suit and donning a red velvet smoking jacket, slinking into the billiard room to pot a few balls, before his first whisky of the day.

In southern Estonia, I took the ferry across the sea to Saaremaa, the tree-covered island where the meteorite fell. Under a cold sky, the ship crossed the sea, and the sky was full of seabirds circling the wake. I drove out into more forests, fine empty forests, along a road without cars which snaked through the island. There was a thick mist falling across Saaremaa; the road slipped away into whiteness. I missed the turn to the meteorite site, and drove on towards a small town, called Kuressaare, where the mist was still thicker. I could see a few houses, and a castle at the end of the street with what appeared to be a drawbridge. There was a health spa on the shore, full of people in towelling robes, where I tried to ask for directions, but the atmosphere was so cranky and medicinal that I left without finding anyone to ask. The mist lingered along the coast, rolling off the pale sea. I stepped into a bar and asked for directions from a pale blond man who was sitting at a table. He pointed me back along the road.

'If I said *tuli* to you, what would I mean?' I asked.

He was nonchalant and friendly. He considered the question thoughtfully, as if people often came to the bar asking him to define random Estonian words.

'You would mean "fire," ' he said.

The second time the mist had cleared and I saw the sign to the meteorite site pointing off the road, towards a patch of woodland. The land was completely flat, until a sudden hill, which swept the forest up at a sharp angle. I walked up the rise, and at the top I could see that the hill was part of the circular ridge of a hole. It was the hole gouged out by a burning rock, when it crashed into the flat soil of Saaremaa. The circumference was impressive, and a lake had formed in the crater. The brown water of the lake reflected the trees, which clung on to the hillsides, hunched towards the lake as if they were sliding slowly down the slope into the water. Everything was focused on the large crater hole. The forest was silent and the mist swept around the sides of the crater, sidling along the branches of the trees. I was blanched out of the meteorite hole, as the mist obscured the view across the waters.

In the *Kalevala*, there was a story about the 'fire from Heaven.' The Old Man of the sky sent fire to the earth, splitting the heavens, spilling a spark of fire through the clouds. Väinämöinen and Ilmarinen decided to go and find out what the fire was that they had seen.

The spark had fallen from the sky, piercing the clouds, and the flame had whirled through lands and swamps, until it plunged into the waters of a lake in Finland. The lake nearly caught fire, and the waters were flushed red from the flame. Three times in a night the lake foamed as high as the spruce trees around its banks, roaring to its brim from the force of the fire, leaving the fish stranded on the shore. At the time, the queen of the north had stolen the sun, so the hero-gods decided to fish for the fire. Settling themselves on a patch of unscorched land, they unravelled a twine into the water and brought up the fire, but the fire escaped, singed Väinämöinen's beard, and disappeared into the distance, setting the juniper heath alight, burning up the spruce glades, and burning half of the north.

A blast with the force of an atomic explosion, Meri said. It must have had a profound effect on the tribes that saw it—a blazing sun falling to the earth, suddenly, without any noise, then a great explosion and a raging fire in the forest, a cloud of dust darkening the sky. The president thought that Thule had been a thing, not a place. Thule was a rare and terrifying event in the history of the Baltic region. It had been the fire which burned in the east, Thule the flame. The ancient Germanic tribes, reeling from the shock of seeing the sun falling to the earth, understood that even the gods could die. The locals, living in the marshes on Saaremaa, muttered through generations about a Great Fire. It was a story in their land, but it came from a particular place, and they offered to show Pytheas where it had happened. They showed him where the sun fell from the sky, but when Pytheas's account of his journey disappeared, and Pytheas's story was made and remade from leftover fragments, later writers thought he had meant the setting of the sun in the land of Thule.

The meteorite fell on the land, and thousands of years later Meri felt it added a layer of irony to Nazi destruction, that the Nazis were desecrating the basis of their myths, the event that spawned the idea of Götterdämmerung. This is where it came from, Meri had said, and in this way Thule was a story about the origins of the German people, though it was far from the 'Aryan' utopia the Nazis had imagined. It was a story of an original trauma, an original terror, which changed the way these early tribes saw the world. All of this was impossible to prove, impossible to justify except as an elaborate fantasy, but Meri's idea worked as well as Nansen's idea about Thule, or Burton's. Meri's Thule was as much of a patchwork of fragments and imaginative reconstruction. Meri wanted the word Thule for his nation, and for Meri, Thule was a purgatorial fire, sweeping across the land. It made Thule less a dream of an ideal place and more an event beyond the control of humans, beyond the understanding of early tribes. The witnesses of this fiery Thule were the shocked locals, staggering from their fields and marshes, seeing the fire blazing into the earth, burning for days, the clouds of ash blackening the sky.

And as I left Estonia I thought of the ancient philosophers of Thule, gathering their sources, batting the story from nation to nation. Thule had been a mystery, an expression of curiosity about the indeterminate edges of the world, part of the urge to complete the map. But the story had long been entwined with power and conquest; Caesar saw the conquest of the last land as a triumph for his empire, Virgil imagined Augustus lord of all the lands, even as far as Thule. Meri had tried to lift Thule out of the scrabbling sets of hands, by suggesting that Thule was something beyond the human world. He saw Thule as a story about the power of nature itself, the force of celestial objects, the terrible energy of fire. One Thule might be swamped by unwanted visitors. Another Thule might be smashed and burned. Another Thule might be destroyed by the Nazis, then by the Russians. Meri had asked for the story back, as if it were a piece of national memory, a national dream, forgotten during the occupation.

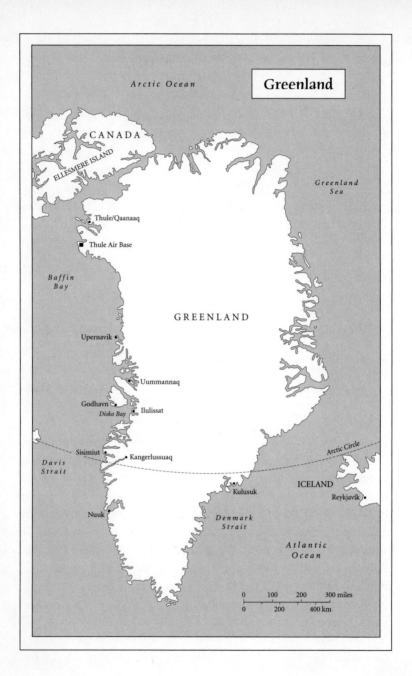

ICE HEART

⸙

North! North into the whirlwind! North to the mocking gale!
Toward the lash of the driven snowflakes where the scourged
    sea-dogs quail!
Saw he no ruby towers? Longed not for softer land?
Aye! But a tenser power gripped and directed his hand!

But rather to go where others have not, to conquer where all
    have lost,
To battle the frenzied hurricane while Hope is a naked ghost.
Such is the power that drives him into the torturing gale;
This is the rugged goal, this the desired Grail!

      "Ultima Thule," Thomas Caldecot Chubb (1899–1972)

It had been a conversation running through thousands of years. There were key players, more strident voices—the classical writers, setting the scene, Strabo writing irritable prose, because he never really believed in Thule anyway, Virgil and Pliny, Geminus of Rhodes and Pomponius Mela, and Tacitus speculating about Agricola, and Ptolemy finding a place for Thule on his map of the world. There were studious kings and clerics writing up the latest findings on the north, from Alfred the Great to Bede to Adam of Bremen, mingling them with classical stories. There were Vikings, ploughing across the oceans, Ottar the Viking, Erik the Red—burly men, covered in scars. There was Petrarch wondering where Thule might be. There were the Spanish and Portuguese explorers finding new worlds and carrying Seneca in their packs. There was Burton,

225

insistent that Iceland was so very obviously Thule, agreeing with Columbus who had sailed up to Iceland and called it Thule. There was Nansen immaculate in spurs, talking about Norway and Thule. Now, there was Lennart Meri in his small country, crafting an ancient past for his nation.

The earlier writers marked out a time when vast plains stretched into darkness, and the sea was an intimation of ancient emptiness, and everything that lay beyond the circle of familiar experience was a playground for all the fabled beings of mythology. Later, others watched the calm and sober lines of the northern landscape appearing, new stories from the north revealing forests and great rivers, ice floes drifting on an empty sea, and the mists curling at the base of ancient slabs of stone. For a time, a simple answer was enough, the simple selection of a country: Iceland, Norway, or Britain. There were agonistic arguments, between self-appointed experts, determined to end the debate. There were parodies, there was Pope grouching about flaccid verse, like the dank offerings of Thule, there was Goethe making fairytales from it, Shelley, Godwin, Poe, all throwing it in for a piece of scene-setting or mere atmosphere.

Sustained talk of silent spaces, the expression of a sense of fascination for snow-bound plains, light falling across ice crystals, forming a rainbow of colours, and a sense of the strangeness of long twilight days, the swart nights, and those moments when the longing for home called like a clarion cry across the ice. There had been a terrible pause, when the conversation had been taken over by brutal rhetoric, but gradually the voices had sounded again. Tentatively at first, growing more confident.

In my mind there was a blank spot, a vast white patch, the most northerly island. I turned to the ice mountains of Greenland. Seeking to draw the strains together, I turned to a forbidding ice-plain, at the edge of the maps, spreading towards the frozen ocean. Greenland had nothing to do with the original idea of Thule. Pytheas could hardly have sailed so far. In all the learned expositions, all the mutterings of clerics and geographers, no one had ever seriously claimed that Greenland was Thule. The ancient ice field had nothing to do with the argument across millennia, with all the writers and explorers and adventurers proposing their theories. But it had everything to do with the twentieth century, and with the recent history of Thule. It had everything to do with the post-war world that Meri had described, though it was still remote, still a distant and almost inaccessible place.

It was a question of modern cartography: on the global map, there are two places called Thule, both twentieth-century creations. In 1910 a Danish explorer called Knud Rasmussen set up a trading post in the far north of Greenland and called it Thule. He named the local people the Thule Inuit and set out to study their traditions in a series of Thule Expeditions. Rasmussen used Thule to define the barren wilderness he called home—a place both remote and domestic to him, a place where he was an outsider, but where the local people tolerated him because he spoke to them in their language, and sold them guns. Rasmussen pinned the word Thule to the whiteness of Greenland, the most northerly land, the largest island in the world, a land stretching as far as the frozen ice around the North Pole.

Thule, a distant place, a settlement at the edge of the world, turned out to be in the middle of the Cold War. In the 1950s, the US Military found that Thule was equidistant between New York and Moscow, as the bomber flies. They built an air base there, and called it Thule. They moved the local Inuit population away to another Thule, a new settlement further north. Thule became a Cold War outpost, at 76° N. Thule Air Base was a staging post for nuclear bombers during the Cold War. It was part of a general trend—it was during the Cold War that the Arctic ice became so useful to the US and the USSR as a great blank hiding place for nuclear submarines, nuclear missiles and nuclear waste; a site for frigid operations, scattered with secret outposts. The frozen ocean around the North Pole became a no-man's-land. The vast ice-heart of Greenland lay at the centre, between hostile nations.

⊶⊷

I flew back from Tallinn to London, and took to phoning around, trying to find a way to the ice island. I sat in the flat in London and stared at the Westway, at the fleets of cars waiting patiently to move forward. As I prepared to travel again, Greenland was no longer a frost virgin waiting for violating footsteps, but it was still covered in a thick and ancient mound of ice, ice so heavy it had crushed the land, forcing it down into the sea. The inhabitants—there were barely sixty thousand—lived along the coasts, in the few ice-free regions. Greenland was an immense ice-plain, and the thought of it fascinated me as a monstrous and indefinable shape might fascinate a child, innocently unaware of the terror it represented.

It was still remote. Getting to the Almost Unknown Country was a major problem. I made calls, and the quotes reached thousands for flights and helicopters, because the regular coastal ships stopped south of Thule. I tried to track down scientific research ships; I tried to persuade the US Military to fly me there in a B-52. But there weren't any B-52s flying to Thule, they said. I began to lose impetus. The city was sliding out of summer. People began to button up their coats as the sun grew paler, as the wind gusted around the streets. I was beginning to think the trip was off, the season was too late, but I still had an urge to get to this Janus-Thule. Following more and more implausible leads, calling up people who failed to disguise their confusion, I finally found an independent scientist who said he might be able to help.

He told me to meet him at his house in Hampstead. It was a house in a quiet street by the Holly Bush pub, its windows covered in dirt, ivy crawling up the walls. I arrived early and the door was opened by a man wearing dungarees, who led me into a small room and told me to wait. I sat shivering as a cold breeze rattled the panes. Scratched wooden shelves lined the walls. There was a woman sitting at a desk in the corner, reading, who nodded brusquely as I walked in. She wore a starched white blouse and half-moon glasses on the bridge of her nose. She was staring at me over her glasses. I glanced at her immense pile of books. *The Behaviour of Reptiles. The Analysis of Plants.*

I picked up a book from the shelves, flicked through a few pages, and meant to put it back on the pile. Then I dropped the book on the floor, and as I leant to pick it up I caught her staring at me again with an expression of fixed irritation. I smiled apologetically and began flicking through the pages again, conscious of her glare upon me. She did not want to leave me alone. She was like a missionary of an uncompromising church, and when I looked up again she was almost waggling her finger.

Someone arrived to fetch me, a thin man with a coat as shapeless as a shawl, slung around his shoulders. The house was full of inexplicable people. The woman sighed as I stood, as if mourning the loss of the fight, and stared me out of the room. I followed the thin man through rows of books, and reached a double door standing ajar. The man wafted me up an unswept staircase, where there were dustballs as big as my fist in the corners of the steps, and intricate cobwebs fastened to the banisters. He walked with downcast eyes, responding in monosyllables to my attempts at small-talk. Nice weather. Yes. Nice staircase. Yes. You work here a lot? Yes.

At the top of the dust-stairs was a map of the Arctic Ocean, the countries curving around the top of the planet, sliding towards each other. The map was decorative; there were pictures of significant explorers stuck to a few of the patches of white—Nansen's head poking out of Greenland, Robert Peary pinned to the North Pole, and Amundsen with an airship. Greenland was a vast country in the shape of a bloated slug, with the word THULE stamped on its north-western coast.

A door opened, a white-haired secretarial head appeared, wearing a tired expression, and an arthritic hand gestured me into the room. The light was dim; a heavy writing desk squatted in the centre. Dwarfed by the desk was the fossilized scholar, slouched on a chair, wearing a tattered suit. He shook hands, but he stayed on his chair, and he murmured so softly I could barely hear him. Andrew was a patched-up relic, living off his early research. The walls were covered with shelves, the shelves strewn with books and files, the desk crowded with papers. It all looked staged, like a film set, and Andrew looked as if he had been deposited there that morning with instructions not to leave. Andrew had been intrepid many years ago; he had spent a while with the Inuit in the far north of Greenland, at Thule. But the years had battered Andrew into his room and now he slumped behind the desk.

He screwed up his face, and whispered into his collar: 'In Greenland the fabulous becomes real. Greenland is the meeting of the real and the fabulous. A super-reality, a hyper-existent image of truth and destiny. In Greenland object and subject are elided. In Greenland we ask ourselves what am I? What do I mean?' And he smiled.

'In Greenland the stars meander through the heavens, forecasting, predicting the future. Everything swirls—the lights, the snow in the wind, the waves as they wash across the bergs. It is a place both beautiful and ghastly; yes, it is a place of contrasts. Only the flexible of mind can understand this immensity; only the immense of spirit can swirl with the beauty of the stars, the ravenous motions of the wind. Rasmussen named his settlement Thule because he understood immensity.'

Andrew slouched in his chair, his head emerging out of the antique folds of his neck, his hands like leather. His chin was almost under the desk. He talked and talked, without pauses, his voice almost inaudible and unhurried. 'Imagine what it was like for the Inuit when the Americans arrived in the 1950s. There are books about it, by a Frenchman. I will find them for you.'

He meant a writer called Jean Malaurie, who had written about the Greenlandic Inuit, in books with titles like *The Last Kings of*

Thule. Malaurie had been staying in the first Thule when the Americans arrived. He had gone over to visit the American base, and found snack bars and barracks buildings and a host of courteous soldiers, a cinema, a powerhouse, telephones, a baseball centre, a radio tower, a restaurant and a hospital. He wandered around, over excavations and networks of piping. Back in the village of Thule, he had watched the helicopters and icebreakers, a 'formidable Armada,' bringing more occupants to the base. The ships were filled with 'bobby-soxers of Thule,' boys from Harvard and Berkeley, who wanted to see the Arctic by working at the base. They streamed across the ice to the Inuit village, swapping cigarettes, axes and footwear for souvenirs.

'And do you think—' I began. Andrew held up his hand.

'Some of the Inuit thought they would be sent away, some thought the Americans had magical powers to control the weather, to make a constant summer. And people were worried; they thought with the Americans came things like the atomic bomb. Really, they were right on that. The Danish government pretended it was not true, but we know that the Americans kept nuclear weapons at Thule during the Cold War. Without the knowledge of the Inuit, of course. But also I think from what was said at the time that somehow the Inuit felt that their place, their Thule, had always been unusual, and now here was the proof, because the great power of America had found them out, even in the remote north.'

Thule Air Base was established on a barren patch of rock. The creation of a permanent military base at Thule had been approved by President Truman in 1950. The agreement was ratified with Denmark as part of the newly formed NATO defence programme. A NATO area was established, called the Greenland Defence Area. Thule Air Base was constructed in secret under the code name Operation Blue Jay. Construction began in 1951 and was completed two years later. US ships appeared on the Greenlandic coast, bringing thousands of men. The Americans banged out a base: 82

miles of road, in a country with virtually no roads, 10 hangars, 122 barracks, 6 mess halls, a gym, a service club, an officers' club, library, post office, a bakery, a theatre, a chapel and a hospital. There were warehouses, power plants, heating plants, a thousand-foot pier constructed from barges towed from the Gulf of Mexico.

The US Military stacked up supplies at Thule. They brought in anti-aircraft guns, surface-to-air missiles and nuclear warheads. Thule became a secret place in Greenland; access to the US Military base was forbidden to those without clearance.

In the spring of 1953, the inhabitants of the Greenlandic village of Thule were moved sixty-five miles to the north, to Qaanaaq or the second Thule.

'And do you think—' I continued.

'It was as if the Americans wanted to pluck the secret from the . . . from the . . .' Andrew lost his train of thought. He picked up a pencil with his gnarled fingers, toyed with it for a moment and then dropped it again.

'And do you think—'

'You know, I went in the 1960s, to Thule Air Base.' Andrew slumped further into his chair, his head pressed so firmly down into his chest that it seemed he would never raise it again. He was almost inaudible as he spoke, and I leaned further across his desk, trying to understand these faint sentences.

'I was young. You weren't born, of course.' He tried to lift his head, but the effort was too great. It dropped down again.

'By the 1960s, it was a big place. Thousands of soldiers there, waiting for the nuclear war, for Russia to attack. You have no idea of the paranoia that existed. They were spending so much money, so many millions. They had flown everything from America, of course. You don't find dynamite and metal and vast quantities of wood in the north of Greenland. You don't find telephones and buses and ha! ha!'—a faint rustling sound was coming from Andrew's throat, which I identified as a laugh—'baseball bats. Not many of those in the north of Greenland. Not many such things at all. They brought it all over. They were nicely set up when I saw them. The soldiers seemed happy. You'll probably find the same, when you go. They even had refrigerators in the houses.'

'And—' I interjected. The trembling hand again, like an ancient policeman directing traffic. I raised my voice: 'And *do you think*—'

Andrew whispered more insistently. 'I must say that I think it was really millions and millions that they spent. You know they only had two months when the sea was not frozen, only two months to bring everything through to the base. It was an astonishing feat of organisation.'

He was old and frail, but Andrew knew how to deliver a monologue. He skipped around a little; he wasn't strictly chronological. But he was determined to finish. I wondered if he was often alone in this room, talking softly to himself, sinking slowly into his chair, waiting for the knock on the door, a reason to draw his head upwards.

'Yet you could say that there has always been something strange about that base, because of its name, because it became Thule Air Base. It gives a different atmosphere to the place I think. I felt it even when I was there. The American soldiers did not want to know their environment when they arrived. They wanted to sit in their gyms and phone home to their parents. But it seized them. I thought even the most obedient soldier came to be in awe of the vastness of the rocks around them. In this respect they were weaker than the Inuit, who understand the antiquity of the stones. Many people disagree with me,' Andrew said, spreading his hands on the desk. 'But I am glad the Inuit kept the name of Thule, so it wasn't just the Americans who had it.'

After this I was given a handshake, told to take a pile of thermals and to be sure to write—and then I left.

Standing outside the tall house with its windows thick with dirt, I felt a strange sensation that Andrew had been laughing at me, laughing at everyone. It was odd that I—who had long been obsessed with the Arctic regions, and with this old tale of Thule—had a moment not really of hesitation but of startled pause. For a moment I felt that I wasn't going to the most northerly island but that I was setting out for the centre of the earth.

⚭

The ship's name was *Aurora Borealis*. If it kept afloat on the ice seas, it wasn't thanks to the captain, who had crashed the ship two weeks earlier, holing the bow on a piece of shore. They had repaired the ship, but the captain feared the worst when he returned to the south. So he was in pre-emptive mourning for his job, though he tried to be cheerful during the voyage.

The ship was a smashed-up icebreaker. The passengers lolled in the saloon, smoking in the afternoons; they drank, they ate, they dozed, they read bumper books about Greenlandic wildlife. Total wilderness, everyone said all the time, it was a chant coming off the boat. It was like a moving convention, devoted to the worship of absolute vacancy. We were heading for Thule, the real-time Thule—the name shared between an Inuit village and a secret US Military base, hidden in the far north of the island. A dark comedy, this dual personality Thule.

The sea route to Thule passed along the western coast through multi-form bergs, cracked and twisted, rising to sharp points, drifting with the waves. Waves curdled around the base of the icebergs, coiling into the gaps in their surface. The haggard grey coasts were empty; the ship moved past black rocks, which looked like sloppy stacks of crumbling charcoal, spilling into the sea. At midnight, the spectral autumn version of the Northern Lights appeared, a sky full of swirling green and white forms, swelling from the horizon like fires. They pulsed at the corners of the sky, seeping slowly across the stars, ebbing to a silent rhythm. I stood on the deck, watching the patterns of the lights moving across the clouds.

There were orderly villages in the south, set up by the Danes. In Ilulissat, in the west, the houses were wooden, painted in bright colours. Four-wheel drives ploughed the dust from the streets and shops sold supplies. There were fields of sledge dogs, chained to rocks, and the edges of the town were a series of dirty wooden shacks, interspersed with rubbish dumps, piles of broken-down cars, engines from boats—junk-yard collections, stacked in people's gardens. There was a Rasmussen museum in Ilulissat, celebrating the life of the Dane who brought the word Thule to this ice island. The museum was in the small house where Rasmussen's family had lived for a while, with a view of bergs drifting on the fjord. Born in 1879, Rasmussen grew up speaking Danish and Greenlandic Inuit; his mother was of partly Inuit descent, and his father was a Danish missionary. Finishing school in Denmark, Rasmussen tried out opera singing and acting, with scant success. He turned to writing, trying out journalism, and was sent on trips to the north, to Sweden, to Iceland. He met another ambitious Dane, Mylius Eriksen, and they decided to follow the Viking tradition, the Viking sailor Erik the Red, and sail to Greenland. It was a conscious imitation of their historical forebears, forebears known only through mythologized accounts: *The Saga of Erik the Red, The Saga of the Greenlanders*. It turned out badly for Mylius Eriksen, who later suffered a frozen death in eastern Greenland. His body was lost for decades, the details of his death known only because another member of the expedition left a note on the ice explaining what had happened. Rasmussen became a writer, sending back reports from northern Greenland, naming the Inuit settlers he found 'the Thule Culture,' and making Thule expeditions across Greenland and into Alaska.

When Rasmussen set up camp at Thule in 1910, the country was still unknown in many places, its frozen coast attracting polar explorers looking for a last camp before they set out further north. Peary had based himself up in the north-west of Greenland, in the area around Thule. He sold the Inuit guns, and left his descendants in the villages of the far north. In 1910, Greenland was inhabited, but its inhabitants were subdued by the enormity of the rocks, the storms raging across the cliffs, the darkness of the winters. For centuries, they lived in turf huts, indistinguishable from the moss rocks. Rasmussen suggested that the remote place he named was an 'Ultima Thule' in the superlative sense, an Ultima Thule of blasted cliffs, an Ultima Thule of ice islands. He had found the Ultima Thule of northerly places, the most extreme and bleak and compelling. His naming had nothing to do with Pytheas, he hardly referred to the musings of Strabo and Pliny and Pomponius Mela. Rasmussen used Thule as it had come to be understood, as a literary term, a piece of scene-setting myth.

It drew together the beauty and terror of an immense ice-plain, it seemed to fit with the strange clash of disconsolation and euphoria I felt in Greenland. Greenland was a beautiful series of cliffs, and then it was a vast uninhabitable ice-plain, the ice crushing 90 per cent of the land. An ancient land, its rocks ravaged by ice, in places nearly four billion years old.

It offered an absolute and unyielding sort of silence. Its physical vastness was matched by its antiquity. Greenland was an enormous plain of ice, the largest island, the most ancient rock in the world. In none of the other places I had been had the concerns of the human world seemed so small. Others had understood this feeling; Herman Melville had encapsulated the strange presence of the empty ice: 'And as for solitariness, the great forests of the north, the expanses of unnavigated waters, the Greenland ice-fields, are the profoundest of solitudes to a human observer.' The solitude of the ice, the solitude even of the deck, the vast rolling ocean, the ship heeling like a drunk, the blank sides of the mountains, the ice cap glinting above.

In Ilulissat there were glacier tours, lines of boats circling the ice-towers in the fjord. There were queues of tourists watching the sea forming into smashed sludge, admiring the pieces of pancake-ice colliding and splitting. There were scattered rags of ice lying on the water, pushed by the wind. There were masses of ice rising out of the sea, stern and solitary, the waves swirling around their bases. The mountains stretched behind the ice, pale in the sun, with contours like muscles along their sides, coloured red with moss. The ice-fjord was mesmerizing: so much ice, and it was only the tattered overspill of an immense glacier, and the immense glacier only a small fragment of the ice cap. It looked idyllic as the boat moved out of Ilulissat. The ice castles were blue and white, the sunset added a rich bloodied shade to the piles of drifting ice, and the bergs made a fine slapping sound as they bounced on the sea. The lights of the small town shimmered on the hills; the inland ice stretched beyond, a white snowfield, glowing red under the sky. The boat moved slowly through the congealed sea. The ice lay in the water; the clear sea showed the submerged forms of the bergs; the blue ice sparkled beneath the surface. At night everything was still, the wind dropped, and the moon rose, large and round. In the north there was still a narrow strip of evening light. To the east, the mountains lay stacked up along the coast, dark against the dusk sky. The bergs floated alongside the ship, forced by the pressure of the waves into fabulous shapes. There was one with stalactites and stalagmites around a great hole, like the mouth of a semi-submerged sea monster, roaring as the sea poured through the gaps between its teeth. Another was like an ice sculpture of a pyramid, its sides smooth and perfectly planed. They were infinitely diverse, thousands of chunks from the ice cap, the oldest bergs a deep blue, their colours reflecting onto the sea.

We passed through this thicket of bergs, ice shapes moving slowly alongside the boat, like a convoy sailing us along the coast. After Ilulissat the tourists faded away, and the emptiness took over, drawing the ship further and further north. Brief stops on the shore increased the sense of distance. I would clamber ashore, onto a silent promontory, seeing the ship small against the mountains out at sea, and feel a sense of complete solitude. I would wander along a coast, my walks constantly curtailed by a jagged glacier, a frozen lake, or the spectral plains of the ice cap itself.

We stopped at an abandoned mine, a relic left on the shattered coast. The ship stopped, and everyone got off. We had travelled along a fjord for hours to arrive at the mine, which lay among vast grey mountains, with ice clambering down their sides. On one of the rocks was a patch of dark ore, shaped like a black angel, and beneath its right wing were two holes, gashed in the mountain high above the sea, with a sheer drop beneath. This was the entrance to a mine, long defunct. The workers had been winched each morning towards the black angel, like a scene in a melodrama. They descended in driving sleet winds into a black mine, and emerged later into the darkness of the winter days.

On the shore opposite the flying fury's mountain were the remains of the mining settlement. There was a low wooden building, surrounded by white rocks layered in piles on the beach. Odd pieces of mining equipment were scattered around. Piles of concrete slabs, shattered bricks, twisted sheets of metal, a shoe, a sweater. Most of the buildings had been burned, but the barracks building had been left to rot. As I walked through the rooms—a small bedroom, a living room with a few chairs left strewn around, a bathroom—I trod on shards of glass. The place had been vandalized. The windows were shattered, the u-bends of the toilets were smashed; the wooden doors had been pummelled and thrown around. It looked as if the miners, who had once been trapped on this exposed piece of shoreline, had made a violent farewell, kicking in the doors of their former housing, smashing the furniture. But most likely, the destruction was the work of winter storms. It was a wreck, lurking under a weird-looking mountain, as the light faded.

The *Aurora Borealis* was moving so slowly along the coast there were days when I thought we had stopped altogether. It was more like a suspension of time than a voyage. The sea contained us; the land offered no escape, only the silence of the ice fields. The rocks changed colour with the changing tones of the sunlight—moving from vibrant purple to a rusty orange. I could sit on the deck for hours, watching the gradations of colour, and then there was the liquid metal of the ocean, boiling beneath the boat. After a few days, the boat was a seething torment of restlessness, as if the stillness of the view compelled us all to action. Rumours started to develop about other passengers: the two biologists who had fallen in love; the man who was troubled, but an artist; the Scottish sisters who were thinking of flying home at the next stop, except they couldn't because there weren't any flights. So they stayed on the ship, glowering through breakfast and disappearing for the rest of the day. Bumping into someone in a corridor by accident became a contest of regret, extended to pass the time. The boat resonated with symphonies of phoney concord, trilling up and down the decks. The sense of unease was critical, as if we were all fading into the view, vanishing into the vastness of the sky. It made us slightly raucous, struggling to keep a conversation going, as if to fall silent would be to disappear.

My neighbours at table were six German scientists. One of them walked with a limp, and he ate nothing but fruit. He wanted to live until he was 130, he told me. He already looked about 110. At first they were all friendly, jovial and welcoming, but after a few days they were bored of my German and wanted to trade puns together. They made their napkins into swans and talked about the weather. Soon they just wanted everyone else to vanish; they said they disliked queuing behind them for food, and passing them life-jackets and waiting while they fumbled for change at the bar. But they kept it up, toasting each other, greeting each other in the mornings like long-lost friends, treading on each other's toes in the queues and then pretending it was all an accident.

We came to a small village, a few wooden houses set against a beautiful red mountain. A cluster of Greenlanders wearing jeans and sweatshirts wandered around. The continuous roar of drilling rose above the sounds of the street; a large wooden and concrete block was being built on the bog at the edge of the town. A light rain fell as I walked across the moss-rocks. I passed the building site, I walked cautiously around the piles of matted dog fur. A few builders were walking back to the village, Danes talking softly, dressed in fleece jackets. They were moving quickly, with a sense of energy and purpose; it highlighted something strange about the place. Everyone else seemed to be swaying as they walked. A gentle motion from side to side, as if they had just been on board a ship for a hundred days. Then I saw a fetid lake, and I turned a corner to find a local leaning drunkenly above a pile of his own vomit. He was staring deep into the vomit, pondering the void, and then with a great effort he swayed himself into a standing position and wiped his mouth. He fumbled in his pocket for a light for his cigarette.

Greenland was no longer a blank space. It was no longer a fantasy plain; the coasts were travelled, dotted with names. It made me think of Conrad: 'It had ceased to be a blank space of delightful mystery. . . . It had become a place of darkness.' The boat was ploughing a lonely course along the coast, and though the ice was beautiful from a distance, arresting in its whiteness, the realities of life in Greenland were stark. Vast tracts still lay untouched; the ice cap had never been crossed before Nansen took his skis to the white ridges. Greenland had defeated the Vikings altogether, though they struggled to live there for a few centuries. In the tenth century the Vikings had arrived, led by Erik the Red. Erik found there were animals for hunting—walrus, whales, reindeer—as well as fish, and fertile pastureland onshore. Erik sailed back to Iceland, with news of the fertile land beyond the ice sea. He called the land Greenland, in a conspicuous piece of euphemism, thinking an attractive name would make people sail there.

Erik took a fleet of boats back to Greenland, and others followed afterwards. Later Norsemen sailed from Greenland to the west, and recorded that they found a utopian land, called Vinland, where grapes grew abundantly. The clerics further south wrote up the new finds, merging their reports with old fantasies about the north. Adam of Bremen wrote that Greenland lay far out in the great Ocean, and that it was possible to sail to the island from the shore of Norway in five or seven days, as likewise to Iceland. The people in

Greenland, wrote Adam, were bluish-green from the salt water, and this was how the country got its name. The Greenlandic Sagas written by the Vikings were equally fantastical, littered with echoes of myths and saint-voyages in the north. The indigenous populations they turned into Norse trolls, calling them *Skræling*, describing them as underground people with large staring eyes.

The Vikings struggled as the climate changed, and by the fifteenth century they had lost contact with the outside world. They disappeared; their settlements were abandoned. What happened to them remained mysterious—later arrivals found a few buildings, a few hunched skeletons, but nothing conclusive. They might have fallen into anarchy, fading into the perpetual darkness of the winter, losing the will to survive. They might have died of disease. They might have been murdered by the Inuit; they might have thrown in their lot with more successful tribes and become semi-Inuit themselves. No one knew for certain.

The human history of Greenland was a series of faint voices, drowned out by the winds, a few ragged settlers struggling to hunt, stumbling across the ice-plains. At some stage in the deep past, a few Inuit came from Canada, dwindling or retreating through the years, to return again centuries later. Much later, there had been hunters along the coasts, European whaling ships firing shots at the seals and walruses, bringing home narwhal tusks which were occasionally mistaken for the horns of unicorns, so mixed up were fantasy and reality in contemplation of the ancient north. There were Inuit stories about these hunters: a Greenlandic tale called "The Man Who Could Not Be Looked At by the Europeans" about a Greenlander who was blessed with a magical quality which meant that the European whalers could not look at him, even when he stole supplies from their boats. It was a story of wish-fulfilment for the Inuit who saw the European whalers sailing off with their hunting spoils. Until the twentieth century, Inuit numbers never rose to more than a few thousand. Guns had helped the Inuit survive, and had allowed their population to increase. They had spent the twentieth century gradually losing their traditions, moving into more modern, Danish-built houses along the coast. But they had continued to hunt and fish along the coasts.

The century had hardly changed the superficial view. Greenland was the whitest land in the world, the most immense ice cap in the north. The ice cap was blank and impressive. The bergs were protean and graceful, rocking gently on the waves. The winters were harsh; the land fell under darkness, though the sky was rich with the Northern Lights. Going up that coast was like travelling back to the Ice Age, when ice rioted across the mountains, when ice was the only presence on the land. The air was frigid and taut. The long stretches of the coastline ran on, deserted, into the glinting whiteness of the ice. On the grey beaches nothing moved, the sea flowed into the fjords, through tight channels of rock. The waters splashed the bergs, the bergs drifted silently alongside the boat. It was the stillness of an implacable force brooding, a force with an intention I couldn't perceive, couldn't recognize. I couldn't get used to it, I saw it all the time, at the edge of vision. I pushed the mysterious stillness away, but I felt it all the time, I dreamt of the ice.

There were no settlements for a few days.

The ship moved through the emptiness, creeping along the coast towards Thule. The birds emitted occasional cries; the glaciers rumbled in the distance. At night, I was sometimes woken by the gun-crack of ice against the hull, as the ship barged through the smaller bergs, which lay almost flat against the surface of the sea. I stood through the hours on the icebreaker, watching the shore for signs of life. There were the same immeasurable rocks, shattered by the force of the ice. The same prismatic flood of colours, staining the rocks. The bergs massed around the ship, hemming it in. The ship hit the bergs like steel against steel, the ice was so ancient and compressed.

Sometimes small things happened, looming large against the stillness. An Austrian became so drunk that he slid from his bar stool and lay pretending to be a seal on the floor of the saloon, laughing until he cried. Because of this, the bar woman refused to serve anyone before 4 P.M., but the scientists came and hammered on the grill, a morning chorus of plaintive voices begging for relief, so she re-instituted the earlier system, which allowed everyone to be drunk by noon. The captain shouted at his son, who was one of the crew. He screamed along the deck, swearing in Russian, and his son looked haughty and offended. Later they laughed and joked and sang drinking songs. The first mate told me he had a feeling for ice. He was from the Ukraine; he spent most of the time icebreaking around the Russian Arctic port of Murmansk. He knew the ice, understood its shifting moods, its rigid quality, he said. Standing upright on the bridge, he said there was a science of ice. And there was a religion of ice. Ice charts, material predictions, and then the less determinate sense of the ice, of what it might do.

There was a red light flickering in the distance while he spoke, which the captain said was a helicopter. Someone else, one of the German scientists, said mockingly, 'Can it really be a helicopter? When we are thousands of miles from the nearest landing strip?'

The captain shrugged. 'Helicopter,' he said. 'Or perhaps Sirius Dog Star.'

There is an exact process, the first mate was saying, an exact process for moving through the ice.

The German scientist was still sceptical. 'Sirius Dog Star?' he was saying. 'You mean the Sirius Dog Star which is not visible with the naked eye?'

There was a pause. The captain grabbed a chart. 'Not Dog Star,' the captain said, rustling his charts, staring at the red shape. 'It is Jupiter,' he added, with certainty.

'Perhaps,' the German scientist said, trying not to smile, 'it might be Mars.'

And the captain laughed uproariously—he slapped the scientist on the back. 'MARS!' he laughed. '*Mars!* You're mad!! You are a crazy German!'

The captain glared at the red shape of Mars.

After a few days of empty coast, there was another small town spreading up the hillsides, with a runway carved out on the flattened mountaintop. A pile of rubbish was burning by the shore; smoke drifted across the beach. The children clustered around a football match, near the kiosk which had a sign saying THIS WAY FOR BEER in Danish. The dogs whined and dragged at their chains, sniffing through the dirt. Outside the houses, objects were strewn across the grass—outboard motors, clothes, boxes, metal parts, fishing nets, boots, kayaks, rowing boats, and then the rubbish, the piles of discarded plastic bags and bottles, hurled at random across the rocks, the brand-labels garish against the grey and green of the moss-rocks.

In the harbour, a Greenlander had just dragged a seal ashore and was preparing to dissect it. The process was methodical: the seal was split open, and the skin was removed, scraped away from the blubber. The skin came off like a coat—the Greenlander cut neatly round the seal's flippers, producing a flat oval-shaped piece of fur, which he threw in a rock pool. It was a deliberate process: after the skin, he turned to the organs, which he piled on the rocks; there was a system, because a Greenlander came to join him, and took a few piles for himself. They chopped the blubber into pieces, and slapped the pieces onto the stone. Gloveless, the man washed his hands in the water, preparing to load the seal flesh into a boat, to take it home. After a gory half-hour, the seal had been reduced to a few piles of flesh, thrown into a few plastic bags. The man's Danish wife sat on a rock, smoking a cigarette, and then she took one of the bags and climbed into the boat.

I admired his swiftness, his practical abilities with a knife. The endurance of the Inuit shamed the inhabitants of the boat, all of us with our need for regular meals, our ill-tempered queuing for breakfast, our desperate struggle to stay clear of the whiteness. Apart from the seal-hunter, in the cold village on the rubble mountain everything seemed vague and incoherent—from the raging drunks slamming their feet on the pavement, muttering at the sky, to the smiling families who would offer me morning coffee with a glass of wine. They seemed static up in the far north, imprisoned in empty space. They could go out to sea in their motorboats, but the distances between the settlements were vast, hundreds of miles of impassable rock and swelling silver waves. There were no roads along the shattered coasts. All the technological advances in transport still left them trapped in their villages.

As the Germans fell silent at dinner, as the hours moved slowly onwards, I imagined we were sneaking past a white-bellied mythical creature, snoring in the distance. Sneaking towards the last frontier, US Air Base Thule. Perhaps it was the remorseless stillness of the land or the endless emptiness of the coasts, but as the occasional settlements became increasingly strange, I began to create a wild fantasy about the voyage. It had a plot like low-budget sci-fi: a secret struggle against an indeterminate threat, set against a studio backdrop of hostile plains of ice, the white paint still drying on the set. I had a thumbnail summary: radio signals from Thule Air Base stop; someone is summoned to the scene to see what has happened; they find atavistic carnage, a few survivors hiding out in their barracks refusing to come out. Somewhere like Kurtz's camp, relocated to 76° N. A fragile collection of people, presided over by a man who has lost his mind, taking on the amoral power of the wilderness. The crazy governor of Thule would be sitting in his metal shack, tended by a few soldiers in ragged uniforms. A white storm would sweep across the base, obscuring everything. Conversations would be in desperate crescendo, screamed above the wind.

———— ✺ ————

There was a violent storm, and everyone fumbled along the corridors, vanishing at intervals to be sick. Everything slid off the tables; people wheezed in the dank below-decks air; waves splashed onto the decks. Later the water froze, making the decks like a skating rink. We moved onwards through a twilight sea, the coast hazy under the night mist. White-flecked waves were crashing onto the black rocks, ice shone on the mountains. The rocks were low above the water, coloured grey and green. The bergs were sometimes fifty metres high, with intricate carvings on their sides. Mountains loomed above the bow of the boat, icebergs drifted along the coast. The whiteness of the sky merged with the pallor of the sea. The season was dwindling towards winter, but the boat still ploughed through the ocean.

There was a murmur of dissent; no one wanted to leave the ship. The captain was bright and optimistic. 'Welcome!' he was saying. 'Welcome to the lovely town of Kulloorrdddsssaaaussag—well, whatever it's called, it's a lovely town! I love this town!' He sat on the bridge, watching the mists swirl around the mountains, with his feet up on the maps.

I joined a party of two, the adulterous biologists, leaving their spouses at the bar. The Inuit children had come to the harbour to watch us arrive; we were so far north that a ship was a major event. The children laughed on the quayside, staring at the arrivals. I could see a few passengers looking through their portholes on the ship, before vanishing back into their cabins.

The shore was covered with debris, the port a piece of wood surrounded by rusting containers. A dead dog was decaying slowly to the left of a pile of boxes. Litter, broken bottles, a few piles of seal innards. The paths were muddy. It was ten in the morning when the ship docked, and the houses were shut up and quiet. A few children moved between the painted houses; the dogs lay with their heads in their fur, as the sunshine spread across the shore. The vast rock pile behind the settlement, rubble rising into a mountain, was coloured a brilliant red, beautiful in the sunlight, and from the first level of the pile there was a view on all sides of silver waves and icebergs. Clouds hung above the mountains, ice covered the peaks, falling into the troughs and crevasses, dwindling across the slopes.

There was a smiling Greenlander coming down the path and because the biologists had vanished behind a pile of rubble he came up to me, his hand outstretched. He spoke a fractured Danish; he told me he was called Lars. Struggling to phrase the question, as I struggled to understand, he asked me to his hut for coffee and wine. His wife, Anna, had baked a cake, he said. I followed him along a path stained with grease and blood. He was small, wearing black trousers, a blue shirt; he was sixty-four, he told me, though he looked a decade or two younger. His house was a wooden shack, painted blue. Lars's neighbours had killed a seal the day before. Its guts lay on his porch, arranged on a plastic sheet, glistening. Lars stepped neatly over the guts, opened the door into a pile of chaos, a house made of scraps, wood hammered roughly into tables piled with dirty plates and coffee cups. He was a hunter, he said, but the season had not been so good. He lived for much of the year by fishing, but he shot seals when he could, and in September the polar bear season began. He showed me his fishing log; he hadn't caught a thing for months. Anna brought out the cake, the coffee and the cups. The kitchen was full of antiquated appliances—1970s plastic mixing bowls, coffee pots, rusty old pans—and the walls were covered in certificates and pictures, gaudy images of Christ, photographs of their children. There were no books, but there was a large TV and a video recorder, incongruous in the patched-up room.

'This,' said Lars, holding up a piece of paper, 'is my certificate, when I came second in the national dog-racing trials.

'I have seven children, four sons and three daughters. I had another son, but he died last year, on the ice. Here,' said Lars, handing me a large picture of his son in a shroud, which stood on the cupboard.

'This is Greenlandic cake,' he said, handing me a slice of stale fruitcake.

'I have two boats, small boats. I never go to Nuuk,' he said, smiling. 'It is too far away. I have heard it is a great city.'

A great city of thirteen thousand people, spilling its metropolitan vastness into the fjord.

'But my brother lives there. He married a Danish woman. I have not seen him for twenty years.

'My son,' Lars said, 'caught two narwhals. That is a wonderful thing. You can become rich, even from one narwhal, because every-one wants to buy the narwhal horn.'

He smiled. Anna smiled. He had built his house with his own hands, he said, then later he said the Danish government had given it to him, as a present. Lars wanted me to stay for the day; it was pure kindness. We could hardly understand each other, but he kept bringing out pictures and cakes while Anna smiled.

'Come again, come again soon,' Lars was saying, as I thanked them and stepped out onto the porch.

It was hard to get a true sense of Lars and Anna. It was hard to get a true sense of anything in the ice island, because of the blank-ness that surrounded everything. The endless whiteness of the ice drained the spectrum, dominating everything. It wasn't just the people who were bleached; it was the objects too. The objects were fainting into pallor. I scrambled up icy rocks, to the peak of a small rubble mountain above the town. I avoided a large hole which had been dug as a rubbish pit, and was already almost filled with bright plastic bags. Then I nearly fell into a narrow ravine, like a gash in the mountain. There were water pipes banged into the rocks in a long line, running up the mountain, and the mountain was like the wreckage of an avalanche. Moss clung to the slopes; there were white birds nesting at the top, and cracked eggs scattered further down the mountainside. Beyond the ridge I could see to the foot of a glacier, the bergs around its base crushed together, forming a mass of ice and snow on the sea.

One evening as I was lying flat on the deck of the ship, I heard voices approaching, and there were the captain and a Philippine sailor walking along the deck. I laid my head on my arm again and lost myself in a doze, though the wind was whipping across the deck and the night was cold. Then I heard the captain saying: 'I don't like us going this far north. Am I the captain or not? The sea-son is changing, the ice gets thicker. We should turn back. They've said we can't even go to Thule Air Base. Permission denied. So why are we going on? Look at this weather,' he said, as the wind blustered and the ship heeled, 'I've seen worse, but this is a small ship, you feel everything.'

Then they both said some bizarre things. The Philippine sailor said, 'But perhaps we could go there anyway.'

And the captain said, 'They're not letting anyone into the air base. It didn't used to be this way. We used to stop off there. Not this year.'

I was wide awake by this time but stayed still, wondering if they had seen me, or if they cared. They were walking off along the ship, sliding around on the deck, as the waves pushed the ship from side to side, a hypnotic lurch, a lurch my body was beginning to grow used to, which no longer made me sick.

I turned onto my back, watching the stars. The sky was dark blue. I heard the captain saying, 'I still think we should turn back,' as he vanished into the bridge.

At Melville Bay the sea was almost flat. The waves were like eels trapped under foil and the water was silver in the pale light. There was a band of blackness on the horizon. The north was under rain, and snowflakes fell onto the ship, lightly at first, becoming thicker. It was mid-afternoon, and the bar was full of people staring at the silent ice, as the sea congealed. The captain had come down from the bridge, and was standing with his hands on his hips, surveying the scene.

'We are not going to Thule Air Base,' said the captain. 'It is not allowed.'

There was a collective sigh. No one really knew where we were any more; the map seemed to bear no relation to the ice cap, glinting in the distance, and the ragged rock piles along the coast. We all kept trying to pin a flag to a part of the map, trying to fix ourselves somewhere on the globe, but the vastness of the island, the silent blocks of empty stone, gave us little to go by. The ship was retreating further north, further into the whiteness. We'd had a change of course, and now we were heading straight towards new Thule. The second Thule, the Thule built for the Inuit when they were moved further north.

When the US Military arrived in Greenland in the early 1950s, events moved swiftly. The Inuit were soon led to understand that they couldn't stay in Thule, the Thule Rasmussen had established, at the foot of the mountain where their ancestors were buried. They were informed that there was a new town waiting for them, a town of purpose-built Scandinavian houses. By these subtle negotiations, a change of location was made persuasive to the Inuit, and they went further north. They had arrived at a still colder place, which they called Qaanaaq in Inuit, or Thule. It was one of the most northerly settlements in the world.

The ship lumbered across the ocean, as the bergs bounced on the waves. There was a strange atmosphere to the evening. The skies darkened and a band of mist stretched across the mountains. There was a dull rumble from the glaciers, rolling across the sea towards the ship. Ellesmere Island stretched away in the distance, a range of white mountains. The ship moved the last miles along the ancient coast bordered by thick white waves, in and out of fjords, with the swell of the sea bullying the boat around, shoving it from left to right. The captain spent every hour on the bridge, dodging the ship around the bergs, which were growing by the day, clustering on the surface of the sea. The waves were harsh on the boat, they slapped the sides, as if they were trying to wake us from this trance-like progress along the coast. I stood on the bridge, with the captain surly in his uniform, staring at the sunset. The night swept across the skies, staining everything dark blue.

I was dimly aware of a worrying noise; it was ice shaving along the sides of the ship, scraping under the hull. The bergs drifted past, rocking on the darkness of the waves. When the ship approached the sea ice, the sound was the first thing I noticed: the distant crash of waves against ice, like breakers on a shore. There was a glow on the horizon, as if the remote slopes of a glacier would soon be visible, bleeding down the sides of a mountain. The ship moved through the ice, as the frozen chunks collided with each other, grinding under the hull of the ship. When the ship hit a low berg, the decks rose and fell, and a gentle shuddering went through the frame.

The ship sailed through the pack-ice, through a frozen sea. The forms of the ice were infinitely diverse, tinted by the sunlight, creating shades of green and blue, like distant flashing lights. All around lay a glittering expanse, spreading as far as I could see, casting a light into the mist, which hovered above the drifting ice. As the night drew on, the sky became cloudy and hostile, and the ice shapes bucked on the shifting ocean.

The morning was pale, as if the day were on edge. When the sun rose there was a creamy fog sitting on the sea, falling along the deck. But then the sun shone slightly through it, and the fog started to sift itself, rising off the ship.

We were at 77° N and 69° W. The last coils of mist hung on the waves, seeping along the shore. This was new Thule, a settlement arranged in tidy rows, with the more recent housing jumbled at the outskirts, falling out of the plan. The mountains lay under a sky of pink and orange. The harbour was one more pile of rubbish, one of the most northerly piles of rubbish in the world: rows of containers, plastic bags lying neglected on the muddy beach, the remnants of fishing boats, with the dogs forming piles of matted white fur. It was a Thule with a touch of the shakes to it; the drunks were shouting from their windows, stumbling along the roads, swinging umbrellas, rummaging through the supplies stacked by the harbour for bottles of beer.

It was the last stop for the ship and the biologists, the beer-struck Austrian, and the German scientists all stumbled onto the shore.

The Austrian was saying, 'Is this Thule?' He tripped on the rocks and almost fell, grabbing at a pile of boxes.

It was a Thule of sorts. This village was one of the most remote places you could find in the north. It was the edge of the world, this land of Greenland; there was little beyond it, only the dark realms around the North Pole. The Inuit of new Thule didn't exactly live in harmony with their surroundings; some of them worked in Thule Air Base, others were supported by subsidies from the Danish government. There were various elements that were additional, various elements superfluous to the simple conditions of hunting and fishing. The previous day a supply ship had arrived, and the shore was covered with boxes: food, drink, electrical goods, a range of necessities and a few luxuries. Theirs was no longer life lived absolutely in the raw, as it had been in the past. But they barely intruded on the vastness around them. It was one of the most unmediated relationships to nature I had seen. A few mod-cons, a radio and a TV couldn't persuade the inhabitants that they controlled the environment around them. The mountains rose above the town and Thule sheltered on a slender piece of flat beach, between the empty ice and the empty sea.

I walked along dirt tracks between the wooden houses towards the moraine mountain, the rocks decorated in swirls and spots of colour, shaded red and yellow and brilliant green. The sun formed a band of orange and red above the horizon. As I climbed the rubble mountain above the town, I could look down on a sea of mist, breathing across the settlement, obscuring the small box houses. I walked across the rocks and moss, trying to reach the edge of the ice. The distances were illusory; the ice receded every time I reached another peak. The ice was a white glow on the horizon, merging with the sky and the clouds. As I climbed each low hill I thought the ice would be on the other side, but the other side was another plateau of rocks. A cold wind was gusting across the plain. As I walked closer to the ice cap the plains became like immense fields ploughed roughly by a giant, the furrows too vast to step across; instead I was walking up and down the sides, stumbling on the rocks. I was sweating, though the temperature was below zero, less from exertion than from a sense of nervous hurry. I was desperate to arrive at the ice beyond the rock plains.

Throughout the journey, I had seen the ice cap in the distance, but I had never walked to the edge of the ice. I was cold as I walked and disconcerted by the empty silence. After what seemed like hours, the ice appeared ahead, a long low plain of white and black, rising gradually into the distance. I trod on the ice and it crackled under foot. The surface had formed into ridges; there were peaks jutting out of the ice further away, the bare rock sharply contrasted to the whiteness. This was the emptiness I had sought, and it stretched ahead of me: a crazy beauty, immeasurable and bizarre. It was the 'other world' the Victorians had expected in Iceland; I felt as unnerved as early visitors to Iceland had felt, trying to grip their feelings in a few deliberate phrases. This was nature performing its strangest turns; this whitewashed country was nature in a truly bizarre state. I had seen many varieties of northern landscape, but I had never seen nature as astonishing as Greenland. To the extent that Thule was an idea about nature that amazed observers, nature that receded into an overwhelming mist, islands that appeared and then vanished again, then Greenland was a sort of Thule. It was the ice world that had fascinated Nansen; it seemed deadly and strange to him. A scientist might have talked me through it, telling me about the micro-organisms hidden in the ice, the chain of reactions which made even this whiteness part of the breathing of the planet, but under a cold sun I was chilled away from the ice cap, frozen back onto the rocks. Everything seemed distorted by the ice; the distances were impossible to calculate, and the way back passed through a valley of emptiness, with no landmarks available, just miles of rubble.

There was a severity to the beauty which I couldn't quite get away from. The ice lolled across most of the country, ice so heavy it had forced the land down, creating a vast trough in the middle of the land, reaching to a depth below sea level. Great rifts of ice, formed into black and white stripes, undulating upwards, ice crushed together. The retreat of the glacier had destroyed the lands along the coast, ripping at the mountains, piling thousands of boulders onto the soil. It left a shattered land, littered with moraine debris, miles of discarded stones. More violent than a raging fire, the ice had wasted the coasts. The ice lurked behind every range of mountains, this immense whiteness. The early settlers could make no impact on the land; they faded away, their turf huts destroyed by winds and storms, leaving hardly any traces of their presence.

As I walked back, with the ice glinting behind me, the sun shone brightly. When I turned around the light was glittering across the ice, turning it silver. It looked like a piece of precious metal, gleaming in the sunlight. I kept turning and staring at the silver ice.

I walked back into the settlement of Thule, a settlement swaying from side to side, shouting into the afternoon. The passengers had disappeared; they'd either thrown in their lot with the Inuit or gone back to the ship. A woman followed me along the beach, muttering in Inuit. I tried to talk to her a little in Danish, but she didn't speak Danish. It was cold in the town; I puffed on my hands as I walked around, feeling my cheeks go numb, the wind blasting at the cracked skin on my hands. No one ever went to Thule; a villager told me that the supply ship only came once a year. And they hadn't expected our ship at all. 'Two ships in two days,' he said. 'That will be it for the year.' It was a Thule struggling against the mass of the ice, where the mist was a dynamic and constant presence, changing its forms as the light changed, spilling waves of cloud across the sea, draping itself around the base of the mountains, breathing across the village, through the untidy streets and the stacked-up containers. It was a Thule where the ice shapes drifted on the sea and the temperature plunged as the day drew on.

Talking to someone in the hotel, the hotel with its back against the ice, I had a sudden idea. Someone mentioned a helicopter which flew to Thule Air Base. It was due the next day, though often the weather delayed it for days or weeks. It was ambiguous news, but once I heard about it I knew that I had to get on the helicopter.

I ran across the smashed glass, around the matted dog hides. I pulled a dinghy from the shore, and set out towards the ship, forgetting to wear a lifejacket and causing the captain to wave frantically at me from the bridge. I scrambled up the ladder, and ran along the corridors, bumping into the other passengers. I found the Austrian sitting in the bar, and I said goodbye.

'You're going?' he said, into his whisky and beer. 'Well, good luck. Farewell.'

I tried to find the captain, but he had disappeared. The first mate was holding the bridge, staring fixedly at the sea, trying to keep the boat away from the drifting piles of ice. 'I do it because I can, not because I must,' he was saying through gritted teeth, as I waved goodbye. Then the captain re-emerged, and when I explained he said he understood. 'If you want to go, you want to go.' He shrugged. If I wanted to go to Thule Air Base, he would try to arrange something for me, he added. 'Use the phone. We'll sort it out,' he said.

I spent the afternoon calling up American soldiers and embassy officials in Denmark, with the captain laughing furiously at the time I was spending on the bridge. When I had something like a plan I dragged my bag from the ship, and rowed it back to the shore. I dragged it as far as Hotel Qaanaaq, a wooden house with a handful of neat rooms. From the windows there was a view of the ocean and the distant form of the ship. There were no other guests, I was told with a smile. I stuffed my bag into the room, and then I went out to walk along the dust streets.

It was cold in the Thule they had hammered to the ice-shore. A coldness that made me sneeze and cough even as I walked a few paces along the beach. Rasmussen lurked behind the evening, a bemused presence, wondering what had happened to his settlement. He had known the Inuit, he had lived with them, written about them; he had called them the Thule people. These people of the remote north had been his inhabitants of Thule, a non-European people, with nothing to do with the Germanic tribes. Now the

Thule Inuit were trapped in this semi-civilization, in a town they couldn't entirely understand. When I walked along the street, asking for directions, they stopped and smiled and tried to help. At night the local drunks came out in strength, weaving between the dogs and the rubbish. Through the mist haze I saw them moving along the beach; some were lugging boxes and bags, others tripped as they walked. There was an Inuit man standing on the shore, holding a guitar. He was tall, with fine features and dark eyes, wearing black trousers and a blue hooded top. It seemed a piece of curious defiance as he sang to the twilight. The multi-coloured rubble rocks loomed behind the town: shadows against the pale sky.

He was singing about the mountain by old Thule, where the Inuit had buried their dead. It was a lament, soft in the stillness. As he played the locals began to sing along, a strange chorus, lifting their voices to the ice-plain. A steady droning of male and female voices, with a few more Inuit coming to join the choir, huddled in their coats. It had a curious effect on my frozen senses—the soprano female voices, the men singing the bass lines, everyone shivering slightly on the beach, the lights of the town glinting up the rubble coast. It was crazy and moving, this faint sound of voices, in this village in the wilderness.

'What do you think?' I asked a local, who was listing slightly. 'It was our home,' he said. 'We feel shame, as if we have been weak.' The Greenlander stood on the beach, among the debris of the shore, the bust-up crates, and the dogs lying like rocks. 'It is very hard here,' he said, suddenly, eagerly. 'We have no money.'

None of them knew anything about a recent treaty which said they could visit Thule Mountain and return to Thule after a few years. None of them thought it would help. It was too difficult to get to their former settlement, they said; they hadn't the money. And they couldn't believe something as abstract as a treaty; it hardly registered as a reality. One of them shrugged. 'Probably it won't happen. No one will make us houses there. It would cost too much to go there. We can visit, like visitors in our old settlement. But that's not what we want. Recently we celebrated the founding of new Thule,' he said. 'But it was no celebration. There was singing, dancing,' he said, 'but I felt sad at heart. We should not celebrate this,' he said. 'It was a defeat.'

Standing in Thule, puffing on my hands, my face chilled by a blasting ice wind, I stared at the rubble rocks and the drifting ice shapes. The light subsided slowly across the mountains. The lights glittered on the metallic surface of the sea.

In the morning the sky was a vivid pink. The people were silent in their houses, sleeping off the night before. As I dragged my bag from the hotel room I heard the thud of helicopter blades. The town was bathed in light, the sun was glinting through the haze, and the dogs were whining along the beach. I walked out of the settlement, towards the flat rock where the helicopter was standing. The pilot was loading a few boxes and a child with a broken leg into the back. He was an upright Dane, and we had a small tussle about my failure to have anything like a ticket. He was irritated by my inability to present the right paperwork, and he nearly slammed his door. Basic stubbornness made me persist; it was the tussle of an hour, and then the helicopter had to leave, so he told me to get in.

When the helicopter lifted into the air I looked down at the small huts of new Thule, spreading across a small patch of land. A few locals were watching the helicopter ascend, and then they turned and walked slowly towards the harbour.

It was a short flight across brilliant whiteness. We banked south towards Thule Air Base. The helicopter pilot showed no trace of strain when the helicopter moved out above the ocean; he was a stocky man wearing a tattered uniform, and he said, 'My father came and worked at the base in the 1950s. He loved it there. Look at that stuff below! Isn't it amazing! Beautiful beautiful ice!!'

'Is everything normal at the air base?' I asked.

He stopped talking, wiped his mouth, and said, 'Normal! Normal! You'd hardly call it normal! Normal!' he said a few more times, and laughed. 'I love the Americans,' he said. 'I love them.

They're great. The Greenlanders, I love them, such a warm vibrant people. I love them so much, I married one! We live in Copenhagen! We have seven children! Seven! I love it here, but I love my wife, my children too. So I work for a month, go home for a month. It's a hardship posting, everyone says that. But if you travel a few days north from here, you'll see polar bears on the ice! How often do you get to see that! I've seen dozens of polar bears! Oh yes! I love it here.'

The child slept behind us. The pilot said, 'People say we are mad to live here. I say to them, "What do you know?" I love it here! A month on, a month off! Perfect!'

We had just turned again when I saw a brown mountain, planed at its top like an inverted coffee cup, with the sea sliding slowly past it. This was the mountain where the Inuit had buried their dead, and further inland stood the silver rows of barracks buildings. There was a long white runway, stretching towards the mountains. The ground was dusted with snow. We hovered above the surface, and then the helicopter came to a halt on the ice.

At the entrance to the base there was a large sign: WELCOME TO THULE AIR BASE. Everything was clean and orderly. A sallow band of light stretched beneath the thick clouds. The rust-coloured slopes of the mountain stood with the pale sea beneath them. Further inland, the ice cap glittered.

The helicopter pilot was waiting for the blades to wind down. 'Remember'—he smiled—'be nice to them, they'll be nice to you.'

There was an exhausted quality to the light; it made everything sepia, as if I were watching an antiquated film, its scenes crackling through the projector, the cast performing jerky movements, everything subtitled 'US operations, Northern Greenland.' I had thought for a while along the coast that I might find a contemporary Kurtz. These fantasies faded at the sight of the trim walls of the arrival lounge, and there was a young first lieutenant shaking my hand, smiling broadly and introducing me to two smart majors who were smiling too, stretching out their hands. They were delighted to see me, they explained. They would be glad to show me around. There was another flight out of the base in a few hours, and it was regrettable but I would have to leave then. But they could show me a few things in the meantime.

The majors were stocky men, almost identical, with their shaved heads and their broad smiles. They pointed towards the tidy barracks buildings; they nodded at the oil drums like white mushrooms, the storage containers, the heating pipes. They pointed me into a van, and dragged the door closed. Driving through the barracks-lined streets, there was no sign of anyone at all. Everyone was inside, staying out of the wind, which was blustering hard now, blowing the dust off the roads. Between the massive pipelines and the white fuel containers, there was a view across the frosted rubble to the pale sea. The sun was sliding across the sky.

Standing in the street for more than a few minutes caused shivering like convulsions, but the majors cracked jokes and laughed, slapped their hands on their knees. We left the edge of the base and the van bounced along a rock track, heading out towards the ice cap. We drove through the rubble towards the ice cap. The majors were immaculate in duty uniforms; when they weren't laughing they spoke in fluent acronyms. They didn't seem cold, though the windows of the van were frosting over and the wind was shaking the frame.

Everything I had seen in Greenland made me wonder why the US Military was still up there. In the Cold War a secret base made terrible sense; the quickest route for an attack on Moscow was across the North Pole. The base had been built for more than ten thousand soldiers; at the height of the Cold War it ran at full capacity. Thule Air Base had been running on a few hundred since the Cold War finished—a frosted shadow of its former self, left in the remote north. Large parts of the military city had been dismantled, many of the buildings taken away. Yet the US Military was still in Thule.

One of the majors said: 'We're here for BMEWS—the Ballistic

Missile Early Warning System. It's actually over there.' He pointed towards a patch of ice in the distance.

'Our mission,' said the other major, 'is to provide North America, the President, NORAD, SecDef, JCS and unified commands with warning and space surveillance. We operate a radar which continuously provides warning of sea-launched and intercontinental ballistic missile attacks against North America.

'We also detect and track earth-orbiting objects. We monitor and control satellites,' added the major.

We swerved along the rock roads, trailing a drift-cloud of dust. The long shining plains of snow, yawning into the distance, were like a force pitched against the majors' certainty. The majors were ignoring them, smiling into the ice-dust, pointing out patches of significance, antennae almost obscured by the rocks and the whiteness, satellites in the distance. They waved their arms at the ice cap.

'There's talk about modernizing Thule Air Base, making it a crucially important place for US missile defence. This is the next phase for Thule. We will alert the Pentagon, should missiles be approaching the USA, and those missiles will be blown out of the sky,' said one of the majors. 'Secretary Powell has been to Greenland now.'

The other major smiled and said: 'You won't see the difference after the upgrade. The base won't look any different. Operations might change a little.'

In the far north, the US Military was watching a band of sky. The purpose of the base had changed: during the Cold War it was a place where nuclear bombers could land on their way to an attack. Now it was a defensive station, watching the world, so the US government could anticipate an attack.

'Watching who?' I asked, and they laughed and shook their heads.

'We watch whatever we are ordered to watch,' said a major, a phrase like a tongue twister, but he showed no signs of stuttering.

There was a pause while we rattled across a pile of stones, and then the other major said, 'We watch for speed. A particular sort of height and speed. We saw the Russians doing missile tests in the Barents Sea a while back. Other than that it's pretty quiet round here.'

He smiled. Behind the robust forms of the majors, I could see the pale blue waters of the sea, and the white mountains along the coast. The barracks shone in the weak sunlight. In the distance a cluster of satellite dishes stood among the ice-covered rocks.

We stood outside the van, while the majors pointed at dusty patches of ice, scattering acronyms across the view, and when everyone was shuddering and clapping their hands in the cold, the majors stepped back into the van and beckoned to me to follow them. 'If you don't mind,' they said, politely. They smiled and slammed the doors shut.

We scuffed along the rubble tracks, back into the base. The streets were made of dust rocks, and the buildings were all stamped with their functions: GYM, RADIO STATION, SHOP. Behind the closed doors, the barracks were full of soldiers, moving from the luxury gym to their posts. A few soldiers, a few purposeful apparitions in uniform, hurried out of one building into another. Community, the majors kept saying. Against the bitterness of the cold, the vastness of the wilderness, Thule Air Base released its key strategy: society, like a military tactic, spun around the men, lifting them above the void. 'We are preparing for a setting of the sun party,' said the major. 'In the spring we will have a rising of the sun party,' he added. 'Fancy dress. Concerts, bands invited. Greenlandic choirs. Leather-making workshops, ceramics workshops, woodwork, pottery societies. You can take the stuff home,' said the major. 'Made in Thule.'

'And anyway we only stay for a year,' said the other major. 'You can't get too sad in a year. It's just one winter, one period without sunlight, and then there's the summer.' And he smiled.

'And the cold? The relentless biting, frigid air, the constant darkness in the winter?' I asked.

They shrugged. 'It wasn't so bad,' they said, smiling.

'In the summer, you can go for long hikes,' said a major. 'In the winter, of course, there are serious storms, so you can't go out so much. But in a way that's when the community is most close, because everyone is around all the time. People can't do stuff on their own. I'm kind of used to this sort of cold—I come from North Dakota. But we still have to be very careful. And in case people get depressed during the long winter months, we have very bright lights, all around the base, so you can go about your business, as if there's ordinary daylight.'

'Do you ever regret coming here?' I asked.

'I do have one regret,' said the other. 'When I came, I forgot to bring a good fancy dress costume. Anyone who comes here, I'd say that's an essential. Everything else you can buy, but a good fancy dress costume, it's worth its weight in gold. If I'd just had a Hawaiian shirt, or a great hat . . .' and he tailed off, imagining the perfect costume.

We walked around the supermarket, which was full of kitchen equipment, mugs and hats and T-shirts with GREENLAND or THULE AIR BASE stamped on them, cut-cost alcohol, tax-free cigarettes.

'Perhaps,' said one of the majors, smiling, 'you might like to buy this?' And he held up a cup which had THULE AIR BASE painted on it, with a picture of an Inuit with a sledge and dogs.

So I bought the cup.

Then they pushed through the doors of another low-rise barracks block, and there was a room lined with portraits of former commanders. In the next room there were photos of the base in 1951, rows of corrugated iron and steel, the same old snow, the blazing colours of the sunrise dulled into black and white. There was a page torn out of the *New York Herald Tribune*, from October 1951: THE US HAS TOP OF THE WORLD AIR BASE. CAN BOMB ANY PART OF EUROPE. In 1951 it was a major scoop.

There were two Danes wandering around the museum, try-

ing to interest me in a bunk bed, part of the original accommo-
dation for soldiers. One of them saw me looking at the newspaper article, and came over. He was about sixty, tall and stocky,
with thick grey hair, dressed in a neat tracksuit. 'When you read
about it now, everyone says it was a secret at the beginning,' he
said, smiling shyly. 'As if no one knew about it. But even the Russians knew, from the beginning; I remember a friend of mine told
me he had heard about a piece on Russian radio, all about the
Thule Air Base, and that was almost the same time as it was being
built.' He had been in Thule Air Base as a young man, he said. 'I
came to make money, like everyone. I was a civilian contractor.'
Now he had returned, for the same reason. 'The money is not as
good now, but it is still a lot. Really a lot.' He laughed and
scratched his head. The other Dane had been circling the room,
looking slightly irritated, but now he came over and tried to
show me the original air traffic control system. But I was walking
straight towards the showpiece—a rusted piece of metal, standing in a room lined with photos. This was the emergency escape
hatch from a B-52 bomber that crashed in the 1960s, spilling
controversy across the ice. It had been carrying nuclear materials
when it crashed. For years, it was claimed that the debris had
been removed, but eventually they conceded that perhaps not
everything had been found. A fragment, a small quantity of plu-
tonium, might have been left on the seabed.

'The crew ejected,' said the Dane with the thick grey hair, 'and
this hatch was found two hours' walk away from Thule Air Base.
We had a fine job getting it back to the base,' he said. He pointed at
the dents and cracks in the metal.

The majors and I were walking along the street again, and I
said: 'Do you feel cut off from world events, stuck up here in the far
north?' They smiled politely, shaking their heads. 'We do whatever
we are asked to do . . . don't choose our posting . . . happy to serve
our country in any way possible,' said one, mumbling slightly. 'Part

of the same operation . . . homeland security, national defence . . .'
And the other nodded slowly. For a moment, neither smiled.

We were back at the security station, and on the runway I
could see the plane was ready to leave.

I wanted to stay longer; I was asking if I could stay a night, a
week, but they all shook their heads.

'Unfortunately . . . completely impossible . . . No one can stay,
not even our wives . . .' said the major, shaking his head.

'Not even our mothers . . .' said the other major, shaking his
head.

'The next plane isn't for a week, so you'll have to hop on this
one,' said the deputy commander, a tall affable man, who had just
emerged from an office in the runway complex. A foot away, someone had taken my bag, and was searching through it. 'Just routine,'
said one of the majors.

'I'd love to talk,' the deputy commander was saying. 'But you
have to go. You say Thule? You're looking for Thule! Well you
found it! You have a good flight now.' He shook my hand, turned
smartly and disappeared into his office.

The winds might blast at two hundred miles an hour, the temperatures might drop to minus forty, but Thule Air Base stayed the
same in the north, watching the sky, waiting for a threat. There were
no desperate messages, crackling out to Washington. Thule Air
Base was a piece of hi-tech military hardware, standing in the middle of the ancient ice. At Thule Air Base, they floodlit the winter, living it out in the gym, staving off lunacy with parties and concerts.

There was no Kurtz; the soldiers were the servants of a more
elusive power. Thule Air Base took its orders from Washington; it
was the northern outpost of a vast military empire. The invisible
figures of the Pentagon controlled Thule from a distance, sending
orders into the ice, which were obeyed without question. Everything was out of the hands of the majors, out of the hands of the
soldiers scurrying through the blasting winds. The instructions
were terse—sit in the north, watch the sky for threats to the USA.

The ebullience wasn't feigned; the soldiers liked the place, the glaciers and the rocks, the frozen ocean. But none of them knew what was going on. Far away, in the south, the generals were dictating the script. Sealed instructions, a sense of driving momentum, nothing could abate it.

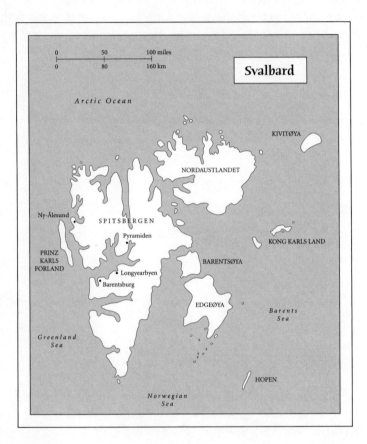

Svalbard

0	50	100 miles
0	80	160 km

Arctic Ocean

KIVITØYA

NORDAUSTLANDET

Ny-Ålesund

SPITSBERGEN

Pyramiden

KONG KARLS LAND

PRINZ
KARLS
FORLAND

BARENTSØYA

Longyearbyen

Barentsburg

EDGEØYA

*Barents
Sea*

*Greenland
Sea*

HOPEN

*Norwegian
Sea*

PROPHETS

⊶✷⊷

With favoring winds, o'er sunlit seas,
We sailed for the Hesperides,
The land where golden apples grow;
But that, ah! that was long ago.

How far, since then, the ocean streams
Have swept us from that land of dreams,
That land of fiction and of truth,
The lost Atlantis of our youth! . . .

Ultima Thule. Utmost Isle!
Here in thy harbors for a while
We lower our sails; a while we rest
From the unending, endless quest.

"Dedication to G. W. G.,"
Henry Wadsworth Longfellow (1807–1882)

The plane flew into a beautiful northern night. The sun had set into the sea, and the sea was as calm as a mirror, reflecting the evening radiance of the sky. Below were the silent plains of ice, the blank spaces unseen for thousands of years. The darkening ocean, the drifting bergs, the sludge-ice beneath were blanketed in clouds and darkness. The flight had been chartered from southern Greenland to Svalbard; I was once again an interloper, having begged a seat from a tour company. It was a modern jet, comfortable and sterile.

The cold sea stretched toward the Pole, as the ice began to close around the northern lands for the winter.

I had travelled in search of silence and a retreat from the city. I had been looking for a quiet and empty land, where everything would be simplified. I thought of it as a walk with Rousseau, disappearing out of the complexity of the city into the virtuous innocence of nature, experiencing a state of childish receptivity to external objects. It was a hunt for an Arcadia away from the seething world below. Yet I found history scattered across the plains and the urge towards rustic simplicity bound up with anti-democratic movements during the twentieth century, with the elitist agendas of the Thule Society. I had been retreating from all the clutter, the litter, until I was confronted with the whiteness at the most northerly edge of the retreat—the vast ice heart of Greenland. A land still magnificent and terrible, though polluted in places by military debris, controversially contaminated by lost nuclear materials. A land as close to absolute wilderness as I had found, still retaining the anarchic force of unbridled nature, even as the US Military sat out the winter on a patch of the coast.

When the remote north was an area of speculation and uncertainty, Thule could be many things. Thule could be pure while it was a fantasy, a place beyond the reach of humans. But now, the human history of the north in the twentieth century was bound up with my sense of Thule. As much as the silent ice and the ancient rocks, the mournful Inuit, the optimistic wilderness-hunters sitting on their slow boats to nowhere, and the US soldiers were a part of the history of the north in the last century. I had seen desperate bleakness, people struggling to survive. I had stared in horror at the silent ice. But amidst it all, I had felt moments of stubborn exhilaration. It was hard to know what to think. Where to stop, with the frozen ocean stretching beneath me?

Every society had some version of the yearning for an Arcadia, for a time when life was simple and everyone lived close to nature. My own entwining of this yearning with nostalgia for the simplicity of childhood was hardly unique. Growing older, growing up, brought all the chaos of adulthood, the pressures of money, the loss of time. Returning to London would bring back the feeling of disorder, loss of control. The state of innocence, the state of simplicity, was a holiday state, transient, impossible to sustain in the real world. As I listened to the low hum of the engines, I thought that knowledge and experience brought ambivalence; things became cloudy and difficult. Things might be better in a myth-world, but the option was not available. As an adult, I had to accept the trade-off—that the fall into experience brought a sense of comparison. It brought the consolations of knowledge, of knowing that others had felt the same way. The state of innocence was static—it lived and breathed and found fascination in small things, but it couldn't choose. Having no knowledge of the alternatives, it couldn't really understand.

The dream of Thule—a virginal untouched land—could never breathe and sweat as a crowded hopeless city or a history-strewn landscape could. Knowledge littered the landscape, changing everything, but it added a world of explorers and travellers and writers and poets to the empty rocks, as well as wars and violence and destruction.

It was easy to look nostalgically at the explorers, with their single goal, the emptiness around the North Pole. They had sailed, skied and flown, Nansen had set off in *Fram*, Amundsen had set off in the *Norge*, determined to discover, to shade in the blanks on the maps. It had driven them mad, this sense of something out of sight, something they didn't know. Nansen had written it out in *Farthest North*— 'Why?' he had asked. 'Why did we continually return to the attack, to the land of darkness and cold, the shore of corpses. To what end?' He answered his own question: 'It was simply to satisfy humanity's thirst for knowledge. Nowhere, in truth, has knowledge been purchased at a greater cost of privation and suffering. But the spirit of humanity will never rest till every spot of these regions has been trodden, till every enigma has been solved.' The explorers would not settle for the fantasy version, the mythical imaginary version, the utopian version of the lands in the far north. Women with beards, unipeds, griffins and Hyperboreans were all very well, the explorers thought, but they wanted to find the real north, whatever it was. They were prepared to lose the old myths in order to discover what was really there. And Thule had changed, as part of this process. Thule had begun as a real place, but Pytheas's account had been lost, and Thule had become a rich fantasy about the north, a word expressing a dream of remoteness and simplicity. Now the lands of the far north had been mapped, sometimes colonised, sometimes used for resources, sometimes for tourist retreats into the wilderness, Thule was something different. It contained imperfection and degradation within its borders. It expressed compromise and experience. Still, the longing for silent spaces, for the unusually empty, for the thrill of the solitary trail, continued to send people to the farthest reaches of the earth. The story would change and change again.

The whir of the engines changed pitch, and we were descending towards the archipelago of Svalbard. Svalbard was a Norwegian colony, once called Spitsbergen, and it was a strange combination of worlds: it was a wilderness, everyone told me, but it was kept clean by tough edicts and restrictions, regulated, divided into national parks, maintained by a strict governor, a person placed by the Norwegian government, granted far-reaching powers to prohibit and restrict. It was my last stop on the Thule-trail, a trip to a place which mingled pragmatism with idealism, wilderness worship with the unsentimental use of resources. And Svalbard was where a colony of scientists fashioned theories about the coming earth, the future of the far north. From Svalbard, these scientists had tested the waters of the Arctic Ocean, and suggested that the physical composition of the ice might be changing. They had predicted the melting of the frozen sea.

Under a soft and tentative dawn, the land of Svalbard emerges below. A landscape of ice and rock, rising from a white sea. Zebra-striped with snow, the mountains are a succession of sharp ridges and dark crevasses, with clouds swirling around their peaks. Further inland, the mountains are flat at their highest points, their slopes like immense ladders, layered with sandstone and slate.

The plane loses pace across the runway, another slender Arctic runway perched on a patch of flat land. When the doors open, the wind blasts into the cabin, rustling the magazines and newspapers. There's no bus, no arrival gate; I step down from the plane and walk into the silence of the valley.

Svalbard is a grandiose and barren place; the mountains like vast crumbling sphinxes covered with patched blankets, their folds falling heavily to the valley floor. The glaciers rise into blank blue walls, spilling ice into the sea. Rock and ice mingle in a two-tone frieze, the granite dark against the whiteness. Seals bask on the icebergs. The sun casts an orange glow across the sea. There is a broad valley that stretches for miles, and reindeer graze in the far distance. Kittiwakes and guillemots gather on the cliff tops, screeching and crying. The dappled patterns of the mountains emerge above the line of the mist, bright against the clouds, their slopes streaked with ice.

The houses of Longyearbyen look out across the fjord, and the fjord is as smooth as a sheet of glass. Across its smoothness show the reflected forms of the mountains. Longyearbyen was created as a coal town in the early years of the twentieth century, and the skeletal shapes of mining equipment are still scattered on the mountainsides. A small graveyard lies outside the town, its crosses coated with ice. I walk along Longyearbyen's main street, past the bright orange and yellow rows of houses. A polar bear skin has been slung over a balcony, claws drooping towards the street. Reindeer shamble through the streets, grazing on the brittle grasses at the edge of the roads. The few tourists sit in the pizza restaurant, eating whale-meat pizzas; they wander into the shops selling piles of seal fur; they flock past the skins and antlers, the mournful stuffed bears and foxes; they stand in the street, watching the evening fall slowly across the mountains.

In Longyearbyen, I watched the sun shining across the water and I thought about the Ancients and Vikings and poets talking and toasting the dream of Thule. Permanently squabbling, locked in a dispute across the centuries. None of the classical geographers had been to Svalbard, none of the poets or philosophers. The Vikings might have come here, but it was uncertain: there were Viking reports of a land called Svalbard—meaning cold coast—discovered in the last years of the twelfth century. This was why the Norwegians had renamed the islands Svalbard, though they had earlier been called Spitsbergen.

At three in the afternoon everything was blurred by dusk, and the shadows crept out from under the buildings. At the hotel the tourists filed to their rooms, where the curtains were flung open. The hotel was a mock hunting lodge, a place of wooden ceilings in pale pine planks, one more stuffed polar bear standing in reception, with the evening's luggage stacked around him. The windows of the Nansen dining room faced towards the shore, where the ragged rocks fell into the fjord. There was an antic feeling to the hotel: in the Nansen dining room the guests were pushing fish steaks around their plates, drinking slugs of Nansen cognac, having just stepped off a cruise ship called the *Fridtjof Nansen*. Nansen had been here at the end of his attempt on the North Pole, after surviving a winter in the ice. He came to Svalbard and found it was changing fast—that was in 1896, after a steamship had started coming to the place, bringing visitors. Even Svalbard, he had muttered, has become a tourist colony. He had watched the tourists at the Svalbard Post Office. Now Nansen was a brand in Svalbard, a label attached to the wilderness experience. He was smiling and waving, beckoning everyone through the entrance gates, turning his mournful eyes towards them.

It was a land a little like Thule, standing before the ice ocean, at the edge of the world. Glaciers covered two-thirds of the land, but the Gulf Stream made the archipelago milder than most places at 80° N, and the summers were sometimes nearly warm. Svalbard had most of the elements of Thule—the midday darkness of the winter, the midnight sun of the summers, the frozen ocean lurking off its coast. The inhabitants lived in their perfect small settlement of Longyearbyen, where there was no crime, where the only menace came from the Arctic winter, the freezing fjords and the sudden storms.

They all wanted to welcome me into the church, the devout adherence to the rules, so I walked with a few trekkers along the valley, and camped under the glacier. We walked in silence, staring at the thick turrets of stone, carved and smashed at their heights. The mountains were like cathedrals—baroquely patterned, with great stone ramparts and intricate friezes carved in the rock. The snow was stacked into the crevasses, shining on the slopes. There were mountains like shards of ice on these islands, rising into vicious peaks, but the mountains around me had been smoothed by the weight of glaciers during the last Ice Age.

It was dark at the camp so we lit a fire, the orange flames gaudy against the night. The crackling of wood and the whining of dogs were the only sounds. Everyone was cold, and the frigid air kept me awake through the night. I felt the blasts of the wind through the holes in the tent; the chill swirled into my sleeping bag. The sledge dogs whined, the temperature slumped, and the wind wailed around the tent. We had guns stacked by the entrance, in case a polar bear shambled into the camp. But nothing disturbed the night, except the dogs dragging at their chains and kicking up dust. The only presence was the icy breath of the cold, sidling up to me, curling itself around me. I shivered, I listened to the rhythmic sounds of breathing, and then I gave up on sleep and dragged the sleeping bag out of the tent, towards the smouldering remains of the campfire. There was a small patch of warm air directly around the wood, and I huddled towards it. Sitting up, propped against a pile of food bags, I watched the fire dwindle, listening to the silence of the valley. After a few hours even the dogs were quiet, heads into their fur, coiled onto the rocks.

The darkness lingered long into the day, and we cooked up porridge on a campfire, huddling at the edges of the flames, trying to stay warm. The others were all silent in their windproof jackets, watching the flames crackle through the wood. Later we walked slowly along the ice, sliding on the rocks, carrying something like a packed lunch. The sun was low in the sky, dwindling quickly, turning the sludge sea orange. It was hard to get a good look at the other people because the light was always fading, casting shadows across their faces. Some of them were new recruits to the wilderness; they had wanted this for years, the silence, the frigid blasting wind. They were the ones with a spring to their step, bouncing across the rocks like children, picking up ancient fossils, ice-smashed bits of basalt.

Later, we left the camp by the glacier, walking the short distance back to Longyearbyen. The scientists shook hands and waved goodbye, stepping back into their hotels, taking each other for pizzas in the small restaurant shacks. I walked down to the docks. The shore was a field of mist, a few motorboats were stranded there, their decks empty.

On Svalbard the governor reigned benevolent over everybody. The governor's civil servants, environmental experts, tourism consultants hardly dared breathe when he let his eyes fall on them. It was a place where the rocks were protected, and occasionally mined, depending on what the governor decreed. The governor threw edicts and boundaries across the land, keeping everything plain and empty. The rocks were tagged with rules, enforcing a state of innocence. The island could not be used for the purposes of war: since World War Two, when Svalbard was bombed and occupied by the Germans, all fortifications and naval bases, secret military sites, missile defence systems were prohibited. Much of the land was cordoned off, kept clear of tourists. The unrestricted use of the island, which nearly wiped out the walrus and the reindeer, had been replaced by a system of national parks, plant-protection areas, bird sanctuaries.

The governor was an autocrat with a fat rulebook. He demanded that travellers remain in official tour groups, that they confine their journeys to the appointed tracks. The rules were pasted to the walls of the hotels and bars: 'Do not disturb animals and birds. Remember, you are a guest. Do not pick flowers. Do not go into the wilderness without asking permission from the Governor. Do not damage or remove cultural monuments. All traces of human activity prior to 1946 are cultural monuments. It is illegal to search for or to attract the attention of polar bears.' The wilderness was too pristine for random hiking strays to wander across it; the polar bears were too fierce for the uninitiated to set off alone. It was the governor's request to the visitor to travel with the herd, to stay on the authorized cruises, the authorized helicopters, the authorized buses. The trailblazer was outlawed from these ice islands; the governor would have politely escorted Burton, Nansen or Amundsen off the rocks. Everyone was asked to leave untouched the untouched glacier, to stay in the settlement of Longyearbyen or to take the official tours.

The edicts were so strict that Svalbard became an invented reality, with something slightly odd at its edges. Still, the governor had environmental necessity on his side, sacrificing the interests of humans to the abiding beauty of the rocks. The visitors became obedient subjects, following the governor's decrees. They had come on their own grail quest, looking for the almost unspoilt and almost empty places of the north, and they hardly wanted to wreck the cold mountains and debauch the fjords. They deferred to the governor, joining him in his enterprise to keep this land pure. For a few days, I relaxed into the forcibly innocent world of Svalbard, innocence decreed by the omnipotent governor. The governor was out of town when I arrived, but I learnt a lot about him. He was the fixed subject of nearly every conversation; half of Longyearbyen loved him like a father, and the other half cavilled violently. Yet they all obeyed him.

Though the governor was trying his best to balance it all, there was little he could do about the creeping processes, the chemical reactions in the atmosphere, the traces of climate change. There was a team of prophets on Svalbard, casting their cards at the future, a regiment of scientists deployed in a small colony called Ny-Ålesund, north of Longyearbyen, north of every other settlement in the world. The scientists were offering up predictions about the coming earth, the warmed earth of the future. They were trying to lasso the indeterminacy of the future, drag it towards the present.

Far below these notables, the resident mine owners seemed to occupy a blank spot in the governor's vision. There were still mines on Svalbard—Norwegian and Russian-owned, like relics from earlier centuries, when the trappers and the furriers and the whalers swarmed on the beaches, in their blubber camps, or in their huts stacked ceiling-high with hides. The coal companies were still allowed to bang away at the rocks; the governor called it cultural heritage, because there had been coal mines in Svalbard for a long time, but really the coal mines were commerce, old-fashioned exploitation. Svalbard was a rich cold coast: the ice-mountains were seamed with minerals, the rocks filled with coal, gold and diamonds. The history was hardly pretty—the preceding centuries showed a line of determined humans, trappers hiding out in the snowstorms, knives poised, guns ready, miners coming to blast the rocks, piling up dynamite. Armies of pragmatists, hardly interested in old dreams, taking what they could from the islands.

It was late in the season for outings but I persuaded a bony-faced man called Anders to take me to the Russian mine at Barentsburg. Anders was wearing bright orange overalls, like a human beacon on the shore. He moaned as he fumbled with the ropes. 'I don't understand why anyone wants to go there,' he said. 'It's a bleak place. Miserable.' Anders's boat was a stuttering motor-cruiser, which moved slowly along the fjord, cracking the sludge-ice as it went. The ice churned under the boat, and Anders stood on the bridge, saying how beautiful the winters were, when the mist rose from the fjord sides and the moon gleamed across the ice. He was surly and unkempt, his hair coated in grease, his hands covered in dirt.

'There's never a perfect place, but I prefer this place to anywhere else,' he said, screwing up his eyes to stare at the mist.

Barentsburg was round the corner from Longyearbyen, along a coast of green rocks, covered in ice. There was nothing to see at first. The town was engulfed in thick mist; the quayside was covered with rusty iron containers stacked up in piles, and the skeletal shapes of cranes. Russian workers stood in small groups, talking. Anders ran up the steps from the shore, and found a Russian woman called Natasha who said she had a spare half-hour and could show me a few buildings. Anders was off to buy vodka, he said, and he moved quickly away towards the local shop.

Natasha was neatly dressed in a red jacket, black trousers, small bird-heel shoes, and she seemed to be speaking an official language. Everything she said jarred significantly with the physical evidence around her, but she ignored the discrepancies. She shook my hand; her hand was cold, and she breathed heavily as we walked up the steps to the town. She said: 'In Soviet times you had to be a member of the Communist Party to come to Barentsburg, but now, it is only necessary to be healthy, to be able to overcome Arctic conditions for two years.'

We passed the piles of steel containers, and Natasha said they were full of coal; in the winter it was impossible to ship anything because of the ice, and the coal was stored on the shore. During the summer it was taken away. We walked past dilapidated wooden houses, standing by the shore, their windows broken. Natasha gestured towards the shattered windows, and said, 'We keep these buildings to remind us of how things were,' and then she said, as if that had not quite explained things, 'We always mean to repair them each summer, but the summers are so short.' It seemed unlikely they would ever be repaired.

'You can come here for longer, if you like, and the average stay is eight years,' Natasha said. 'There have not been so many changes here since Soviet times, and the conditions are still hazardous. But there are positive benefits, all meals are supplied, and we have a small café for further purchases. But,' she said, suddenly, 'you must not look the men in the face, you must not go too close to the people, you must not talk to them.'

Through the mist, I saw the Russian miners coming and going, sometimes on their own, sometimes in pairs. They walked past, saying nothing. They were the real representatives of the town of Barentsburg, and their faces were blank, impossible to read. There were no women on the street, no children. It was the end of their shift, and they walked into the canteen, a vast black-and-white building by the quayside, with a putrid smell rising from the kitchens. Above the entrance was a poster of a bearded Russian standing in front of an Arctic snowscape and a poem in Russian, written out large, saying:

So, wherever you now travel
On the threshold of any Spring
You will think of Arctic ways
You will dream snowy dreams.

Dream the Arctic dream—even the Russian Arctic Coal Company was saying it to its employees. Natasha thought I shouldn't go inside the canteen. The men were busy in there, dreaming the Arctic dream, and they couldn't be disturbed. In the winter, when the sun had failed, the men would emerge from the darkness of the pits into the darkness of the afternoon, with the winds blasting across the frozen expanse of Grønfjorden. The lucky ones had their photos hammered to a board in the centre of the town, photos taken against luminous orange curtains, which stripped the colour from the subjects. Some of the men had put on suits and ties and tried to smile; others squinted miserably at the flash.

'These are our best employees of recent days,' Natasha said, though the photos looked as though they had been hanging there for decades. 'We have visitors who ask if the people who come here have done anything wrong, but of course they haven't.'

Once Natasha had summoned the spectre of Siberia, the tone was irreparably altered. The high-rise brick and tile, the decaying wood, the memorials paying homage to the dead—the victims of mining disasters, of plane crashes, of a dust explosion in 1997—created a strange atmosphere in Barentsburg. There was a Denisovich air to the miners slouching slowly from the pithead to the bar. If they were the lucky ones, they knew their country was in trouble. If this Arctic desert was a privileged life, they were men without illusions that things might improve.

Brooding over it all, there was a bust of Lenin, with a sign behind his head saying ARCTIC COAL. He was the most northerly Lenin in the world, said Natasha, laughing him off. But he made the place look trapped in the Communist past, trapped in Communist colours, Communist functionalism, fading away in the far north. In this land trapped in the past, Lenin was still presiding. One devastated brick façade had its date etched above the door, 1977, the year time stopped in the settlement, stranding the workers in a continual 1970s of dull orange and fading yellow. There were great holes in the roofs; the walls were streaked with dirt. It was impossible to disguise the fact that the town was poor. Most of it was made up of crumbling brick buildings, standing on shattered paving slabs.

We walked from Lenin along the main street, past the sign for the hotel, and the peeling paint of the post office. There was an old wooden church, compact and elegant against the sprawling block buildings. We stopped briefly in a yellow-tiled bar, studiously decorated with Arctic art, faded pastels of Barentsburg under ice, everything for sale. There was a small museum, with a collection of minerals, a reconstructed coal mine, and a gallery full of paintings of miners.

As Natasha said goodbye I tried to ask her why she had come to Barentsburg, what she did during the days, whether her husband was a miner. But she smiled and avoided every question. She told me she loved it there, but she looked tired and cold. It was impossible to tell. The Russians never came to Longyearbyen, Anders said, sotto voce, as we prepared to leave the Russian mine. Anders had become loquacious in my absence; perhaps it was the trip he had made to Barentsburg's bar. He lit a cigar, puffing the smoke into the mist. He said that Barentsburg was a closed place. Through the mist we watched the workers stacking the steel containers, dragging boxes around on the quayside.

'The Russians won't be honest about Barentsburg,' said Anders, in a cloud of smoke. 'You can't talk to the people much; they don't want to say anything. It was worse before, but it's still bad. They earn much less than the Russian officials say they do. That's just one of the reasons why they tell you not to talk to the workers. The other reason is that they are all alcoholics.'

There was a last sound of the crash of steel along the quayside, and then we passed the receding shapes of the containers, blurred by the mist.

'The hotel is full of rats,' Anders said, as we left, 'and the workers drink. The workers cannot leave Barentsburg, once they arrive; there is no transport available. If they leave before their contracts end,' Anders said, 'they lose all their money.'

The boat slid back along the coast, and the moon rose. The air was cold and the mist swirled around. The governor left the Russians to their frozen rocks, and hoped one day the coal would fail. Meanwhile he let the Norwegian Coal Company blast away, because Svalbard coal was the cleanest in the world, they claimed. The governor let the coal go; the companies exported their fossil fuels. Then the governor sponsored a scientific research base at Ny-Ålesund, to research the effects of fossil fuels on the Arctic. It was a paradox, a tidy story. It had a beginning—the Coal Companies—a middle—the Scientists—and an end—the Coming Earth, the future. Despite the blasting of the mines, the melting of the ice was a nightmare Svalbard was trying not to fall asleep into. The governor thought the mining could continue, so long as he sponsored the scientists in the north.

Flying from the mining town of Longyearbyen to Ny-Ålesund was a trip from cause to effect. As the mist breathed across the mountains the light aircraft shuddered along the runway, and rose suddenly into the air. The passengers sat among the crates of scientific equipment, with "fragile" scrawled across the boxes. The plane moved above the azure depths of Isfjorden, towards the mountains of Oscar II Land. Beneath lay vast glaciers, spilling ice into the fjord. They were named Nansenbreen, Sveabreen, Borebreen on the map; from the sky they were another crazy vista of ice and rock, the distinctions between places impossible to discern. Ny-Ålesund stood on Kongsfjorden, where icebergs drifted from a pale blue glacier.

Ny-Ålesund was little more than a few yellow, red and beige painted wooden houses, in a loose circle around a central mess building, with a broken train track at the edge, rusting into the tundra. There were no hospitals, no schools, just the wooden huts, made for scientists. There was a hotel for visitors, which was where I was taken, deposited by a friendly scientist and told to unpack and find my warmest clothes. There seemed to be no one else there. The corridors were silent; the living room was polished and empty. Paintings of ice-mountains hung on the walls. There was a notice saying: 'Attention! Please take the polar bear threat seriously!'

The fjord was pale blue; the glacier fell in frozen cascades towards the edge of the water; the mountains rose above, a mist curling around their peaks, too light to obscure the contours of the rocks.

The scientists all ate in the mess room, talking about the melting of the ice, tucking into Scandinavian buffets. They were a sombre collection, sitting in their cramped huts making diagrams about the coming earth. The melting of the ice, they said, was a possible result of global warming. There had already been thinner ice cover in the Arctic Ocean during the summer in recent years. It might be related to global warming; it might be a trick of nature. If the ice began to melt more intensely there would be lots more water around, and what this would do was uncertain, they said.

Sometimes the scientists sat in the sea between Svalbard and

Greenland, watching the changing of the ice. Or they sat in their small huts on Ny-Ålesund, writing papers proposing that climate change might be causing a retreat of glaciers in the Arctic region. Some of them said the global sea level was increasing, an effect of the melting of the ice. The scientists stayed cautious, even as they quoted their statistics. They were reluctant prophets, talking only of 'climate change scenarios,' things that might happen. Knowing that in the past definitive theories had been proved to be ephemeral, the scientists scattered their reports with qualifications, insisting that everything was merely hypothesis. Everything was laced with un-certainty, though most of the scenarios seemed to be varieties of dis-aster. They wouldn't tell the international corporations what to do; they wouldn't tell the governor to kick the coal bosses off his idyll. They monitored and assessed.

Running around the base was an Englishman called Jeremy, constantly cheerful, greeting everyone he met with great warmth and enthusiasm. The winds were always biting, but he still stopped on the paths, shaking hands. His hair was always perfectly parted, even in driving gales, and he always wore a fleece jacket in blue, brown windproof trousers, a striped shirt like a city banker, and large boots, which he stamped on the ground as he said, 'Well, lovely, really lovely to see you, must be off'—this to a scientist he had seen ten times already that day, and would see another ten be-fore the day's end, there being only one path in the settlement, only one dining room, and hardly any scientists.

I shook hands with Jeremy, and I learned that he ran a scientific station, one of the huts glazed with ice, lashed by the winds. Weaned on stories of Scott and Shackleton, Jeremy had decided from an early age that he wanted to work in Antarctica. He realized, he said, that he had to get a skill which would be useful on expedi-tions, so he trained to be a carpenter. After a few years, he became an administrator in British Antarctica, overseeing scientific research bases in the south. Then, he said, he was offered the chance to come to Svalbard. 'I thought, I've never seen the remote north,' he said. 'So I thought, why not! Beautiful place, really extraordinary to work here. And gosh it's cold today'—as the wind slammed us both against the wall of a hut—'let's go inside, my gosh, let's go inside.'

I respected his striped shirt; I respected his ungloved hands. His constant affability was an achievement in this place, which was nothing more than a dozen huts by an almost frozen fjord, the icebergs drifting slowly through the sludge, the deep blue glacier rumbling in the distance.

Everything in the scientific research station was orderly—huts, equipment, the small quayside with the motorboats lined in rows. The mess was open for breakfast, lunch and dinner, and the scientists ate together. One day Jeremy said: 'You should of course meet Alice.'

Alice knew all about the coming earth, he said, though like all the others she was reluctant to commit herself. But she could spin a riddle or two, offer up an augury, as long as no one asked her to stamp it as definite. 'Alice is a very remarkable person,' said Jeremy.

Suddenly there was a murmur of voices. A scientist had fallen into the ice fjord. He was Olav, he had been out looking at the bird cliffs, making notes about the end of the season. He had hit a patch of ice in the fjord, and his boat had buckled like a crashed car and thrown him in. Murmurs of concern broke out among the scientists, and the mess immediately emptied. Jeremy said 'I'm awfully sorry, I must go and see if there's anything I can do. I'll tell Alice about you—' and he ran out.

The settlement was in a state of shock from the near loss of a scientist to the elements. No one talked much, and Jeremy was nowhere to be found. I sat in the hotel, leafing through information packs and rule-books, and then I walked along frosted train tracks towards the edge of the fjord.

———⦵———

Later I went out on the fjord with Alice. I was slightly nervous because of what had happened to Olav, but Alice put me in a luminous survival suit and told me to blow a whistle if anything happened. Alice was small and compact, wearing jeans and a large sweater, with grey-blonde hair and an expression of rapturous calm. She didn't want to be adamant, she said, but some things looked very worrying indeed, and it was hard to know what to say. She had not found so many signs of good news, she said, vaguely, deliberately vaguely. But things might change, she added, lending me a hand as I climbed into the small boat.

The boat was a nautical midget under the towering bergs. The sludge-ice massed around the hull; the pancake-ice scratched at the paintwork. Under a twilight sky Alice steered the boat into the icy centre of Kongsfjorden, past the icebergs drifting from the glacier, swaying on the waves. A bearded seal yawned on its iceberg and flopped into the water. From a distance, the glacier looked serene, edging towards the fjord, a gentle slope of clear white and blue ice, the mist romantically encircling its base, softening its fall towards the water, and the icebergs looked pure white and blue. Out in the middle of the fjord, the boat hit the waves and lurched sideways as Alice swerved to avoid an iceberg.

Alice steered the small boat through the massing chunks of ice to the bottom of the glacier, stopping at a stretch of ice-littered sea twenty metres away. The glacier chilled the air around it, adding further depths of coldness to the evening. It was a squat glacier, dribbling ice into the fjord. The ice in the bergs was muddy, greased with dirt. For a few minutes, we sat in the boat and listened to the roar of the glacier, the groaning of the ice. As we listened, a loud boom came from the glacier and a great chunk of ice dropped into the sea before us, shaking the boat. Then everything was calm again, except for the lapping of the waves, causing the bergs to sway and rock in the water.

Sitting in the boat, staring at the glacier, Alice explained to me that it was sometimes difficult to be happy, knowing what she did about the ice-plains and their coming doom. She was not a mystic, or a novelist, she wanted to emphasise, but she thought some things were so worrying and probable that it was worth talking about them. In recent years, there had been bad tidings from the archipelago, from the scientific researchers on Svalbard. Chemicals from Russia, from North America, from Europe had circled in the air and water and moved towards Svalbard. The ice might melt, at some stage, and no one was predicting a sudden improvement in conditions.

'Let us just say,' Alice said, dropping the tiller and sitting upright in her survival suit, 'that there are man-made chemical compounds found in high concentrations on Svalbard, and they seem to cause damage to those animals in which they accumulate. They come by air, they come by water, and they are changing the wildlife on Svalbard. The Arctic wilderness,' Alice continued, after a long pause, 'might be under threat from the chemicals of more southerly civilizations, chemicals carried by air from Europe and North America, or by water across the oceans—from Siberia to Spitsbergen.'

Alice stopped talking while she manoeuvred the boat backwards, because we were being lapped towards the glacier, drawn into its coldness. I sat quietly, shivering violently, waiting for her to resume. Alice said: 'This business of drift, the Arctic drift, you mentioned it earlier. Since the 1980s there have been systematic changes in the ice around the North Pole. Nearly all scientists now agree that this is very unlikely to be caused just by nature,' she continued. 'It is the speed which makes the change different from before. There have been very low sea ice measurements and these yearly lows have strangely coincided with years when there has been an unusually large transport of ice from the Siberian Ocean towards Canada.

'Many of the travelling chemicals are carried westwards by the current that Nansen hoped would take him to the Pole,' said Alice. 'They come from the Ob, the Lena and the Yenisey, as the torrent pours into the Arctic Ocean. There are ships operating in the Barents Sea, and there is prospecting for oil and gas in the region. The Russian military installations also present a source of pollution.

There is nuclear waste; there are chemical and biological weapons and other military equipment,' said Alice bleakly.

And I thought of Nansen's *Fram*, drifting towards the infinite shadows of the North Pole, prow held high, drifting into darkness. Sailing towards the pure ice-plains, untouched by humans. I thought of Nansen, standing among the rocks, obscured by the mist. His journey prophetically outlined some of the future problems that areas such as Svalbard would later be confronted by. Alice told me that Nansen's Arctic drift theory was now the basis of modern research into the passage of pollutants from Siberia across the Arctic region. Now this current moved chemicals around the far north, dragging the overspill of Russian rivers into the ice. A torrent of waste, drifting across the silent ice. It was a distressed version of Nansen's theory of polar drift—the Arctic Ocean dragging polluted waters towards a formerly unknown region around the Pole.

'And now,' Alice resumed, 'the ice is warmed by polluting currents and melts into the ocean. No ice, no polar bears,' she added, firmly. 'This is already happening in North America. Polar bears are specialists, they specialize in killing seals, and of course we know where seals live. The polar bear lives and hunts and eats on the ice. The female bears only stay on land to give birth. If the ice were to melt,' said Alice, 'then the polar bears would lose their habitat, they would lose the seals. They wouldn't survive.'

Alice paused to listen to the glacier. The rumblings were heavy and ponderous now, promising a minor explosion of ice, a swell in the waves. We moved away from the ice wall, back towards the bird colonies, where Alice paused to glance up at the spiralling guillemots. She nodded, scarcely perceptibly, at a crowd of squealing birds.

'And these chemicals I told you about,' Alice said, 'they are drifting in the seawater from the Russian coast, and they are carried by air from Europe and North America. They come from so many places—but there are persistent organic pollutants—we call them POPs—which end up in Svalbard in high quantities, and they are stored in the fat in an animal's body. The more fat you eat, the more pollutants you get. So, a polar bear, at the top of the food chain, receives the highest quantity of these pollutants. Some of the polar bears—the females—are growing male organs. Whether this change in hormone balance also changes their behaviour, we are not yet sure. Perhaps it will.'

The hermaphrodites of Thule. The victims of an unplanned experiment, the introduction of man-made chemicals into an Arctic wilderness. The animals were changing, becoming grotesque and outlandish, more like the mythical beasts once thought to stalk across the northern lands.

'And it's not just the animals, of course. The Inuit have a far higher level of POPs than other humans, because they eat seals,' Alice said slowly.

There was another long pause, as we listened to the noise of the birds swelling around us. 'I assume this is not a good thing,' said Alice. 'And then there is global warming, which might cause the melting of the ice around the Poles. Well, we have already seen parts of the ice shelf breaking off, drifting into the sea, and lower levels of sea ice than usual. We don't know,' she was saying, 'we don't know what will happen. But we can guess at some things. As the earth loses its white surfaces, its ice, then it gains more dark areas, and the dark areas absorb more of the sun's radiation, so this makes the earth hotter. So it might get worse still, if it gets worse.'

'None of this is a crazy fantasy,' she said. 'None of it is science fiction, or outlandish. It's now respectable science, performed by trusted scientists, by cautious people. I think it is completely possible that the ice around the North Pole would one day melt. It might be possible to avert this, but we don't seem to be trying very hard.'

There was a final pause, as I shook with the cold, and then Alice said: 'I think we should return to the shore,' and she gripped the tiller with resolution, speeding us past the muddy icebergs, back towards the lights of Ny-Ålesund. Alice lived in suspense, in the northern scientific base. Scientists were usually cautious, and Alice was as cautious as any. Her conclusions were partial. Some things had been improving in recent years, she said, they might continue to improve. At the same time, Alice discerned something she couldn't control, a creeping threat to the natural world she observed.

At the harbour we kicked off our luminous suits, and shook hands.

The past and the future lurked at the edges of the daytime dusk. Walking back to my room I passed a bust of Roald Amundsen, his head cloaked in a hood. It was one more Arctic shrine, and I stood for a few minutes in the freezing wind, reading the inscription. Behind him, there was an orange wooden building, now housing the small sanatorium, which had once been Amundsen's house. I found that I didn't want to go back to the hotel. I walked from the circle of buildings across the tundra, where a rusting mast stood at the edge of the fjord. I wasn't sure if I needed a gun, so I watched the surrounding hillsides nervously, imagining each pale rock was a bear. The mast looked like an electricity pylon, but a sign had been hammered to the metal:

AMUNDSEN-ELLSWORTH-NOBILE TRANSPOLAR FLIGHT 1926 HONOURING A GLORIOUS ACHIEVEMENT OF HUMAN ENDEAVOUR TO ROALD AMUNDSEN LINCOLN ELLSWORTH UMBERTO NOBILE AND THE CREW OF THE AIRSHIP NORGE N1 WHO FOR THE FIRST TIME IN HISTORY FLEW OVER THE NORTH POLE FROM EUROPE TO NORTH AMERICA OPENING THE POLAR ROUTE. TAKE OFF: SPITSBERGEN 11 MAY. LANDING: ALASKA 13 MAY 1926.

The airship had been anchored to this mast, and it stood as a memorial. Amundsen had flown in an airship above the ice fjord, above the glinting whiteness of the glacier, and across the North Pole, hurling flags onto the ice. It was his last great piece of exploration.

The mast stood, surrounded by the vastness of the mountains.

———⊗⊗⊗———

In some of the stories, Thule lay between the earth and the world of the gods, somewhere beyond the reach of mortals. Past and future lurked at the edges of vision in Svalbard. The future was an untouched continent; like Nansen in the ice we were drifting towards it, on a temporal boat called *Forward*, perfectly passive, waiting to arrive. When all these formerly mysterious places were mapped, the future seemed to me as the blanks on the map must have seemed to the explorers: out of reach, impossible precisely to imagine however much we might speculate. Anyone might guess, but absolute certainty was impossible. As the scientists, experts, explorers of earlier centuries threw out ideas about what might lie in the remote north, so the scientists on Svalbard were trying to calculate the future.

Svalbard looked like a dream of a perfect place—an idyllic empty land, with the ice gleaming like diamonds and the sky a perpetual dusk-dark blue. Without these scientists, I could have slipped into the silence of the mountains, admiring the metallic waters of the fjord and the mottled bergs, watching the sun dying across the mountains. In Svalbard the quest for knowledge lurked behind every drifting cloud of mist, every soft sound of the waves lapping on the shore. The scientists could have packed up and gone home, with a scientific *Que sera, sera*, accepting that their predictions would fall on deaf ears, that their tentative conclusions would be used to argue for inaction. Instead they kept churning out their charts, stacking up statistics and scenarios. They kept working in sub-zero winds, in forgotten outposts, as determined as the explorers had been, trying to shine a light into the darkness ahead.

I was standing on the edge of the frozen fjord, thinking of the writers and explorers and cartographers, with all their theories and their certainty. Each in their own way had been certain; each had stood at the transmillennial debate with a glass firmly in their hand, toasting their version of Thule. 'Peace,' 'Ice,' 'Scotland,' 'Iceland,' 'Norway,' 'A retreat,' 'The last land of the world,' 'An interim land between humanity and the gods,' 'Home of the Hyperboreans' 'Gothic fantasy,' 'A wild, weird clime' they had all toasted, convinced of their rightness.

I had found no single answer, no grail glinting on the rocks. But I understood what Thule might mean to me. For me, Thule was about the northern lands, the clouds drifting across the northern sky, the flickering green of the Northern Lights, the whiteness of the ice creeping across the mountains, the pale lakes and semi-frozen seas, the mountains like cathedrals, baroquely patterned. Thule was an ancient fragment, representing thousands of years of discovery in the north. It was an ancient human fragment, a piece of story-telling about the far north. It expressed the ambivalence of the human relationship to nature, as I felt it—the desire for space, the appreciation of grandeur and beauty, the sense of unease in hostile, uninhabitable nature, the need to make use of nature to survive, the perilous balance between survival and exploitation. It expressed the ambivalence of the human relationship to perfection: a desirable but impossible state, a state glimpsed and occasionally seized, for a fleeting moment, but doomed to transience. Thule was ambiguous, available for use or corruption. Thule represented all the explorers and writers imagining and travelling and trying to understand. They knew the worst, they knew the desperate struggle and the terrible cold, but they had watched the play of colours across the ice, they had been struck by the beauty and silence around them.

Svalbard lay under a pale sun, the ice fragments drifted across the fjord. I understood that it was inevitable that as the lands of the north became part of human history, they would lose the plainness of perfection, the sheen of purity. The yearning to return to a blank space, a space allowing endless fantasy, was utopian and impossible. It was regressive; it sought to forget the desperate struggles of the explorers. The question was how far we wanted to go, how much we wanted to transform these ancient tracts of ice. Humans had always had the power to transform the scenery by acts of imagination, to make symbolism of a barren rock, or mystery of a sluggish sea. Humans had always hunted and lived in the remote north. But now humanity could fundamentally alter the balance of natural elements, maybe even melt an ice-shelf or two. All the remaining remoteness of the north couldn't save it from chemicals that drifted in the oceans, or pollution that was brought on the wind, or a gradual shift in global temperature. The pragmatic colony of Svalbard was a place where fantasy and beauty existed alongside nervous prophecy. No one was bellowing certainty from the rocks. The scientists all said their talk of future destruction might be just another theory. It might be mocked by later generations as one more dream of the ignorant. Or it might be an accurate forecast of the coming world. The future was shrouded in darkness, as the maps once were. But the rumbling had been heard in the distance, the frozen ocean might one day be nothing more than an old fairytale, a story from a vanished world.

The birds circled above and the mountains shimmered in the mist. The moon was shining across the glacier. I stood at the edge of the fjord, thinking of the ice swirling into the darkness around the Pole. It was a beautiful night. The glacier was groaning gently in the distance, the bergs were moving slowly along the fjord. From the runway above the settlement a light aircraft lifted into the sky, drifting towards the ice mountains. There was the sound of propellers beating across the settlement, and then the noise died away, leaving just the silence of the ice and the moon glinting through the clouds.

. . . ONLY THE PAST IS IMMORTAL.
DECIDE TO TAKE A TRIP, READ BOOKS OF TRAVEL
GO QUICKLY! EVEN SOCRATES IS MORTAL
MENTION THE NAME OF HAPPINESS: IT IS
ATLANTIS, ULTIMA THULE, OR THE LIMELIGHT,
CATHAY OR HEAVEN. BUT GO QUICKLY . . .

"PERSONAE," DELMORE SCHWARTZ (1913–1966)

ACKNOWLEDGEMENTS

For supplying the ideal environment in which to finish the book, thanks to Sir Alistair Horne and also to Sir Marrack Goulding and the Fellows of St. Antony's College, Oxford.

For formal and informal briefings along the way, thanks to President Lennart Meri, President Vaira Vike-Freiberga, former Prime Minister Mart Laar, Minister Kristiina Ojuland, Commander Neil Rasmusson, David Hempleman-Adams, Borge Ousland, Roland Huntford, Jasper Griffin, Arne Naess, Heather O'Donoghue, Geir Wing Gabrielsen, Frederic Hauge, Liz Morris, Bragi Olafsson, Olav Orheim, Per Egil Hegge and Tiina Peil.

For logistical support, many thanks to the Norwegian Embassy in London, particularly to Ambassador Brautaset, Mrs. Elisabeth Mohr Brautaset, John Petter Opdahl and Anne Ulset. Thanks also to the International Press Centre in Oslo, the British Antarctic Survey and the US Embassy in Copenhagen, particularly to Alistair Thompson.

Thanks to Kim Witherspoon and David Forrer at InkWell Management and to my editor, Carolyn Carlson.

Various editors supplied me with the best kind of employment for the peripatetic writer—flexible commissions which allowed me to thrash out ideas and steady my bank balance when I'd spent too much money on trains and boats and 'planes. For this, many thanks to: Robert Silvers and Barbara Epstein at the *New York Review of Books*; Mary-Kay Wilmers and Paul Laity at the *London Review of Books*; Claire Armitstead, Giles Foden and Andy Pietrasik at the

Guardian; Robert McCrum and Stephanie Merritt at the *Observer* and Andrew Johnston at the *International Herald Tribune*.

For generous deeds, discussions, reading of drafts, thanks to Brian and Peggy-Lou Martin, Eyjólfur Emilsson, Arna Mathiesen, Beate Elvebakk, Hallvard Fossheim, Per Ariansen, Oystein Ska, Jonas Jølle, Ragnheidur Kristjansdottir, Svavar Svavarsson, Tim Garton Ash, Avi Shlaim, Felix Martin, Kristina Hemon, Rory Stewart, Sophie Breese, Arho Anttila, Katri Krone, Robert Macfarlane, Erik Rutherford, Beccy Asher, Tristan Quinn, Katherine Shave and Abigail Reynolds.

Many thanks to my parents and to my brother Daniel.

And most of all to Barnes.